Praise fo

"Clearly the best book on conflict I've ever read. Woolverton takes us beyond conflict management or resolution and shows us the type of leadership that uses conflict to not only grow but multiply the kingdom. It's thoughtful, scholarly, and full of biblical examples. If you're looking for a book on how to constructively lead in the midst of conflict, look no further."

—Bill Easum, founder and president of the Effective Church Group; author of *Dinosaurs to Rabbits: Turning Mainline Decline to a Multiplication Movement*

"Jesus promises, 'In this world, you will have trouble.' And we do, and often it comes in the form of conflict. Within our disputes and disagreements, Woolverton sees possibilities for growth and chances for development. As a pastor, he wants what Jesus wants: for us to grow and develop as we are found in Christ and on mission for his church. Drift no longer; read *Mission Rift*."

—Kyle Idleman, senior pastor, Southeast Christian Church, Louisville, KY; author of *Not a Fan* and *Don't Give Up*

"'Our job is not to resolve conflict.' With that opening salvo, Woolverton grounds conflict resolution in discipleship formation rather than surface tension management. The result is a book that addresses conflict by understanding it rather than merely providing tips for quick fixes. Elegantly written and brimming with gentle, direct wisdom, *Mission Rift* has the clarity and urgency of a crystal bell. It will be on church leaders' desks for decades to come. I'll be using it in my classes, effective immediately."

—Kenda Creasy Dean, Mary D. Synnott Professor of Youth, Church, and Culture, Princeton Theological Seminary; author of *Almost Christian: What the Faith of Our Teenagers Is Telling the American Church*

"Every church experiences conflict. But why? We often miss important lessons in the tension of conflict, and *Mission Rift* reveals them. Woolverton offers a unique perspective on how mission-driven churches are shaped rather than paralyzed by conflict. The strain of conflict can be painful. *Mission Rift* shows you how it can be fruitful."

—Sam Rainer, president, Church Answers; lead pastor, West Bradenton Baptist Church, Bradenton, FL

"Woolverton's book could not be more appropriate for these days. Conflict is present in every pastor's life at levels never before experienced. As I read *Mission Rift*, I wanted to send it to thousands immediately. Woolverton writes from personal experience but also with excellent research and from his own earned academic credentials. His writing is compelling, and one can identify with many of the scenarios. This is not a quick fix conflict resolution book. It brings new light to Scripture and the final goal of transformation for all. I love the words of the benediction prayed by Woolverton's mentor as he moved to his new church assignment: 'May you be sufficiently overwhelmed in ministry as to always find yourself on your knees in utter dependence on the Lord Jesus Christ. Amen.' May it be so for all of us."

—Jo Anne Lyon, general superintendent
emerita, the Wesleyan Church

"Are you, like me, tired of managing church conflict? Are you, like me, tired of being afraid of conflict and even running from it? Woolverton, a respected and experienced church leader whose wisdom we tap as a faculty member at Evangelical Theological Seminary, has some wonderful news for us. In this helpful book, he encourages us to reframe conflict in light of our divine mission mandate. 'Would we address it differently,' he asks, 'if we knew that its presence actually means we are doing something *right*?' When we view it not as a problem to be solved but as a marker of healthy, biblical leadership, then it can be not managed but led. This volume contains the wisdom we've been looking for, and thus I recommend it to students, grads, colleagues, and scholars alike."

—Tony Blair, president, Evangelical Theological
Seminary, Myerstown, PA; executive partner, Kairos
Project; author, *Leading Missional Change: Move Your
Congregation from Resistant to Re-Energized*

"Woolverton is one of those authors who practices what he preaches. The wisdom he shares in this book is the same you see expressed in his day-to-day dealings with people. In his writing, Woolverton helps us see the intricate, exhausting, depressing, and transformational nature of conflict. While providing down-to-earth examples the reader can understand, he weaves together deep insights, helpful practices, and encouragement for the journey. You and your ministry will be well served by *Mission Rift*."

—Greg Henson, president, Kairos University; coauthor of *The Council: A Biblical Perspective on Board Governance*

"Let's face it: most pastors want their congregations to be happy and content. Disagreements and quarrels in the pews and the committee rooms indicate that something must be resolved, managed, and fixed. But a peaceful church is not a faithful church; God's call disrupts the status quo and disturbs the placid. Drawing on years of pastoral experience and thorough research, Woolverton challenges pastors to embrace the discomforting and anxiety-provoking elements of congregational life. In *Mission Rift*, the faint of heart will find encouragement and insight to tap into the energy that comes from chaos and conflict, and they will learn to use it as a catalyst for moving forward in God's mission for the church."

—Peter de Vries, pastor of Old Union Presbyterian Church, Mars, PA; coauthor of *Soccer Mom in Galilee*

"Writing from a pastoral perspective, Woolverton has crafted an excellent leadership manual for the missional church. It is unique in its fresh approach to conflict, cutting-edge principles for congregational leadership, and systematic presentation of practical illustrations. For him, a good leader can 'stir up healthy conflict,' as conflict is a vital process for spiritual growth and development. *Mission Rift* is an essential text for church administration and leadership."

—James Z. Labala, dean, Gbarnga School of Theology, United Methodist University, Monrovia, Liberia

"Conflict. The average pastor's blood pressure rises at the mention of this word. Headlines regularly provoke our emotions as we read how pastors and their church parishioners fail at understanding and approaching conflict personally and organizationally. Woolverton, an expert practitioner, reframes conflict as a challenge that unleashes incredible spiritual and leadership growth opportunities. *Mission Rift* provides research in a readable style. More importantly, it is written with integrity. I have known the author for twenty-five years as a loving mentor, fearless rescuer, pastor's pastor, and constant friend. He has personally modeled everything he has written in this book with humility and honor for the Lord Jesus Christ. Every pastor, seminary, and Bible college should add this book to their required reading list. Readers, expect radical transformation as you integrate this book's insights into your life!"

—David Coryell, executive director, Christian Endeavor; general secretary, World's Christian Endeavor

"Courage, focus, and curiosity will be cultivated within you through this fresh approach to the storms of church conflict. Others might shut down, but you can remain open by using the framework and tools Woolverton provides. From his wealth of experience, he shares the challenge of discipleship thinking, a scholarly framework, biblical examples, and personal stories to activate and equip you. This essential manual will help you not only lead but also grow your congregation through the catalyst of conflict. Prepare to be stretched by and to grow through these truths so that you may guide others along steps you have already taken. Renew your humility and confidence as you embrace your high calling to lead."

—Jesse Gill, psychologist; author of *Face to Face: Seven Keys to a Secure Marriage*

"Nothing raises blood pressure quite like the term *congregational meeting*. I'll never forget one where emotions ran high and a few tempers flared as people prepared to air and defend their entrenched positions on major changes proposed for worship. At one point, then associate pastor David Woolverton stood up and looked tenderly over the crowd. 'It's important to acknowledge tonight,' he began, 'that what many of us are really feeling is grief.' With that insightful, elegant word choice, the atmosphere softened, passions were defused, and we began to honestly share with each other so that our congregation could finally move forward. As a friend and colleague in ministry for eight years, I have watched Woolverton enter countless situations of conflict and stress as a nonanxious, ever-loving, warm, and instructive presence. He not only embodies and makes a life practice of the principles of *Mission Rift*; he is able to teach them. I highly recommend this wonderful book not only for clergy but for parishioners as well. It is a lighthouse and course correction desperately needed everywhere in society right now."

—Alisa Bair, composer; author of *Grief Is a Dancer: A Memoir*

"Whether you are a new pastor or leader seeking to develop your abilities or a seasoned leader looking to challenge yourself, Woolverton's book provides infinitely valuable wisdom and insight that will open leadership doors for years to come. He focuses on a need so many leadership books ignore: dealing with the hidden roadblocks, traps, and saboteurs in our own hearts so that we can actually change and become the leaders we long to be. His wisdom, insight, and application are hewn from his own personal pursuit to fulfill this call, so his words ring with an honesty and authenticity that awaken in me a hopeful calling."

—Sean Rajnic, licensed professional counselor

"Woolverton brings years of experience and wisdom to a must read for every pastor. These chapters and their insights will transform your ministry. Whether you've been in ministry for twenty years or two months, this book will help you lead better and, more importantly, teach you how to not just navigate conflict but leverage its reality for the growth of your church and the effectiveness of your ministry."

—Daniel Gulnac, lead pastor, Palmyra Grace Church, Palmyra, PA

"This is a good book—fresh, useful, and well researched. Woolverton cuts through the jargon and takes us straight to the heart of struggles that are so prevalent in churches today. This practical work skillfully encapsulates biblical insight to illuminate the landmines of conflict and how to stay on mission. His understanding of family systems theory is thorough and brilliantly applied to real-life happenings. This much-needed work makes an excellent resource for pastors and boards to study and learn together."

—Steven Trewartha, senior pastor, FaithPoint Lutheran Church, New Prague, MN

"Written by a seasoned leader who was seminary trained in theology but acquired leadership training on the streets and in church board rooms, *Mission Rift* challenges our assumption that church conflict is bad. As a result of years of pastoral experience, Woolverton encourages leaders who are exhausted or even leery of church conflict to instead pivot and lean into the storm. What if the very conflict we are trying so hard to avoid is the final ingredient necessary to bring about spiritual growth in our church family? *Mission Rift* just may be the reminder we need to grow from church conflict rather than to run from it."

—David Ashcraft, senior pastor, LCBC Church, Manheim, PA

"*Mission Rift* equips both pastors and lay leaders with practical and profound tools to work through congregational conflict. Woolverton teaches spiritual communities how to work through divergent opinions rather than choosing one side or the other. If you are searching for a fresh perspective on discipling and leading churches in the twenty-first century, read this book, and then buy it for your leadership team."

—Ken Henry, head of staff / pastor, Westminster Presbyterian Church, Charlottesville, VA

MISSION
RIFT

MISSION RIFT

Leading through Church Conflict

David E. Woolverton

FORTRESS PRESS
MINNEAPOLIS

MISSION RIFT
Leading through Church Conflict

Cover Design: Brad Norr Design

Print ISBN: 978-1-5064-6477-0
Ebook ISBN: 978-1-5064-6478-7

To Kristine,
who every day reveals to me the heart of God

Contents

Preface
Conflict That Kills, Conflict That Cultivates Growth

AS A PASTOR, I HAVE FOUND THAT EVERY CONGREGATION I HAVE served over thirty years has had to navigate through conflict as we sought to "make disciples who make disciples." Learning to welcome the unchurched, dropping established programs, developing new leaders, realigning ministries toward our mission, letting go of staff members who didn't want to change, putting limits on sabotaging behaviors, giving away our Christmas Eve offering to meet the needs of our unchurched neighbors . . . all brought about conflict, sometimes seismic in scope.

At the risk of sounding like a reductionist, after more than thirty years as a pastor and fifteen of those as a church and clergy consultant, I've come to the conclusion that there are two types of conflict in congregations: conflict that kills and conflict that cultivates growth.[1]

Conflict that kills—that damages or destroys teams, ministries, missions, vibrancy—occurs when we as the people of God forget who we are, why we're here, and where we're going in carrying out the divine mission. Yes, people disagree, even in the church. Indeed, whenever "two or three are gathered" in Jesus's name, it seems like there's bound to be a fight. Yet when we begin to focus more on ourselves—our wants, our needs, our preferences—and less on the wants, needs, and preferences of our sisters and brothers in the faith, not to mention those we are trying to reach with the gospel, the ensuing conflicts can be deadly for a congregation. We start to "bite and devour one another," the way the apostle Paul describes the church in Galatia (Gal 5:15). Over time, these chronic conditions push out leaders who have the capacity to reset the congregation's values and redirect its mission. Many of these leaders leave disillusioned, exhausted, and reluctant to engage in further ministry. In the subsequent leadership vacuum, church "bullies" gain control of the flock of God, as they hijack the emotional safety of the congregation and run the church like mob bosses, protecting their sacred turf.

Conflict that cultivates growth—in teams, ministries, missions, vibrancy—often looks similar to conflict that kills, because it begins with the same scenarios. The difference, however, is found in how leaders function. They ask different questions. They focus less on the *content* of the individual conflict scenarios and more on the *context*—why that conflict is present. They focus on creating a healthier, proactive culture that includes mutual accountability, best practices for outreach and mission, and appropriate relational boundaries. Conflict is seen less as something to be resolved or mediated because it makes people anxious and more as a context for learning how to live together as a people called to transform their neighborhoods, schools, and workplaces.

Pastors and other leaders can help faithful followers of Jesus understand conflict as an opportunity to remember who they are in Christ, why they're here, and where they're going on their mission. Successfully leading through conflict toward a transformative end will always bear exponential dividends, empowering a congregation's witness within its community and beyond.

My Story

Even though I had an excellent theological education in preparation for ministry, my seminary courses did not teach me how to lead—especially in seasons of church conflict. Most of what I know, about leadership as well as about conflict, I sought out personally over the years because I was living with conflict in ministry, was serving growing churches, and desperately needed to figure out what to do.

To begin my journey of learning about leadership and conflict, I spent the better part of three years doing basic and advanced levels of clinical pastoral education (CPE), primarily in emergency rooms and trauma units, and caring for persons with acute life-threatening conditions. Studying and ministering to people in crisis and exploring my own feelings and pastoral identity in the midst of it all radically changed my perspective on what it means to minister in a broken world.

The focus of my training was in the growing genre of family systems theory—specifically, the framework espoused by rabbi-psychiatrist Edwin Friedman, who uniquely applied to church and synagogue the systems theories of psychiatrist and Georgetown University professor Murray Bowen.[2] Years later Friedman would write what I consider one of the most important leadership books of our time, *A Failure of Nerve: Leadership in the Age of the Quick Fix*.[3] Friedman's work has influenced much of my perspective on conflict in congregations, shaping my own leadership and consultative work.

After CPE, my journey took me back into the congregational setting where, in addition to dealing with all the "normal" pastor stuff of preaching, teaching, and leading, I had to figure out who I was through the transitions of a growing church (we grew from three hundred to over two thousand in worship attendance over ten years), how to work with a larger staff, and how to manage all the dynamics of change and resistance. Working with colleagues and team members whose leadership styles were quite different from mine and whose levels of security and insecurity in their roles often brought friction created an environment that challenged what I thought ministry was supposed to be.

In spite of all my clinical training, I internalized and personalized the stresses of ministry and had a heart attack at the age of forty-one. While I would not wish that experience on anyone, it became a defining moment for me—a time of reenvisioning leadership, discipleship, and my purpose in the grander mission movement that I believe God intends for the church. I decided to get further training in conflict and began doctoral work in conflict management. The more I learned, the more I realized I did not know and the more I was compelled to pursue further education and research. I sought out strong mentors—like pastor, consultant, and author Bill Easum and leadership expert John C. Maxwell. Their voices broadened my capacity as a leader and sharpened my personal missional perspective.

I began to ask different questions about conflict—especially the kind of conflict that results from deliberate attempts to do mission. For example, what would happen if we changed the way we look at conflict in the church? Would we address it differently if we knew that its presence actually means we are doing something *right* to advance our divine mission? What if conflict was seen as inevitable—indeed even *essential*—in order for a congregation to embody God's mission of engaging the community with the gospel and impacting its unchurched neighbors?

During the past fifteen years, I have taken that education to a new next level. While taking doctoral courses, I began to teach my colleagues what I was learning. The more I taught, the more I was invited to consult with both clergy and congregations, illustrating the great need among pastors and leaders for intervention and guidance. The more I consulted, the more I realized I needed to learn . . . and what I learned, I taught and used, practicing the principle my piano teacher told me in my very first lesson in the seventh grade: "What you do over and over often becomes automatic."

Today, in addition to being a full-time pastor, I continue to guide clergy and congregations in navigating what I call "conflict leadership." I also am an affiliate professor of leadership studies at Evangelical Theological Seminary in Myerstown, Pennsylvania, as well as a faculty mentor in the Kairos Project at Sioux Falls Seminary. My goal in doing so is to share as much as I can of all that I have learned about conflict from ministry in the trenches of brokenness and renewal—my own as well as that of the congregations where I have served.

One of my most important learnings is that one cannot learn to be a peacemaker during times of peace. I learned about conflict from *within* conflict. My hope is that you, too, can learn by sharing in my journey and daring to delve into conflict yourself because we serve a God who redeems it all.

The Why of This Book

Church conflict has been researched and written about for years. Conflict management resources abound, demonstrating that countless clergy and lay leaders are eager to know how to resolve the dilemmas that arise. Many of those resources have formed and shaped my own ministry over the years, and I am grateful for them. So, with so many resources already in print, why write this book?

In *Mission Rift*, I pose questions not typically asked about conflict—namely, what is the conflict's *context*, and why is it occurring *now*? By doing so, I'm looking for the larger, systemic issues that the conflict indicates we need to address. In other words, I'm arguing that conflict actually may be a symptom of something deeper at play in the congregational systems.[4] And if it is a symptom, to what is it pointing? Therefore, I'm less inclined to resolve conflict too quickly, lest we inadvertently sabotage the potential such conflict has to draw the congregation toward appropriate spiritual growth. In fact, paradoxically, I have often found that a *lack* of conflict may be a symptom of missional decline rather than congregational unity. I do not presume that conflict resolution is the goal. Rather, when the church pursues *first* its divine mission, conflict actually may become essential for defining its mission priorities.

The Who and the How of This Book

My aim in writing this book is to assist pastors and other church leaders in leading their congregations through conflict and on toward the mission they were called to serve. Specifically, I'm writing to those pastor-leaders who are *scared*, *beaten down*, *exhausted*, or *challenged* because a current or recent church conflict has suddenly made them aware of their need for training in dealing with conflict. They may be experiencing a post-traumatic emotional and existential crisis as they try to regain a sense of grounding after their conflict experience. They may be looking not only for information and insight but for inner peace and strength to help them through difficult leadership scenarios. They also may be *motivated*, for sure, wanting to prepare to lead people through change and growth by engaging the conflicts in more creative ways.

In *Mission Rift*, I seek to reorient our view of congregational conflict. In part 1, I explore conflict from a theological and ecclesiological framework, offering a different perspective as to why conflict is essential to our discipleship and mission. Then in part 2, I present six principles of missional leadership—each personally vetted the hard way—by which I challenge pastors and other leaders to define themselves within the frameworks of spiritual formation and family systems and then to create environments that facilitate growth within the communities of faith they serve.

Defining Terms

Throughout this book I use several phrases in particular ways. While I expound on their implications in the body of the text, you will find it helpful to know, in broader terms, what I'm referring to when I use them.

DIVINE MISSION

This term refers to the two-pronged mandate given to Jesus's disciples (and thus to the church)—what we know as the Great Commission in Matthew 28:16–20 and the Great Commandment in John 13:34–35. Together they form the core job description of every Christian congregation. Each congregation has its individual slant on mission, but the fundamentals of making disciples and loving God and neighbor are nonnegotiable. Throughout this book, I talk about this divine mission in terms of "remembering who we are, why we're here, and where we're going." This mandate is foundational to guiding people through conflict in the church.

DISCIPLESHIP MINDSET

I view a disciple as an apprentice. In the simple terms of learning a trade, we watch our mentors, listen to their teaching, integrate the learning into who we are, and then multiply what we've learned by mentoring others. This model is illustrated in the relationship between the apostle Paul and his protégé, Timothy. In 2 Timothy 2:1–2, Paul writes, "You then, my child, be strong in the grace that is in Christ Jesus; and what you have heard from me through many witnesses entrust to faithful people who will be able to teach others as well." In conflict situations, how we lead is being watched—not only by our congregations as a whole but also by the teenager who has been nurturing a call to ordained ministry, or the young adult sitting in the back pew who is just beginning to open up to the possibility of making a confession of faith in Christ, and by the neighbors living next door to the parsonage who you've been reaching out to for the past nine months. A discipleship mindset involves being intentional about developing both systems and leaders for carrying out the divine mission. Even in painful situations, we need to be mindful of what behavior we model for others.

NEW COMMUNITY (OF CHRIST)

This term refers to a congregation of Jesus-followers who intentionally gather around select core values, hold one another accountable to healthy patterns of behavior, and live together within the covenantal parameters of love and forgiveness in order to carry out the divine mission. This community is the church—at its best when we remember who we are, why we're here, and where we're going.

Conflict has a way of causing so much stress for pastors and other leaders that it can negatively impact their physical, emotional, and spiritual health. Yet I do not believe God desires us to have a heart attack or cancer or migraines as a result of carrying out our call to ministry. Nor does God want us to self-medicate with overeating, alcohol, drugs, pornography, affairs, or vacuous television or internet activity. Nor does God desire that we self-sabotage in order to save face. God has called us to advance God's missional movement, the church. God equips those who are called to this great task. My prayer is for this book to equip you, empower you, and encourage you to move forward in faith.

PART I

Who We Are,
Why We're Here,
Where We're Going

CHAPTER ONE

Who We Are

If any want to become my followers, let them deny themselves and take up their cross and follow me. For those who want to save their life will lose it, and those who lose their life for my sake, and for the sake of the gospel, will save it.

—Mark 8:34-35

IN THE CONGREGATIONAL SETTING WHERE YOU SERVE, NO MATTER what else God is up to, God is doing two overarching works: First, God is using your unique gifts, skills, personality, character, and attitude to work with the congregation to carry out God's mission in the community. Second, God is using this particular local church and all its issues—the good, the bad, and the ugly—to equip you and the congregation for even greater mission and ministry opportunities.

Let's face it: church conflicts can be scary. They can strain your marriage and family, disrupt your ministry agenda, challenge your personal sense of call, forever alter your perspective on church and pastoring, and quite honestly, make you hate being around people . . . especially Christians. Everything that originally birthed God's call to ministry in your life may be called into question. Conflicts in the church can make you so disillusioned that you want to quit—quit the particular congregation and quit ministry itself. The stress related to navigating church conflicts can cause you to understand deeply the full spectrum of your body's "fight-flight-or-freeze" adrenal reactions.

You may have seasons of depression and times when you feel painfully alone. You might self-medicate with your drug of choice—whether alcohol, nicotine, pornography, or pain medications—or you may find yourself binge-watching late-night episodes of *Family Feud*. There may be times you work harder and longer, believing that doing so will somehow change your circumstances. You might have trouble falling asleep or staying asleep or getting up to start your day.

You may become more easily angered and reactive, at times making (or at least thinking) inappropriate comments. You might have imaginary battles in your mind in which you "call down fire" on those who are making your life miserable. And then, because you're a follower of Jesus, you may live with the cognitive dissonance between your self-justification and guilt about what you're going through and doing.

And you will be in good company.

A Voice Calling in the Wilderness

For many, conflict can be scary. It's so easy to assume that each and every conflict is a cosmic battle between good and evil—especially when we position those who disagree with us as "villains." Such clashes, in fact, are the foundation upon which many a bestselling book, television show, or blockbuster movie is built. *Star Wars*, the Harry Potter series, *Mission Impossible*, *The Jerry Springer Show*, *The Real Housewives of New Jersey*, *Dog the Bounty Hunter*, and programs on the Hallmark Channel demonstrate how society even views some conflicts as entertainment—at least when they don't involve us *personally* and when they are resolved by the end of the show. But conflicts can reveal so much more if we dare to look beneath their stormy surges.

I must admit, that's one of the reasons I like the Old Testament prophet Elijah. If you look at his life journey through our twenty-first-century "church" perspective, Elijah is much like a local church pastor. People come to him for advice and expect wisdom. People come to him with their ailments and expect him to heal them. People come to him with their poverty and expect him to provide. People come to him with complaints about his ministry, and he must somehow not take them personally.

Elijah is just like you and me. In spite of the miracles God performs through him, he is fully human—having the full range of normal human reactions to the confrontations and threats that come his way. Take the aftermath of Elijah's battle with the priests of Baal on Mount Carmel. You know the story. Elijah has just seen and led one of the most amazing battles of faith in the Bible. He has watched God's powerful hand of judgment wipe out hundreds of false prophets to prove to King Ahab and Queen Jezebel that nothing will impinge on God's mission. Now Elijah faces Jezebel, who is the prototype of people we know in our very churches, and must battle his own emotions in order to continue leading. In response to Jezebel's threats, Elijah runs. He flees in fear—in spite of the God who will not be intimidated. He gets severely depressed and wants to die.

Have you ever felt that way? I have. If you're like me, when you feel that kind of anxiety, you will do almost anything to regain a sense of peace. Elijah tries too.

Exhausted, Elijah runs "a day's journey into the wilderness" (1 Kgs 19:4) and finds refuge under a broom tree, where he collapses in self-pity.

Notice that Elijah's encounter with God begins *in the wilderness*. Often, it is there, in the wilderness, that God sharpens the character of those whom God calls to service. Elijah, Abraham (Gen 22:9–12), Jacob (Gen 32:22–31), Moses (Exod 2:11–25), Paul (Acts 9:1–9; Gal 1:11–24)—even Jesus (Matt 4:1–11); it's one of the things they all have in common. For each, the wilderness is an experience of facing and shattering their idols and misconceptions about leadership and God's call to ministry.

5

In the wilderness, our pride is exposed, and we are found wanting. Our definitions of strong leadership are confronted, and we emerge limping and are given but a staff and a Word to compel us. In the wilderness, we are stripped bare, tested, sharpened, reoriented, and then sent back out into the world of brokenness to be a vessel through whom God redeems the world. In the wilderness, God equips us—*you*—to prepare God's people for divine transformative work.

Why is that important? Sometimes we forget who we are, why we're here, and where we're going.

Conflicts in communities of faith are not new—even when they are new to us. The fact that people in your congregation may be fighting is not a surprise to God. Perhaps that's why God sent you there! While God recognizes the exhausting nature of leading in conflict situations, the Lord of Life challenges us to remember the call on our lives, to find strength in that call, and most specifically, to keep moving forward in the faith that the One who called us will lead through us.

We Are Not Meant to Go It Alone

To remind Elijah of his call, God shows up in a penetrating "sound of sheer silence" (1 Kgs 19:12).

In the summer of 2018, my wife, Kristine, and I traveled to Olympic National Park in Washington for ten days of vacation. I had just spent the better part of two years serving a new church appointment, navigating through repeated conflicts dealing with everything from personality clashes among congregation members to "worship wars" to the aftermath of my colleague's extramarital affair with a church member, along with the normal stressors of leading a large congregation. I was exhausted. Four days into our vacation, I was still tense, reactive, and sarcastic—and feeling overwhelmed by the death of our beloved dog just a few weeks prior. I was not very fun to be around.

Then came the Shi Shi Beach hiking trail in the park's Makah wilderness. Within moments after beginning the hike, I was overcome by the "sound of sheer silence." Surrounded by a cathedral of tall trees, this segment of creation was devoid of all sound, including anything natural. No birds chirping, no crickets calling mates, no squirrels rustling in the underbrush. I was overcome by the presence of the Almighty. I remember stopping a quarter of a mile in and feeling the physical release of the weight I had been carrying in my soul. Inside I wept with a sense of freedom as that divine silence reminded me both of how small I really am and that God is totally and immeasurably in control. I felt naked, exposed, and vulnerable . . . yet very free.

This sound of sheer silence is important for us in ministry. We must put ourselves in positions where we can hear it, repeatedly, especially in seasons of conflict. Ironically, it is in such moments of God's self-revelation, in the sheer silence of God's presence, that we are reminded that we are not, nor were we ever meant to be, alone.

Following this encounter, Elijah receives instructions from God: "Go, return on your way to the wilderness of Damascus; when you arrive, you shall anoint Hazael as king over Aram. Also you shall anoint Jehu son of Nimshi as king over Israel; and you shall anoint Elisha son of Shaphat of Abel-meholah as prophet in your place. Whoever escapes from the sword of Hazael, Jehu shall kill; and whoever escapes from the sword of Jehu, Elisha shall kill. Yet I will leave seven thousand in Israel, all the knees that have not bowed to Baal, and every mouth that has not kissed him" (1 Kgs 19:15–18).

What God says to Elijah, in effect, is "Go, surround yourself with a team." It's the power of anointing that equips Elijah to now multiply the impact of what God can do through him, especially as he begins the final chapters of his own ministry. Alone, he remains exhausted; with a team, he finds strength, fortitude, and endurance.

Hazael and Jehu become significant partners with Elijah in carrying out God's mission. Elisha becomes a protégé of Elijah, preparing for the next wave of that mission. The mission of God is central to the entire metanarrative of Scripture. Therefore, it must also be the central heartbeat of every local church.

If you are the pastor of a church, one of your primary jobs is to build a team of leaders who will help carry out God's mission. Additionally, from the get-go, your job is to start multiplying yourself, mentoring others in leadership who will succeed you. No matter how conflicted your congregation may be, God is raising up a group—however small or large—of those who are faithful to the call of Christ. God's words to Elijah speak to God's ongoing mission through the church to the world: "Yet I will leave seven thousand in Israel, all the knees that have not bowed to Baal, and every mouth that has not kissed him" (1 Kgs 19:18). There are people in your congregation whom God has been preparing for this chapter in the church's history—faithful people who have hearts for God's mission and for God's Son. God has been raising them up "for just such a time as this" (Esth 4:14). You are not meant to lead alone. You need to build your team.

Goal Shift: Not to Fix Conflict but to Lead through It

Our goal, first and foremost, is to equip disciples for mission-focused ministry. When conflict arises, it's not our job as pastors and leaders to fix conflict. The notion of fixing conflict implies that first, a specific conflict can be fixed; second, the people involved in the conflict want to be fixed; and third, it's important to resolve the conflict in order to carry out our mission. In reality, we try to fix the things that cause us anxiety, and conflict raises our anxiety. We are afraid that we will lose relationships, status, respect, power, rights, privileges . . . and control. Conflict and its ramifications can make us anxious, and when our anxiety goes up, we will do whatever it takes to reduce it.

Our job is not to resolve conflict. Our job is to develop healthier ways for our congregations to carry out our divine mission of making disciples of Jesus Christ and showing our neighbors that love can, in fact, transform the world (John 13:35; 17:25–26). Conflicts actually are contexts within which that equipping and discipling can take place. We need to change the way we view conflict in the church. Instead of looking at the conflict's *content*, we must turn our eyes to the conflict's *context*. What are the unhealthy relational systems that are breeding grounds for dysfunction (e.g., closed power groups or bullies)? In what ways has this congregation been neglecting its mission mandate and consuming itself (Gal 5:15)? What is this conflict revealing about the congregation's lack of discipled leaders? What are the patterns of repeated conflicts telling you about unresolved grief or unrepented sin?

If we resolve conflict too quickly, we may sabotage the very opportunity it presents to realign the congregation to the mission God has intended for it within its community. Our task is not to fix conflict; our task is to lead through it. Instead of allowing our own or the congregation's anxiety to determine how we react to conflict in the church, we can have the courage to face and lead through the conflict.

But where can we get that kind of courage?

Amid Any Church Conflict, God Starts with the Leader

One of my favorite verses of Scripture is 1 Samuel 17:48: "As the Philistine moved closer to attack him, David ran quickly toward the battle line to meet him" (NIV). The context is the well-known story of David and Goliath. Ever since I was a child, I have loved this Bible story—certainly because my name is David but also because I am vertically challenged (I'm 5′5″). These wonderful words have helped me face quite a few Goliaths over the years.

But I don't think this iconic story is primarily about David facing Goliath. I think it's about something much more enticing. I think it's about David remembering who he is, why he's there, and what God's mission for Israel has been all along—and then asking the Israelite army to do the same thing.

In response to Saul's palpable concern about David's youth and inexperience in facing the much more experienced warrior, Goliath, David recounts with pride stories of how God has helped him defeat a lion and a bear and then asserts his confidence that "the Lord, who saved me from the paw of the lion and from the paw of the bear, will save me from the hand of this Philistine" (1 Sam 17:37). He's not really focusing on Goliath at all.

By doing so, David illustrates an all-important axiom for those who lead in the midst of conflict: a leader's greatest asset within any conflict situation is their capacity to self-define apart from the emotional tensions of the conflict. In his posthumously published book *A Failure of Nerve*, rabbi-psychiatrist Edwin Friedman portrays what he identifies as the "well-differentiated leader": "A well-differentiated leader is someone who has clarity about his or her own life goals, and therefore, someone who is less likely to become lost in the anxious emotional processes . . . someone who can separate while still remaining connected . . . who can maintain a modifying, non-anxious, and sometimes challenging presence . . . who can manage his or her own reactivity to the automatic reactivity of others . . . and therefore be able to take stands at the risk of displeasing others."[1]

The well-differentiated leader can stand within the storms of conflict and lead because they know who they are and what they are called to do, and they choose to move forward regardless of the anxiety of others. Friedman posits that healthy transitions within organizations fail most commonly when the true leader allows the anxiety of others to sabotage the mission of the organization.[2] The leader has "a failure of nerve" to go against the emotional processes of the anxious system.[3] The challenge, therefore, is for the leader to self-define.

One of the best pieces of advice I received in ministry came in late fall 2002 from pastor, author, and church growth expert Bill

Easum. Bill was conducting a ministry audit and consultation at the church I served at the time—the third such audit in a decade. I had just received notification from my district superintendent that I should anticipate a new church appointment in the coming year. So I asked Bill a very important question: "Bill, what advice would you give me as I start at a new church?" His answer radically impacted my ministry and life from that point forward: "David, take the time now to define the priorities of your call—what you know, specifically, about what God has gifted and called you to be as the pastor of that church . . . and then lead from those priorities. Structure everything else around your call."

I received word of my new appointment in late January of the next year and immediately took a week off to pray. I spent eight hours each day journaling, reading Scripture, and discerning what those priorities of my call were. By the end of the week, I had a list of eight items. When I started at my new church, at my first meeting with our personnel committee, I defined how those eight priorities were going to frame what they as a congregation could expect from me for 80 percent of my time with them.

Nine years later, I had the opportunity to be coached by Bill for an entire year. As we began that relationship, his first question to me was "What are the priorities of your call?" Proudly, I shared with him my eight-item list and reminded him of my story. His response: "David, you certainly know what you're called to, but your list is way too long. You need to knock that list down to three to five items. Anything more than that threatens a leader's ability to focus." Three to five? I had a difficult enough time getting the list down to eight! My first attempt at complying was to combine items—my creative way to avoid pruning anything from my list while giving the impression that I had more focus. But after some coaxing, I narrowed the list to five. Truly, it was difficult for me to do so, since I tend to be a workaholic. But the process—and the final list—was freeing; I felt more focused, more energized, and excited to begin. When I shared my final list with Bill, he was pleased, and we proceeded through an incredible year of personal and professional growth.

In January 2016, I received yet another appointment to a church of "great potential" that was dealing with significant conflict and in need of turnaround strategies. As I prepared for this new venture, I heard Bill's words in the back of my mind: "Define the priorities of your call . . . and then lead from those priorities." At this point, I had been in ministry for about twenty-eight years. I had learned a lot, studied a lot, taught a lot of clergy workshops, received doctoral-level training in conflict leadership, and done numerous church and pastor consultations. So, instead of beginning from my five priorities, I took another week of prayer and repeated my defining journey.

When I emerged from my week, I had but *one* priority. I recognized that this one priority not only had defined all my ministry to date but was the fuel that would reignite my call for this next chapter in ministry. That one priority was this: I am called to "mentor and multiply." Everything I do involves equipping leaders and potential leaders who will multiply exponentially the impact of the Jesus Movement. That one simple phrase has helped me decide how I will spend my time, in what and in whom I will invest, how I will equip systems, how I will respond to conflict situations, and how I will shape the strategic direction of the staff and ministry teams I lead.

There is great clarity and freedom in discerning one's call to ministry. How we lead in stressful times must be based in that call, not in our personal feelings, not in how others want to define us, nor in how church traditions or expectations would have us lead. God puts us into our ministry context and equips us for that ministry so we can withstand the anxious storms of our congregation and lovingly move the community of faith into carrying out its divine mission. We must remember who we are, why we're here, and where we're going.

The young David defined himself *prior to* engaging Goliath. In many respects, by the time he faced Goliath, he already was a self-differentiated leader. I would argue that this quality was shaped in him in the wilderness while he was taking care of his sheep. His decisions about God's abilities and God's faithfulness were made within the crucible of prior conflicts (with a lion and a bear and perhaps within the sibling rivalries of his earlier years). I don't know about you, but if I were to fight a lion and a bear and win, not only would there be quite a bit of praying going on, but my trust in the God of the Impossible would skyrocket. David's confidence in heading toward Goliath had nothing to do with Goliath and everything to do with what was formed and shaped within David well before he showed up on the front lines of battle.

Being self-differentiated, mission-driven leaders does not mean we are not afraid. It means God's mission trumps our fear. It means we believe we have been called to ministry—anointed, even—for such a time as this. It means we believe the pain of living paralyzed by fear is greater than the pain of facing our conflict and its ramifications.

David's victorious moment with Goliath, however, would lead to even more conflict as he went on to attain glory, power, and position once assigned to Saul. Jealousies, theological discord, closed power groups, family rivalries, and turf battles abound, indeed. The history of God's people is replete with illustrations of how we turn on each other over seemingly inane issues. New wineskins (projectors and screens) replace old ones (bulletins and hymnbooks). New expressions of worship replace staid and stalwart strophic hymnody. Newer members assume leadership positions once occupied by long-tenured controllers. Cell phone text-to-tithe options begin to replace boxed offering envelopes. Young upstart "Davids" take to the "stage," no longer wearing clergy robes and eschewing the traditional pulpit.

Yet God calls and equips women and men of faith, people like Elijah and David, to be leaders for a divine mission, a movement of God's Spirit to transform the world. Leading through conflict starts with *you*. God wants *you* to be the leader God has called you to be. God placed *you* strategically into your context for a reason—a reason that is bigger than the conflicts you will experience. The question is, Do you know who you are, why you're here, and where you're going?

CHAPTER TWO
Why We're Here

> The sheepdog forcibly maneuvers the sheep, whereas the bibli-
> cal shepherd simply calls as he calmly walks ahead of the sheep.
>
> —Dallas Willard, *Hearing God*

IN JUNE 2003, I WALKED FOR THE FIRST TIME INTO THE SANCTUARY
of the church to which I'd just been appointed and wondered to
myself, "If these walls could speak, what would they tell me?"

The only thing I really knew about Second Street Church was
that it had been experiencing explosive conflict for some time,
climaxing just a few months prior to my arrival with the sudden
departure of multiple families, including quite a few of the congregation's leaders.[1] The story shared with me was that the administrative board had decided to house a before- and after-school
program in the church facilities after the program had been
"unfairly evicted" from its prior location. The board had made
the decision, it appeared, rather quickly to respond to the urgent
needs of the program and its sixty-plus children. The perception
of many in the congregation was that the decision was "railroaded
through" by the leaders without seeking approval from the rest
of the congregation. I was told this program did not have a good
reputation in the community, mainly due to the perceived ineffec-
tiveness of its director, so the congregation was concerned about
what they were inheriting and what ramifications the program
would have for the church's facilities.

As a United Methodist congregation, Second Street Church uses a representational model of governance through its administrative board. Leaders are free to make decisions within the normal checks and balances of the denomination's *Book of Discipline* without seeking congregational approval for all of their actions.[2] Yet, since the decision caused such upheaval within the church, many sought to voice their complaint through congregational voting.

The final straw for some members of the congregation occurred when the before- and after-school program used the church van for one of its trips and "left the van a mess, disrespecting church property." The van was used most frequently by the Travelers Group for its outings to restaurants, entertainment venues, and other outside programs. The Travelers Group was led by long-tenured people of influence in the congregation. They attempted to make their appeal to the administrative board, culminating in a demand that the children's program be expelled "before they destroy all our property."

When speaking at board meetings did not result in change, the leaders of the Travelers Group wrote a petition and got over a hundred signatures from church members demanding that the board accommodate their plea. The board, however, refused to acknowledge the demands and called the petition "out of order," resulting in significant animosity among many of the church members.

I remember my first Sunday worship service at the end of June. In the service, there was a time for "sharing the peace of Christ with someone standing near you." I introduced that greeting time with joy and excitement, inviting people to greet one another with a warm handshake or hug. No one moved. The tension in the room was palpable. I later found out that there were people on the left side of the sanctuary who did not speak to people on the right and that people who were once close friends would exit out of different doors so as not to interact with each other. I knew that I had my work cut out for me.

Two months into my tenure, I received an invitation to breakfast from one of the couples who led the Travelers Group. As breakfast got underway, Harry shared the story of this conflict from his perspective. As he finished, his wife, Jane, pulled out a manila envelope from her purse and held it over the table, offering it to me. It was the petition with all the signatures.

"I want you to see all the people who signed this petition," Harry invited.

"I don't want it," I replied, continuing to eat my eggs.

"Really . . . we want you to have it." The envelope dangled over my toast.

"I don't want it." I was calm yet assertive.

"It's OK. We *really* want you to have it."

Putting my fork down and looking at both of them, I replied, "How about this. How about I tell you why you felt the need to start a petition, and if I'm right, you drop this whole thing and we see what God wants to do to heal this church."

Pulling the envelope back reluctantly, Jane said hesitantly, "OK . . ."

I summarized what I understood of the conflict as they had described it, letting them know that I had heard their concerns. I then said, "When you felt that no one in leadership was listening to your concerns, that no one was doing anything about the issues that were important to you, you tried to get their attention by involving more people, applying more pressure to be heard. The petition was an escalation of a lot of frustration that came from not being heard. And yet it seemed like your attempt was rejected by board members." And then I added, "How am I doing? Am I understanding correctly?"

"Yes . . . ," said Harry, eyeing me rather strangely.

"I don't believe in petitions in church settings. In fact, you won't need a petition to be heard. I *will* hear you. I am a pastor who listens. You need to know that there may be times when I may not agree with you . . . and times when you may not agree with me. I hope that we will be able to respect each other in those times.

Regardless, I will always listen to you. I will hear what's important to you. Would you be willing to do the same?"

On Being Subversive

Matthew 6:33 says, "But strive first for the kingdom of God and his righteousness, and all these things will be given to you as well." Though they are captured in the Sermon on the Mount, often seen as one of the most pastoral and comforting interactions between Jesus and the common people, I find these words of Jesus to actually be some of his most subversive. Clearly, these words are subversive not only politically (i.e., with regard to the Roman Empire) and religiously (such as to some of the sects of Judaism of his day) but also personally (to each of us who allows his words to define the mission given to us). Politically, Jesus reframes the believer's loyalty toward a different type of citizenship within the domain of God: the Lord of lords has a different playbook and uses a different language to shape his people and their neighborhoods. Religiously, Jesus refocuses the crowd on an entirely different liturgy—giving voice to their oppression, their hopes, their needs, their worries—and portraying a God who hears, cares, sees, knows, and has responded incarnationally. Personally, Jesus upends the idols we have used to define our priorities, challenging the lies that have long convinced us that we are what life is all about.

I would assert that Jesus's words in Matthew 6:33 are intended not to comfort us, but rather to call us to repentance, to a new way of life rooted in the mission God had for Matthew's readers—and for us. This same Jesus began his ministry with an invitation-command: "The time is fulfilled, and the kingdom of God has come near; repent, and believe in the good news" (Mark 1:15). I hear "strive *first*" as a subversive challenge to the listener to turn away from a life of self-focused sin and toward the very mission that gives life. "Christianity is a relationship with Jesus the Christ," Leonard Sweet and Frank Viola write. "When things go wrong, it's not because we don't understand certain doctrines or fail to follow particular commands. It's because we have lost our 'first love'—or never had it in the first place."[3] The integration of the Great Commission in Matthew 28 and the Great Command-ment of John 13—what I call throughout this book the "divine mission"—must be *first*. God's righteousness—God's way of self-giving love—must be first. This divine mission of God must be the way of life for each one who chooses to follow Jesus.

In Matthew 18:15–17, one of the Bible passages most often used to establish both boundaries and grievance processes within congregations and other ministry settings, Jesus seems to be laying out an appropriate plan for how his followers are to address offenses (conflict) within the family of God ("If another mem-ber of the church sins against you . . . ," v. 15). We start by going directly to the person who has committed the offense, and our goal is restoration of the offender back into the family ("If the member listens to you, you have regained that one," v. 15). If that plan doesn't work, we bring one or two other believers with us "so that every word may be confirmed by the evidence of two or three witnesses" (v. 16). At this level, the confrontation escalates into documentation, what I call "establishing a paper trail." But if the offender still refuses to listen, the church is to be involved (v. 17); if that is unsuccessful, the offender is to be treated as "a Gentile and a tax collector" (v. 17)—namely, removed from the fellowship and open for reevangelization.

Yet, for biblical integrity, Matthew 18:15–17 must be seen within the framework of all of Matthew 18, or it may be misunder-stood,[4] misappropriated,[5] or even abused.[6] Verse 1 establishes the setting for conflict when Jesus's own disciples confront and then fail at a principle Jesus has been teaching them for two-plus years. They ask among themselves, "Who is the greatest in the kingdom of heaven?" (v. 1). By asking this question, they are illustrating that they are not yet ready for the world-transforming mission for which they are being apprenticed.[7] While God's long-awaited plan indeed is at hand, it is not yet residing in them.

So Jesus brings a child into their circle and proceeds to invert their thinking. In the New Community—the gathering of those who identify with Christ—we come with innocent expectations, we share toys, we share power, we enjoy the moment, we play together. By his action, Jesus issues a paradoxical lesson: "Truly I tell you, unless you change and become like children, you will never enter the kingdom of heaven. Whoever becomes humble like this child is the greatest in the kingdom of heaven" (Matt 18:3–4). Human values and behaviors are inverted in this discipleship-minded movement, setting the stage for how followers of Jesus are to treat each other especially in times of offense. Humility, selfless love, forgiveness, unmitigated grace—these are to be among the interpersonal assumptions for citizens in God's New Community.

In fact, responsibility for and mentoring of such values fall on those who should know better, those who have been on the journey with Jesus longer. "If any of you put a stumbling block before one of these little ones who believe in me," Jesus warns his disciples, "it would be better for you if a great millstone were fastened around your neck and you were drowned in the depth of the sea" (v. 6).[8] Don't miss the hyperbolic contrast. A lot is at stake. Those who would carry out the divine mission must remember who they are, why they're here, and where they're to lead the people. Whatever is in them—or among them—that gets in the way of their carrying out that mission must be sacrificed for the greater cause (vv. 8–9).

That mission, most significantly, includes going after those "sheep" who have "gone astray" (vv. 10–14). After all, God, who is "merciful and gracious, slow to anger and abounding in steadfast love and faithfulness" (Ps 86:15), is a God who champions the weak (Ps 82:3), the lost (Luke 19:10), the broken (Ps 34:18), the oppressed (Ps 103:6). This means that the broader context of Matthew 18 is not so much about how to mediate conflict, per se, but about how to reconcile with, reconnect with, or restore those who have strayed from the values, behaviors, and divine mission of the New Community.[9] Even amid disagreements, we must keep God's mission before us.

In other words, before we go off accusing our sister or brother of an offense (vv. 15–20), however justified it may be from our perspective, we better examine—through the sieve of self-giving love within the context of who we are and why we're here—our own lives, our own motives, and our own sinful choices until we discover that at the foot of the cross of Christ, we stand in as much need of grace as the one who offended us.[10] Then our motive within confrontation becomes *first* one of reconciliation and restoration (as opposed to discipline and excommunication) for the sake of our witness to the world. God's mission must trump even our own offenses.

Finally, in an effort to understand this inverted teaching, Peter asks, "Lord, if another member of the church sins against me, how often should I forgive? As many as seven times?" (v. 21).[11] In response, Jesus tells a story about a servant who refuses to forgive another despite the astronomical amount he himself has been forgiven (vv. 23–34). With the king's memorable concluding line—"Should you not have had mercy on your fellow slave, as I had mercy on you?"—Jesus's mandate to forgive is established. And the penalty for ignoring or violating it is significant: "So my heavenly Father will also do to every one of you, if you do not forgive your brother or sister from your heart" (v. 35).

Matthew 18 also must be read through the filter of Matthew 6:33: "Seek first the kingdom of God" (NKJV). God's mission must be first. God's Great Commandment, lived out within God's Great Commission, must be the way of life of the disciple. God's mission must be more important than anything else for the ones who identify as followers of Jesus Christ. If, in fact, the divine mission is the primary work of the church, then the body of Christ must subject itself ultimately to the values and sanctifying qualities that define life as citizens of that movement. Every fight among Christian brothers and sisters, therefore, has an impact not only on those personally involved but also on the entire community of faith connected to them. In her article "Forgiveness and Life in Community," New Testament scholar Susan Hylen posits that the parable of the unforgiving servant in Matthew 18:21–35 actually stresses the importance of community within the exercising and failures of interpersonal forgiveness. It is the community rather than the individual, she feels, that holds the power to bind or loose within the praxis of accountable forgiveness.[12]

Every act of offense and every response of forgiveness (or the withholding of forgiveness), therefore, has ecclesiological and missiological ramifications: when Christians fight with one another, the church as a whole is implicated, as is its mission in the world.[13] Through his subversive strategy of self-giving love, Jesus has come to set people free, and he has called his followers to do the same.

So how does the church engage in these subversive strategies of Jesus when it comes to our congregational conflicts? We need to reorient our view of conflict as a context for both personal and corporate growth as we engage in God's mission.

To start, we need a working definition of *conflict*.

Defining Conflict

Some treat conflict as "what happens when things are opposed—when different interests, claims, preferences, beliefs, feelings, values, ideas, or truths collide."[14] Others define conflict as incompatibility, a "lack of fit . . . between two or more people, ideas, feelings, or things"[15] or "a felt struggle between two or more interdependent individuals over perceived incompatible differences in beliefs, values, and goals, or over differences in desires for esteem, control, and connectedness."[16] What these various perspectives have in common is simply the understanding that conflict is a clash between opposing forces.

Here I get to apply my high school physics lesson on Sir Isaac Newton's third law! This law—"For every action, there is an equal and opposite reaction"—articulates well the interactions between "opposing forces" in personal relationships. Newton's law states that the "size of the force on the first object *equals* the size of the force on the second object . . . [and] the direction of the force on the first object is *opposite* to the direction of the force on the second object. Forces always come in pairs—equal and opposite action-reaction force pairs."[17] For our purposes, what this basically means is that in every conflict situation, there are action and reaction forces that oppose each other.

Perhaps the most enduring (and most simply stated) definition of conflict, for me, is the one originally offered by Speed Leas and Paul Kittlaus in their book *Church Fights: Managing Conflict in the Local Church*: "Conflict happens when two pieces of matter try to occupy the same space at the same time."[18] Over the years, I have chosen to modify this definition ever so slightly to bring, in my opinion, a less clinical, more relational slant to it: "Conflict happens when two *bodies* of matter try to occupy the same space at the same time."

As was modeled for me in my own training, when I teach this definition in workshops, I typically engage the services of a volunteer—especially one who is much taller or broader than I. I position myself on a "spot" on the floor, and I say to the volunteer, "I'm standing on this spot. You want to be on this spot. What are some ways you might go about trying to obtain access to my spot?"

Interestingly, nine times out of ten, the very first response is "I can push you off," spoken as they demonstrate. (Why the first response among Christians is one of violence requires additional research . . . and perhaps therapy!) Other ideas begin to emerge, each one demonstrated for the visual learner: "I can . . ."

- ask you to move,
- bribe you,
- make you feel guilty for standing there,
- distract you with an emergency,
- distract you with something else,
- lure you off with cookies,
- shame you by pointing out how you're always the one who gets the special spots,

- intimidate you (demonstrated by the tall person towering over me), or
- stand really close to you to make you spatially uncomfortable.

As the volunteer's brainstorming begins to fade, others in the group start participating, adding a few more creative measures for supplanting me, such as "I can pretend you're not there and just take over the spot." To demonstrate, I invite the volunteer to stand in front of me, turn her back to me so that she is facing the group, back up, and step on my toes, without acknowledging me. I then ask the group, "Metaphorically speaking, does this ever happen in the church? Do any of these options happen in the church?" The response is universally affirmative.

After a while, someone in the group will say, "Why can't I just tell you why that spot is important to me?" That moment is holy; there's usually a pause that is pregnant with awareness of the profound simplicity of the question's truth. "Why can't I just tell you *why* . . ."

Everyday versus Missional Conflicts in Churches

Now think of my preferred definition of conflict (two bodies of matter trying to occupy the same space at the same time) as well as the implications of Newton's third law. In conflict situations, action-reaction forces result from the interactions of people, ideas, beliefs, values, needs, spatial frames, emotions, or desires trying to occupy the same space at the same time. Have you ever seen this definition of conflict at work in your congregation?

Since the congregation is a relational hotbed of these inter-actions, conflict can be expected. In fact, in every church I've served and every church with which I've consulted, conflict has been a staple of life. For example, some of the most typical church conflicts seem to revolve around issues like the expectations of the pastor not being met, confusion as to who has "authority" or "control" over the parsonage, how longtime member Tilda is upset (again) that the ladies' sewing circle had to give up their room for the youth group's fundraiser, how the leadership style of the new pastor is not what the congregation is used to, how the chairperson of the trustees doesn't think red is the best color for the carpet in the main auditorium and is now threatening to leave the church unless she gets her favorite color, and those involving money—too little or too much—that end up consuming the pastor's emotional energy.

Yet, if we're honest, none of these issues really engages a congregation on the life-giving adventure that the gospel of Jesus Christ was meant to inspire.

Yet there are conflicts that might. Consider the following examples.

SOMEONE UPSETS A "SACRED COW"

In order to accommodate a growing children's ministry that wanted to do creative things in worship on Sunday mornings, as well as in their dynamic weekday children's outreach ministry, the leaders of a church I served some years ago decided to remove the Communion prayer rail that circled the chancel and then to expand the chancel platform. For years, we had heard complaints from brides and grooms who found it awkward to maneuver around the rail during their processionals and recessionals and from families that had to navigate awkwardly around it to get to the baptismal font when their children were being baptized. The proposed design would accommodate for all of those needs as well. After months of discussion, planning, sharing, and promoting, the renovations began.

Soon into the renovations, a very concerned longtime member came to me and told me how upset he was that we were taking down "the prayer rail." He shared with me stories of all the people who had been married at this rail, all of the funerals and decisions for Christ that had taken place there . . . and all of the people who had prayed at this rail. "Where, pastor?" he asked. "Where will people pray now?"

SOMEONE UPSETS THE MATRIARCH OR PATRIARCH

My first summer at Second Street Church, I experienced their annual all-church picnic. I had been the pastor there for only about two months, so I was still getting to know people's names and backgrounds. As I meandered through the park where the picnic was being held, I randomly started conversations with people. I saw an elderly woman sitting off by herself at a picnic table underneath one of the pavilions, so I went over to her, sat down, and began to chat. Mary was a widow, and the church had always been her and her husband's main focus in their life together. Historically, she had held many positions of leadership, though presently, she was not on any committee.

As she and I chatted under the pavilion, George, the chairperson of the trustees, and his family walked by. I had been in two meetings with George up to this point and was really impressed with his leadership skills. Interrupting the topic at hand, Mary interjected, "That guy there—he should not be in leadership."

"George?" I asked. "How come?"

"He's not been a member of this church very long. He should not be in leadership."

"How long has he been a member here?"

"Only twenty years," she replied.

I thought she was joking, so I chuckled, and then I realized she was quite serious. Intrigued, I then asked her, "Twenty *years*? I know I'm new here, so maybe you can help me understand something. Exactly how long does someone need to be a member of the church before they're allowed to be a leader?"

She looked at me as if sizing me up. Then she changed the subject. I decided right then that I was going to start adding younger and newer church members to positions of leadership. Within three years, I had successfully discipled and repositioned people, gradually realigning the leadership infrastructure. Mary was not happy and made it known in various circles. Even though she was not in a position of leadership, she had influence as a church matriarch, and she used that influence to try to garner control. Sadly for her, the people who were placed into leadership developed a strong sense of team. Frustrated at the loss of her influence, she started attending a nearby church instead.

WHEN DIVERSITY IS NOT SO DIVERSE

One church with which I consulted was experiencing their very first female pastor—an intentional decision on the part of the assigning bishop based on both demographic and philosophical parameters. On the surface, most of the parishioners seemed to be OK with their new clergyperson, but changes in attendance patterns and a significant drop in financial offerings made it apparent that something was not quite right. Four months into her tenure, Pastor Nancy was confronted by the long-tenured lay leader—a male—who, in no uncertain terms, made it clear that their failing congregational health was a direct result of her "living in disobedience" to God's word: "Women, after all," he said, "should not be pastors."

The issues connected to women in leadership—either clergy or lay—join the deeply embedded biases related to race in challenging both our theological underpinnings and how we love those who are different from us.[19] A church member in one congregation that had just dismissed its "ineffective" pastor said to me, "They better not send us a pastor who is Black . . . or a woman either! If they do, I'm out of here!" Racism and gender biases, each worthy of their own books on conflict, are at the root of many congregational disputes, although for many, such issues are not always explicit.

Additionally, intentional cross-cultural pastoral hires, cross-cultural church plants, types of other cross-racial or cross-cultural transitions in churches and communities, or sharing of worship facilities with cross-racial or cross-cultural faith communities can create contexts for conflict.[20] A once vibrant, primarily Caucasian Episcopal congregation, presently struggling for sustainable financial resources to maintain their minimally used three-hundred-seat auditorium, decided to rent out their sanctuary to an Ethiopian congregation on Sunday afternoons. Tension in the arrangement arose when some of the members of the vestry became upset that "those people" were "leaving their songbooks and drums in our altar area." Communities, indeed, are often far less diverse than they think they are.

WORSHIP WARS

Finally, of course, there are also worship wars. When I was appointed back in 2016 to the church I currently serve, the main presenting issue that was shared with me was that this church had "great potential . . . if it would only get over its twenty-plus-year battle over worship styles." Arriving, I discovered that they had two noticeably distinct sanctuaries—one for traditional worship with an organ, a pulpit, a lectern, a chancel choir loft, paraments, and pews and the other with a stage, keyboards, drums, guitars, atmospheric lighting, and video projection screens. There were people in each service who did not interact well with those who attended the other service. Past hurts, judgments, entitlements, jealousies, and personalities from up to twenty years prior had created ongoing division between them, causing a significant breakdown in their sense of unity. Stories of animosity and hurt were shared with me from both sides, along with a yearning from others for a more peaceful interaction. The conflict was at a stalemate. Mediation had already been tried, unsuccessfully. A different strategy—and mission—would be necessary.

When Conflict Is Useful

What if we take the matter of conflict one step further?

Sometimes friction can be a good thing. The action-reaction process of conflict actually may help generate the sufficient energy to produce essential growth—if we navigate through it with good conflict leadership skills. Some examples of when conflict might be essential include the following:

- to catalyze (bring about) change in the status quo
- to develop a positive, unified direction
- to expose or remove "power hoarders"
- to expose unhealthy patterns or vulnerabilities
- to clarify values, identities, or boundaries
- to grow deeper in relationships
- to break through impasses in communication
- to grow in holiness and dependence on God

If we are too quick to resolve conflict in our pursuit of peace and harmony, we may end up sabotaging the very forces that will assist in what God is trying to birth in the congregation. In fact, according to conflict mediation expert Mark Gerzon, when a conflict arises, our very first response really needs to be to do nothing.[21]

Within the context of discipleship, I contend that growth requires conflict—provided that the conflict is processed well. We need conflict. This side of heaven, it is one of the primary forces that pushes against complacency, and discipleship does not occur without God smashing our idols of self-worship. Learning to recognize those moments when new birth is preceded by labor pains, as well as when to harness those forces toward their transformative end, is the key.

It Starts with Leadership

Setting aside the "normal" clashes of personalities and familial positional games[22] (each of which has a role to play in a systems approach to conflict leadership, by the way), I find that most conflicts in congregations come from two main sources: (1) Christians forget who they are, why they're here, and where they're going, and (2) leaders retreat in the face of anxiety—their own as well as that of their followers.[23]

Our divine mission must be the priority. It's our job as the church of Jesus Christ. When we take our eyes off our primary purpose, we drift off course, behaving as if the church is all about us.

We have probably all heard these or similar laments:

- "Pastor, you didn't visit me when I was in the hospital!"
- "Do we have to serve Communion by intinction? What about germs when fingers go into the grape juice?"
- "Why are we giving money to missionaries when we need those resources for our own church?"
- "Pastor, you don't need to keep telling us what to do with the visitor info cards at the start of worship; those of us here every week have all heard you and know what to do with them."
- "How come we don't sing any of the songs I like?"
- "Contemporary music is evil; we need to worship the way Jesus did . . . with the organ!"
- "Pastor, you should be in your office and available for us when we call, not out in the community!"

The book of Acts and the letters of Paul, Peter, James, and John illustrate the amount of energy that must be exerted in the church to keep it from going off course from its intended mission. Inevitably, without consistent course corrections, we human beings will pull the organization and mission of the church toward ourselves. I would argue that this is one of the main reasons mainline denominations seem to be on a trajectory toward extinction: we have allowed the Great Commission and the Great Commandment to become supplanted by spiritual-sounding personal agendas.[24] The human race has way too much practice doing so. We must keep the divine mission at the forefront, however, intentionally bringing it before the congregation—both in teaching and in testimony—*every week*. Otherwise, we will forget who we are, why we're here, and where we're called to lead God's people.

Those whose job it is to bring that mission forward each week are the leaders—both clergy and lay. Therein lies the second problem: leaders who retreat in the face of reactive anxiety—their own as well as that of their parishioners. Rabbi Edwin Friedman argues that the "heart of the problem" affecting leadership today is "a regressive trend . . . where the most dependent members of any organization set the agendas and where adaptation is constantly toward weakness rather than strength . . . thereby leveraging power to the recalcitrant, the passive-aggressive, and the most anxious."[25] Friedman believes that this "failure of nerve" on the part of the leader inadvertently sets the stage within the organization for chronic sabotage of anything that promotes movement beyond status quo, regardless of how the organization complains about its own condition. He says, "There's a widespread misunderstanding of relational destructive processes . . . that leads leaders to assume that toxic forces can be regulated through reasonableness, love, insight, role-modeling, giving of values, and striving for consensus; rather than setting limits to the invasiveness of those who lack self-regulation."[26]

Often, good leaders with great methods for discipleship enter our pulpits only to discover that the powerful forces of the status quo are comprehensive, seemingly self-renewing and interminable, and impressively unyielding. And these leaders eventually give up, often surrendering to the pains of isolation, trauma to their family, and burnout.

I've been there.

But here's the thing. The presence of conflict within our congregations may actually be a sign that leaders are doing the right thing.[27] Perhaps what is needed to reengage the congregation in pursuit of its divine mission is a leader who is able to stir up healthy conflict—by virtue of mission and vision—and then stand nonanxiously in the midst of the storm while the system works itself out.[28]

Within the framework of missional leadership, might conflict actually be *prescribed* for the overall health of the congregation? Would knowing the typical progression of conflict actually help pastors and other leaders remain nonanxiously present long enough to foster the conflict's benefits?

A Rhythm of Growth and Transformation

Many organizational theorists posit their own understandings of how conflicts develop and then progress.[29] Many of these researchers argue that the severity of conflict can be tracked through progressive "stages." They suggest that we can determine interventional strategies based on how emotionally reactive the participants are at each stage of the conflict, as well as whether the conflict, in fact, *can* be mediated within those stages. They all make solid points.

I have found, however, that a set cyclical design does not best accommodate the unpredictable patterns of behavior that occur when people are in an emotional crisis. Every person has a story and therefore reacts uniquely to any given stressor. In fact, people seem overly reactive to offense in today's society.[30] The social and ethical parameters of what some have called the culture's moralistic therapeutic deism[31] make personal experience, personal happiness, and personal entitlements the focus of many a conflict, making hyperreactivity normative. Additionally, I don't believe a one-size-fits-all model accommodates for ethnic and cultural diversity. Specifically, cultural or social patterns or traditions may not necessarily fit neatly into such a model's linear process.[32]

But what if resolving conflict is not the primary goal? What if conflict is actually an essential part in the natural growth and spiritual development of the congregation?

Within such a framework, I have found the "developmental sequence" model presented by social psychologists Bruce W. Tuckman and Mary Ann Jensen most helpful.

In their model, Tuckman and Jensen argue that groups progress in their development through five specific phases: forming, storming, norming, performing, and adjourning.[33]

Over the years, I have used these developmental sequences to assist groups and entire congregations in navigating "turnaround" strategies, as well as the struggles that accompany those strategies. When I coach younger clergy, Tuckman and Jensen's model is my go-to tool. I find it normalizes conflict within a natural developmental process of growth, relationally and spiritually, and supports a pattern that has predictive benefits for conflict leadership, ultimately lowering the pastor-leader's own anxiety.

Tuckman and Jensen's sequential model begins with *forming*. It is the season of "testing and dependence"—a time when group members try out the group, learn the expected behaviors and boundaries of group life, and test which of those group rules can be pushed against. It is the defining phase of group life, where relational connections are formed and group members begin to discern affinities.

Tuckman and Jensen's second developmental sequence is *storming*. It describes what they call "intragroup conflict." Now that the group members have developed their affinities, cooperatives, and partnerships, some will likely become hostile toward one another and their leader as a way of "expressing their individuality and resisting the formation of group structure."[34]

The third sequence in Tuckman and Jensen's model is *norming*. It is the development of "group cohesion." In this phase, the group members accept each other along with their respective unique qualities; they become a "family" or "team." There is synergy around the defining parameters of the group's identity, parameters that the group participates in establishing or refining. Culture is established, and participants begin to buy into the cultural norms that characterize groupthink.

The fourth developmental sequence is *performing*. It describes "functional role relatedness." The group is now ready to become a problem-solving task force—where people function within delegated roles, interweaving their unique giftedness and skills for the common good of the group's goals. The emphasis in this phase is on solutions and constructive action, and group members discover synergy as they work toward that common goal.

The final sequence in Tuckman and Jensen's model is *adjourning*.[35] This is the phase of endings and new beginnings. It is the time when the group deals with the seasons of anxiety about

separation and termination and reflects on the pending adjustments related to the loss of members or the ending of the group
as a whole. Adjourning is about transition and evaluation. Done
well, adjourning gives birth to the next *forming* stage.

Tuckman and Jensen's model is predicated on the observations that groups develop sequentially. Conflict, therefore, is
predictable—and necessary—within group (congregational) life
in order to advance group cohesion and dynamic performance
(mission).

From a discipleship-mission perspective, those who lead
groups that are in conflict seek to harness the emotional energy
of that conflict and reframe it within the spiritual formation of
the congregation. Peggy Reynoso, a missionary with Navigators
World Missions, writes, "Spiritual formation often occurs in the
refining crucible of suffering. Our inmost selves are revealed
in affliction, and as we learn to commit ourselves more deeply
to the redemptive purposes of God, we grow in our capacity to
exercise faith, hope, and love in the midst of troubles and trials.
God uses adversity to shape our souls—and thus to spread the
aroma of Christ."[36]

With this in mind, conflict can be seen as a context for discipleship, providing the essential impetus for getting the congregation to engage or reengage the divine mission—in spite of
how painful conflict may be.

And it's the job of the leader to shepherd them toward that end.

CHAPTER THREE
Where We're Going

Do not think that I have come to bring peace to the earth; I have not come to bring peace, but a sword. For I have come to set a man against his father, and a daughter against her mother, and a daughter-in-law against her mother-in-law; and one's foes will be members of one's own household.

—Matthew 10:34-36

EARLIER I MENTIONED NEWTON'S THIRD LAW, WHICH I LEARNED IN high school physics, and its application to conflict situations. There is another fundamental principle in physics that I find applies to both discipleship and change dynamics in the context of congregational ministry. It's called the law of inertia, and it is Newton's first law of motion. Formally, the law of inertia states, "An object at rest stays at rest and an object in motion stays in motion with the same speed and in the same direction unless acted upon by an unbalanced force."[1] In its most basic form, it is often framed as follows: "All objects resist changes in their state of motion—they tend to keep doing what they're doing . . . unless acted upon by an unbalanced force."[2]

A lot can be said about how this principle applies to the church: resistance to change, homeostatic paralysis, "unbalanced" pastors! It certainly is easy to understand how a congregation's growth, both spiritually and numerically, can be predicated on its willingness—or unwillingness—to engage a process of motion.

Indeed, the gospel of Jesus Christ creates a *movement* of the Holy Spirit. The Spirit transforms, and transformation causes a shift in the status quo.

At its beginning, the church had that spiritual fervor. Then something happened. We settled.

In my fifth year at one of the churches I served, the leadership gathered in a circle of chairs in the fellowship hall. We had just begun the initial phases of our first ministry audit under the direction of church consultant Bill Easum. While we engaged the material of the audit, I noticed that several of our leaders kept pushing back against the discussion, seemingly resistant but not overtly challenging. Up to that point, the church had been growing steadily in worship attendance, and we were needing to address specific changes in order to accommodate the growth. As the senior pastor led the group discussion around those changes, there was obvious silence coming from one side of the room. I finally looked at one of the leaders and said, curiously, "I'm noticing your silence . . . and the silence on the part of others in the room as we talk about these issues. What's going on? What are you thinking?"

The leader seemed hesitant to speak but finally said, "I'm just unsure about all these changes. I'm not sure we should be doing them."

Having known this man for several years and known him to be a solid person of faith and a humble leader, I knew that something was bothering him to make him withdraw like this. So I asked, "Can I ask you a question? Do you *want* our church to grow?"

I was young back then. I probably could have asked it in a better fashion. As soon as it was out of my mouth, I wondered even if I was being disrespectful. The long, thoughtful silence awaiting a response didn't help.

"No," finally came the reply. "I don't. At least not yet. I think we need to grow spiritually ourselves before we grow numerically."

His stating it out loud actually allowed us to acknowledge some of the uncertainty that was packaged underneath the group's

silence: "What are some of the things that scare us about growing? What do we think we will have to give up or take on if more
people start to attend here?" These questions, plus many others,
became important discussion points that night and many other
nights as we talked out our hopes and fears.

Naming those fears also had the effect of engaging all of us in
the discernment process. To their credit, just about all of those
leaders became highly involved with the next phases of implementing our plans—and many of them are still very active in leadership roles to this day. On the congregational level, however, the
ministry audit and its subsequent strategic initiatives raised
the anxiety—and ire—of quite a few people. In congregational
meetings, there were impassioned pleas to not change "the small-
church feel of the congregation" (at that point we had a worship
attendance of about four hundred!), to not grow so big that "we
no longer know everyone." Quite a few families left the church as
we implemented those strategic changes.

Yet many, many more people started to attend. Over the course
of the next ten years (and two more Easum audits), we grew
to around two thousand in worship.

And with that growth came a boatload of conflict.

Resistance, Rebellion, or Movement?

From my experiences in ministry over the years, I've come to
the conclusion that if you are a genuine leader and you have been
called by God to the ministry of the gospel of Jesus Christ, sooner
or later your leadership, and the gospel's message, will *cause* conflict in the church.[3] As stated in the previous chapter, the message
of Jesus was—and is—subversive.

Actually, I contend that Jesus *necessarily* causes division (see,
e.g., Matt 10:34–36). The good news of Jesus Christ is setting
people free from that which has held them in bondage, and the
powers that be, both natural and spiritual, are trying to sabotage
it.[4] In fact, there are people in churches all over the world who

are seeking to preserve the status quo of their congregations, thinking that they are leading a movement that's "for the best interests of the church." Most, in my opinion, are only leading a rebellion against the divine mission in favor of personal interests.

Within my context of missional leadership, a movement develops when a group forms around a cohesive, life-expanding purpose that generates not only impassioned adherents and sustainable resources but also a multiplication of leaders who are able to articulate and reproduce the group's mission for the next generation of participants. Specifically, within arenas of Christian ministry, movements

- are established around the divine mission (in other words, the mandate to live out the Great Commission and the Great Commandment), which they take very seriously;
- have strategic leadership that takes risks in reaching the group's stated mission;
- inspire sacrificial commitment to the missional cause, thereby generating sustainable resources;
- operate within a framework of shared values that shape their vision of hope in a better future; and
- reproduce themselves by multiplying and developing next-level leaders.

On the other hand, rebellion—or, to use a different word, resistance—arises when a group of people comes together in *reaction* to something going on in an organization. A rebellion is not a *genuine* movement. People are reacting to something with which they disagree or within which they feel constrained. A genuine movement takes people out of their status quo and on toward a new destination. While it certainly destabilizes the status quo, a rebellion or resistance actually is an emotional, or psychodynamic, reaction to someone else's agenda.[5]

A rebellion, or resistance, certainly can *become* a movement. It can shape itself around a collective value system and shared goals, which, under the direction of a cohesive mission (purpose) and appropriate, self-defined leadership, can influence a shift in the status quo of the organization, altering its trajectory.[6] Yet by itself, it is born as a reaction to someone or something else. It emerges through the choice of some to stand apart from the established parameters of the organization and operate independently. Its purpose, therefore, originates from within someone else's priorities—whether good or bad, positive or negative.[7]

In my experience, many conflicts in churches are really born out of people's reactions to change and transition—perhaps, most poignantly, when those transitions are strategic initiatives meant to realign the church toward its divine mission.[8] From the seemingly benign to the most controversial, conflicts emerge when two bodies of matter try to occupy the same space at the same time. A leader initiates a change in the status quo, and suddenly the cries of "We've never done it that way before" or "All Pastor Joe wants to do is make us into one of those megachurches" or "We don't agree with this or that theological framework" or "She's certainly not our beloved Pastor George" begin to reign in the minds of those who are against the proposed way of doing things.

While working with people in volunteer organizations such as churches often comes with battles of personality and will, most of us pastors imagined ourselves as helping advance the Great Commission rather than being drawn into seemingly interminable discussions on whether it's appropriate to use rye bread for Communion, whether drums are acceptable in the sanctuary, or if Brother John's new potato salad recipe is going to be allowed to displace the thirty-year tradition of using Sister Sarah's Amish recipe at the annual congregational meeting.

Yet leaders lead. And by nature of their leadership, they stir up conflict when they ask people to give up where they are and what they have for a mission that is greater than themselves.[9] As leadership consultant Reggie McNeal puts it, "Kingdom leaders agitate by fomenting dissatisfaction with the status quo."[10]

Shepherds lead sheep to where they don't realize that they need to go. Sometimes sheep rebel.

In the language of discipleship, without conflict, there can be no growth. The gospel message asks people to deny themselves, sacrifice their own agendas, and give their lives to a mission greater than themselves. Conflict can emerge on any of those platforms. The church desperately needs disciples who put first in their daily agenda the spiritual movement of God's mission. There is nothing more important.

What sets a congregational movement apart from rebellions, resistances, and other types of reactions? As a movement built around following Christ and carrying out his mission, the church inspires a resurrection-empowered hope, a passion to set people free from that which imprisons them, a willingness to transcend personal loss, and life-altering fruit that multiplies the movement.

A Discipleship-Focused, Mission-Mandated Movement

The apostle Paul understood the nature of conflict within the arena of church life. He saw almost every one of the conflicts about which he wrote as an avenue of discipleship and growth in Christ—certainly for the individual believers, but most especially for the church as a whole. In fact, nothing was more important to Paul than carrying out the mission of the New Community movement. Writing to the believers in the conflict-ridden Corinthian church, for example, Paul repeatedly emphasized the nature of that movement and the sacrifices required for partnering with the Holy Spirit in carrying it out:

> But we have this treasure in clay jars, so that it may be made clear that this extraordinary power belongs to God and does not come from us. We are afflicted in every way, but not crushed; perplexed, but not driven to despair; persecuted, but not forsaken; struck down, but not destroyed; always

carrying in the body the death of Jesus, so that the life of Jesus may also be made visible in our bodies. For while we live, we are always being given up to death for Jesus' sake, so that the life of Jesus may be made visible in our mortal flesh. So death is at work in us, but life in you. (2 Cor 4:7–12)

Beyond its organizational infrastructure, what sets a discipleship-focused movement apart from its reactionary cousin is, first of all, its leader's goal of cultivating Christ-centered hope in the congregation and, through the congregation, in the community.[11]

In anticipation of his visit to the church in Rome, Paul sends them a letter laying out the full scope of the gospel message. After methodically destroying any sense of personal hope of salvation wrought by virtue of being particularly moral (Rom 2:1–16), being Jewish (Rom 2:17–3:8), or indeed being human (Rom 3:9–20), Paul unleashes his climax: no one is deserving of salvation—not one; all people deserve death as a penalty for their identity in sin, all people stand in need of God's grace, and the only one who can save humanity is God, which God has done via the crucified and risen Jesus Christ (Rom 3:23–26). In the course of this explanation, Paul presents a grand mosaic that will define soteriology, ecclesiology, eschatology, and missiology for the church for generations to come. It is a plan rooted in a new kind of hope. In Romans 5:1–5, Paul writes, "Therefore, since we are justified by faith, we have peace with God through our Lord Jesus Christ, through whom we have obtained access to this grace in which we stand; and we boast in our hope of sharing the glory of God. And not only that, but we also boast in our sufferings, knowing that suffering produces endurance, and endurance produces character, and character produces hope, and hope does not disappoint us, because God's love has been poured into our hearts through the Holy Spirit that has been given to us."

This new "hope of sharing the glory of God" is what redefines the future for the follower of Jesus. That hope beckons the believer

forward through sufferings, through challenges, through persecutions, through hardships, in a movement empowered and
directed by God's Holy Spirit.

As followers of Jesus, as leaders for his movement, we are
first and foremost to be purveyors of hope. Without hope, without a vision of a future purchased by that hope, we simply stand
in resistance or rebellion to anything that threatens our present identity.[12] With that hope, however, we shepherd God's flock
to greener pastures and places of justice, genuine reconciliation, and peace, and we do so inspired by the resurrection of
Jesus Christ and its promise for all who are called by his name
(John 17:24).[13]

The problem with rebellions and resistances is that because
their leaders lack an inspired mission of their own, they succeed solely in colluding with people's pain and engendering
anger, despair, resentment, and reactionary unity—not hope.
One might push back and ask, "Well, isn't there hope in naming one's pain, in pushing against those who cause that pain?"
My response would be this: within the theological framework of
conflict leadership outlined in this book, only when a therapeutic intervention moves people toward their redemptive purpose
within the agenda of God's mission does naming our pain produce
the hope Paul talks about in Romans 5. When it is done simply to
justify our own sense of violation or entitlement, however trend-
ing that is within our culture, I contend that it only serves to
reinforce a person's enmeshment to their brokenness. God does
not call us to the *appearance* of freedom; God calls us to be "free
indeed" (John 8:36).

Hope gets people moving. Henri Nouwen, in his classic book
The Wounded Healer: Ministry in Contemporary Society, writes,
"Christian leaders are not leaders because they announce a new
idea and try to convince others of its worth. They are leaders
because they face the world with eyes full of expectation, and
with the expertise to take away the veil that covers its hidden
potential."[14]

Because we as leaders are purveyors of hope, our job is to "take away the veil that covers [the] hidden potential" of those who join us on God's mission. Within our leadership amid church conflicts, we must point people to both the cross of Christ and the resurrection event and bear witness, by our actions, that here and now we hold to the hope of the life yet to come.

A second quality of a movement made of disciples of Jesus is that its mission (purpose) is born out of a passion to set people free from that which imprisons them. This is critically important. Remember that while rebellion and resistance are reactions against something or against someone else's agenda, a genuine movement creates its own agenda. A discipleship- and mission-centered movement moves people toward the life that God intends—a life of freedom, hope, forgiveness, love, and grace and release to the captive, recovery of sight to the blind, freedom to the oppressed, and the proclamation of the Lord's favor (Luke 4:18–19).

Such a movement connects people to the grander mosaic of what God is doing in the world.[15] It asks great things of its followers. It asks us to live a life of self-sacrifice when it comes to our own wants for the sake of God's redemptive plan and purpose for humanity. It asks us to lead against the currents of social structure and uphold a value system that doesn't make logical sense in our culture's normal way of operating. It calls us to walk as Jesus walked, love as Jesus loved, value what Jesus valued, forgive when it doesn't seem to make sense to do so, offer grace to those who don't deserve it (though what is grace if not *undeserved* favor?), and by such actions, invite people into a life worth dying for. "Kingdom engagement," Reggie McNeal writes, "thrusts us into situations where abundant life is threatened, compromised, or missing, so that we can serve as advocates for the life that God intends for people to experience."[16] All of which is certain to cause some conflict.

In Mark 8, Jesus gathers his followers—both the crowd and the Twelve—and lays out for them the markers of true discipleship:

43

"If any want to become my followers, let them deny themselves and take up their cross and follow me. For those who want to save their life will lose it, and those who lose their life for my sake, and for the sake of the gospel, will save it" (vv. 34–35).

What exactly did Jesus mean when he said, "Let them deny themselves and take up their cross"? All the followers of Jesus needed to do was watch him.

In fact, a few verses earlier, Peter momentously proclaims Jesus to be the Messiah, to which Jesus responds by telling the Twelve that he "must undergo great suffering, and be rejected by the elders, the chief priests, and the scribes, and be killed, and after three days rise again" (Mark 8:31). As the leader of this divine-agenda'd movement, he was meant to embody both the hardship and the hope he expected his followers to experience.

Walking with his disciples, Jesus spoke "quite openly" about this, but Peter "took him aside and began to rebuke him" (Mark 8:32). Then, in an amazing moment within the account, Jesus turned, looked at his disciples, and rebuked Peter: "Get behind me, Satan!" he said. "For you are setting your mind not on divine things but on human things" (v. 33). Notice how Jesus's *follower* tries to shift the agenda of the divine movement Jesus himself was leading. While we may want to focus on the word *rebuke* here—the same word used again to describe how Jesus responded to Peter in verse 33—I'm drawn more to the body language of this exchange. First, Peter "took him aside" (v. 32). The word choice in Greek insinuates that Peter grabbed Jesus by the arm and pulled him away from the group in order to admonish him. What would make Peter do such a thing? Was he concerned that the other disciples would get scared by Jesus's words and want to leave? Was he upset that Jesus was not conforming to his expectations of the Messiah he just confessed? Was he himself scared of what Jesus's words meant for his own future?

Regardless, Jesus instead "turn[s]" away from Peter and toward the other disciples (v. 33). While gazing at the other eleven, he rebukes Peter. In order for Peter to take over leadership of the divine movement, he must first surrender his right to shape its direction and its consequences. Otherwise, he will convert the movement to a resistance or rebellion against Rome or against the Jewish leaders, just as Judas would eventually try to do. A movement that loses sight of and connection to the grander mosaic of God's mission will simply become yet another of the many reactionary phases of people working out their own stuff and calling it godly.[17]

A third quality of a discipleship-focused, mission-mandated movement is the willingness of its leader to transcend personal loss. More specifically, the leader must have the broad capacity to navigate their people through the grief that inevitably accompanies change to the status quo. Anyone can initiate change. A true movement leader serves as an ambassador for the redemptive work of God's love as it mediates the losses brought about by such change. The leader of such a movement bears the scars of one who has endured the cause of Christ—personally. Such a leader does not ask their followers to do anything that they have not done.[18]

For the past fifteen years, I have led by a particular axiom: *A catalyst produces change. Change produces transition. Transition produces loss. Loss produces conflict. Always.*[19]

A real issue in many church conflicts is that generally, people don't like pain. Or loss. Or grief. When we experience pain or loss or grief, the emotions of that experience imprint themselves on our memory.[20] Any time from then on, whenever a situation closely represents those emotions, we pull away, or we push back; we react—usually in an "equal and opposite" way. (Remember Newton's third law.) In fact, we may not actually resent the proposed change at all, but we resent the emotions we feel that are associated with the change. Therefore, the change is perceived as a harbinger of more pain, loss, or grief. So we resist.

The leader of a discipleship-focused, mission-mandated movement, therefore, must not only become solidly equipped with the skills of grief care but also respect—indeed, value—the people whose losses are deeply felt, are both tangibly and intangibly real, and are intrinsically appreciated as part of God's greater mosaic. After all, Jesus said, "Blessed are those who mourn, for they will be comforted" (Matt 5:4). In writing out of a postconfrontational experience with the Corinthian church, Paul also reminds us that we serve a God who is "the Father of compassion and the God of all comfort, who comforts us in all our troubles, so that we can comfort those in any trouble with the comfort we ourselves receive from God" (2 Cor 1:3–4 NIV).

But here's the thing. While a mission-minded leader compassionately understands and values the redemptive nature of people's pain, loss, and grief, they must definitively guide people through their grief toward the next phase of personal and corporate discipleship. This is the work of spiritual formation and of missional leadership.

In his preeminent book *Managing Transitions*, organizational consultant William Bridges instructs all leaders to ask a fundamental question prior to introducing significant changes to an organization's status quo: "Who stands to lose what?"[21] Whether we realize it or not, there is an emotional price to pay for any significant change a leader instigates. That emotional price is most intimately felt as grief.[22]

According to Bridges, the psychological processes of going through change cause people to react negatively. He calls those emotional processes "transitions."[23] Bridges's theory is that transitions have three phases: endings, neutral zones, and new beginnings,[24] and one cannot enter fully into a new beginning without going through an ending.[25] In order to move forward, one must leave where one is. For example, in order to embrace adulthood, I had to move out of my parents' home. In order to take up residence in Pennsylvania, I had to leave New Jersey. And indeed, in order for the church to which I belong to welcome new visitors to worship, I have to give up ownership of "my" pew.

Endings are an essential part of discipleship.[26] Endings, both realized and anticipated, cause us to feel grief at the prospect of losing what has been our "normal." Even if that "normal" was dysfunctional, it is what we have known; as such, it is a place of perceived security. Bridges refers to the Hebrew scriptures story of Moses and the exodus to illustrate the point.[27] In order for Moses to get the people of Israel out of Egypt, he had to convince them—using God's supernatural power of persuasion—that the slavery, pain, and death of their present captivity were infinitely worse than the fears and unknowns that lay before them (Exod 4:11–12; 4:29–31).

Then, once they had left Egypt, Moses had an entirely different challenge—how to get Egypt out of the people. Their wilderness journey, according to Bridges, became what he called their "neutral zone"—the next phase in their transition process.[28] They had been enslaved for centuries. It's what they knew; slavery was their "normal." Generation upon generation cried to God for freedom; children grew into adults whose grandchildren heard their prayers for deliverance. Then one day, God sent Moses as the deliverer. God answered the four-hundred-year-old multigenerational prayer, the people experienced genuine freedom for the first time, and their new identity apart from slavery scared them. They wanted to go back to Egypt and the "security" of slavery (Exod 14:11–14; 16:3; 17:3).

Before we judge them too harshly, we must recognize that we do the same thing.

We don't like loss. We hate anxiety. We try to manage it when it happens, but we resist pain on so many levels. We will even sabotage new beginnings (new pastors, new worship services, new styles of worship, new building campaigns) so as to bypass the perceived negative emotions of the grief and anxiety we anticipate. And we are good at making our resistance look spiritual—by justifying that our complaints are for the good of the church.[29]

Yet in order to live into the new beginnings of growth—both personally and corporately—we must traverse the ways of loss and grief and the anxiety and fear related to the transition. In fact, we cannot grow in discipleship—we cannot forgive, we cannot be forgiven, we cannot draw closer to God or to others, indeed we cannot engage fully the hope of eternal life—unless something in us dies. Every member of our congregations will face the hard choices of letting go of the old in order to live into the new (2 Cor 5:17). Every significant decision of leadership made to move the church on toward its divine mission will require both personal and corporate losses. Resurrection, after all, requires that there be a dead body to be raised. What's more, the resurrected body will necessarily be *different* from the one that died.

To accommodate that grief process, Bridges describes how to move through the neutral zone.[30] The neutral zone is that period between the ending and the new beginning when the anxieties of having left the familiar are at their peak.[31] Anxiety, of course, doesn't feel neutral. But this period is neutral in that it is the *in-between* phase of growth where we challenge our leaders, threaten our followers, sabotage our missions, abort our causes, all because our fear of what is about to emerge is greater than our fear of what we are being asked to leave behind. Or because we are so overly zealous for the new beginning that we consider the neutral zone a waste of time. Ironically, it's also the phase where the potential for creativity is at its highest, providing great opportunities for personal and corporate growth. Here, in the neutral zone, is where missional leadership—incarnational leadership, to be more specific—is most needed.

What Is Incarnational Leadership?

The gospel accounts tell us about a God who came to humanity *as* a human. God took the initiative, took on flesh, and "tabernacled" (John 1:14 TLV) with us. Jesus, the Son of God, the Lord of life, entered into a human body and into human culture. His words were spoken with a human mouth. His deeds were done with his own human hands. He laughed with people on the hillsides. He ate with those his social structures told him not to. He reached out to touch the untouchable. He hugged lepers. He danced at weddings.

He washed other people's feet. And he walked slowly through the crowds—ultimately leading to his own death as "a ransom for many" (Mark 10:45). And he asked his followers to do the same.

Incarnational leaders enter into wherever people are, whatever they are dealing with, to bring a message of hope and new life—and to move those people toward it.

While the concept of incarnational leadership is not new, I personally began to explore it in two distinct ways while in seminary. First, needing to take a theology course, I decided on one that focused exclusively on Dietrich Bonhoeffer. The course required that I read all of his books. I fully engaged *The Cost of Discipleship* and *Ethics* and was devotionally impacted by *Life Together*. Yet the book that inspired me more than all the others was *Letters and Papers from Prison*. In those pages I saw Bonhoeffer's faith so embody a devotion to Jesus that, on behalf of the greater cause of Christ and the church, he was willing to face into the atrocities of Nazism—into the evil it espoused, even to the point of losing his life—in order to represent Christ-centered hope for both the church and the world and to do so, in his own way, as "a ransom for many." For Bonhoeffer, it was a matter of fully living what he believed, no matter what. As I read his words, I wondered, *Would I be able to be such a fully present leader?*

I also engaged the realities of incarnational leadership while serving as a clinical pastoral education (CPE) chaplain—especially while doing my clinical residency in one of the busiest emergency departments in West Philadelphia. Late one night, a local college football player was stabbed in the heart by a random street gang member, and the entire football team and cheerleading squad showed up in the waiting room. Each person reacted in their own way to the severity of their friend's injuries—some vengefully angry, others already counting him as dead and mourning his loss, still others coming in and out of the hospital in increasing states of grief-stricken drunkenness. I was in way over my head. With the crowd having nothing to do but worry and wait, I went from person to person, group to group, and simply created space for prayer and hope—eventually gathering them into the chapel for a prayer service until the doctor appeared with positive news.

Then there was the time when a gang war brought multiple gunshot victims in, and it was my role to somehow differentiate between biological family and "gang" family—with everyone sharing space in the waiting room and grieving and the rival sides just one remark away from further violence. (Thank God I wore a clerical collar back then!)

While there were many times when I simply did not know what to do in response to the intensity of people's emotions, I learned time and time again about the power of presence—simply being with people as a nonanxious (at least outwardly displayed!) anchor in the midst of their emotional storms—as a sign of hope.

And in the emergency department and trauma bays, as at any time of crisis in both congregation and community, such hope is priceless.

Listen: it is exactly *into* the fray of anxiety that the pastor-leader must go, into the neutral zone of the person's, group's, or congregation's transitional conflict, in order to lead them toward transformational growth in discipleship. To do so requires that we be willing to embody Christ-centered hope while we walk with people through the turbulence of their anxiety (and ours).

As incarnational leaders, we are first missionaries—sent not to "convert" the people of our congregation and community but to "be with" them, to love them, to embrace them with the good news of a God who, by virtue of the cross and resurrection of Christ, has *already* forgiven them. As missionaries, we must learn the "language" and customs of the people we are called to serve, value their culture, and walk nonanxiously amid their fears and foibles. As ambassadors of hope, we embody the grander mosaic of God's redemptive story that gives voice to our congregation's and community's cries for social justice and pleas for fairness—or their lamentations when fairness is far from realized.

As incarnational leaders, we must learn to love our people before we can lead them, walk with them before we can preach to them, cry with them before we can confront them, and trust them before we can ask them to follow us toward a new beginning. We need to do life with them in the trenches—their trenches—confident in the One who has called them (us) to new life.

Incarnational Leadership Always Produces Conflict—and That's a Good Thing

It is the incarnational leader—the one who trusts the process of transition enough to enter into the anxieties of the others—who can lead people toward what God is calling them to become, whether they realize it or not, whether they realize they need it or not. This is our shepherding role. It is our job to catalyze the anxiety of those involved into a creative process of discipleship that fosters genuine spiritual formation and growth.

It will not be easy, but it is essential.[32] And doing so will most certainly lead to conflict. Yet conflicts are actually some of the best contexts for the Holy Spirit to help both individuals and communities of faith grow. If in our churches there is no conflict inspired by the divine mission, then we might wonder if people are really engaged in a discipleship process at all. If there's no conflict, might it be a sign that the congregation has not heard a challenging invitation to participate in mission? Might it be that no pastor-leader has modeled what living the mission looks like for their community of faith? Could it be that no one has been challenged beyond the proverbial "We've never done it that way before"? Indeed, if there is no conflict, might it be that there is no engagement of the dynamic tensions between love and justice that shape the character of believers (Rom 5:1–5)?

Incarnational leadership is quite certain to lead to conflict at some point . . . and that's a good thing. If we, pastor and congregation alike, are doing our job well, if we are living out our call with spiritual fervor, if we are embodying the gospel of Jesus Christ, then we are going to be invading subversively the territories of the enemy of love in order to inaugurate a movement of reconciliation and new creation.[33] For Jesus, nothing—absolutely nothing—short of the transformation of the entire world will do. God is in Christ, and Christ is in the church, reconciling the world to Godself (2 Cor 5:18–19). The type of leadership that takes up that movement necessarily begets conflict—conflict that is born out of the subversive use of the values and principles that define life in the New Community.

So what do we do with that conflict? While the rest of this book addresses specific principles of missional leadership within conflict situations (most of which I have learned the hard way), here are a few practical—incarnational—responses you may wish to put into your proverbial tool belt to get you started:

- "It sounds like you're having a rough time with some of the changes here at the church. Can you share what specifically is bothering you?"
- "You sound really upset with our decision to no longer offer children's Sunday school. Can you help me understand what's bothering you more—the fact that we won't have a children's Sunday school or the fact that we can't get enough volunteers to staff it?"
- "You've shared that you're disappointed in the decisions the leaders have been making regarding outreach. What specifically would you do differently that would help us as a congregation connect with the unchurched in our community?"

By their words, actions, attitude, and presence, incarnational leaders point people toward the divine mission. How can the divine mission now help redirect our congregational conflicts toward the new beginnings that God has in mind for the church?

PART II

Leading through Conflict

Principles of Missional Leadership

CHAPTER FOUR

X Rarely Marks the Spot

Those conflicts and disputes among you, where do they come from? Do they not come from your cravings that are at war within you? You want something and do not have it; so you commit murder. And you covet something and cannot obtain it; so you engage in disputes and conflicts. You do not have, because you do not ask. You ask and do not receive, because you ask wrongly, in order to spend what you get on your pleasures.

—James 4:1-3

LEADING THROUGH CHURCH CONFLICT IS NEVER EASY. WHENEVER two bodies of matter try to occupy the same space at the same time, it can be difficult to discern between genuine issues and personal agendas, between stubborn personalities and deeply felt values, and between post-traumatic reactivity and honest, albeit raw, emotional expression. In conflict—especially in congregations, where our expectations of love and community are high—we can forget who we are, why we're here, and where we're going. So how do we get started?

It has been my experience over the last thirty years of ministry, as well as within the church consultations that I've done, that some basic principles about church conflicts tend to play out consistently—principles that can assist us in reframing conflicts into opportunities for discipleship and mission. While the six principles I present in this book are not all that could be shared, they provide important starting points for us as we engage in missional leadership within conflict situations.

The first principle of missional leadership is that *X rarely marks the spot*. When a conflict arises, I have found that the anxiety related to the "real" issue follows a natural path of least resistance. Therefore, it will show itself in ways that are relatively "easier" for the participants to process—revealing to us where the true need is. Conflicts, therefore, are symptoms that tell us very important information about what is going on in the relational dynamics of the church as well as within the overall health of the congregation.

It is helpful to view X as the *presenting issue* that comes to the attention of the pastor-leader directly or indirectly. It may be something significant in and of itself, or it may seem inherently benign, but it presents itself as the reason for the conflict. Generally, however, rather than being the source of the conflict, X is the *symptom* or *symptom bearer* of something else going on in the relational systems of the congregation.[1]

In its classic definition, a symptom is a "physical or mental feature which is regarded as indicating a condition of disease; or a sign of the existence of something, especially of an undesirable situation."[2] In conflict contexts, I define a symptom as a person, situation, issue, or problem that points to something else going on in the relational dynamics of the congregation. In family systems theory, we call it the "presenting problem" because often it "presents" itself in ways that make us think it is a primary reason for the conflict.[3] While significant in and of itself, a pastor having an extramarital affair with a church member may be symptomatic not only of a breakdown in the pastor's own marriage but also of how insecure the pastor feels about how the church has grown beyond their capacity to lead. Complaints made about a pastor's integrity may actually be symptomatic of a lay leader's fear that the pastor's new proposed missional strategies will make the layperson's role irrelevant.

When engaging a conflict situation, generally it is good practice for the pastor-leader to ask, "Why this . . . and why now?"⁴
Such questions presume that the presenting issue is representing
something else going on, but that there is also a reason that it is
emerging at this particular time. What triggered the presenting
issue? Who are the people involved, and what might be going
on in their lives to bring about this particular situation? What
might be the emotional tenor of the congregation for which this
situation is now symptomatic? How is the reactivity of specific
people symptomatic of the anxiety of others?

Similar to symptoms in our physical bodies, congregational
conflicts can point us to genuine sources of relational or systemic
dysfunction.⁵ I would even argue that such symptoms are one of
the congregation's ways of drawing our attention to what's been
preventing the church from living out its mission mandate. In
Habakkuk, for example, God confronted Israel's attempts at hiding their sins of injustice by saying, "The stones of the wall will
cry out, and the beams of the woodwork will echo it" (Hab 2:11
NIV). When conflict erupts, what stories might it be telling us?
What is the conflict actually exposing?

Symptoms versus Sources of Conflict

Symptoms tell part of the story, so we need to look at them for
what they are and listen to them for what they have to tell us. In
fact, if we allow them to speak, they may guide us in determining
what is needed to facilitate further spiritual growth and mission.⁶
Discerning the difference between symptoms and sources of
conflict, however, can be confusing. Some symptoms are easily
confused with sources of conflict, since culturally, we are used to
focusing on the presenting issue as the "real" problem. Generally,
when we address a conflict situation and it appears to resolve only
to reemerge in a different way later, or we begin to see a repeating
pattern to the conflict, we're more likely dealing with symptoms

rather than sources. However, there are some clear markers that differentiate the two—some common and others more oblique.

TYPICAL SYMPTOMS OF CONFLICT

In the box below, I list several of the most common symptoms of underlying conflict within a congregation.[7] These symptoms may occur within staff teams, ministry teams, leadership groups (e.g., elders or deacons), subgroups within the congregation, the church as a whole, or even denominational gatherings. Clearly, the list is not exhaustive, but it illustrates dynamics present within congregational systems that disconnect on either relational or missional levels.[8] A congregation that elicits a tendency toward cliques or factions may, for example, assume that a conflict is sourced in power dynamics related to closed power systems, when in fact, under further investigation, the presence of such factions may indicate a lack of missional direction created by a void of leadership during a transition of pastors.[9] Or an embedded relational animosity between congregational cliques might be symptomatic of long-entrenched bitterness from a mismanaged accountability process regarding an act of pastoral sexual misconduct.

Division in the staff, as another example, initially may look like a problem of personality differences, but under closer examination, it may point to a power play from a disgruntled, insecure associate pastor challenging the loyalties of other staff toward the senior pastor whom the associate seeks to overthrow. The presence of congregational polarization may be rooted in a dislike for the pastor's leadership style, or it may be illustrative of genuine theological or missional differences that have become irreconcilable. Repeated "parking lot meetings"—gatherings after the official meeting where members voice opinions that were more appropriate for the official meeting—might indicate a distrust in the empathetic responses of leadership, or it might be a symptom of a failure of leadership rooted in conflict avoidance and insecurity.[10]

Common Symptoms of Conflict in Congregations

fighting among staff/congregation members

pastor/staff looking online for new jobs

progressively decreasing attendance in worship or activities

cliques or divisive factions

"us" and "them" language

a win-lose attitude

unfocused, generalized anger

displacement or a disagreement as to the real "problem"

passive-aggressive behaviors

overgeneralization of issues (e.g., "many people feel . . .")

members leaving

increased attendance at leadership meetings

meetings outside the meeting

polarization

increased gossip and ostracizing of members

animosity among members or groups

anxiety—specific or generalized

paranoia and suspicion

pastor or staff persons exhibiting acting-out behaviors (abuse of alcohol, drugs, pornography, etc.)

physical, emotional, or spiritual exhaustion or illness

sabotage (of self or others)

the presence of relational/emotional triangles

shifting of relational alignments

Symptoms point us toward the dysfunctions at the root of conflict—conflict that ultimately disrupts discipleship and delays the multiplying movement to which the congregation is called. Addressing them may quell some of the anxiety connected to the conflict; however, without engaging the true source of the conflict, the emotional energy of the dysfunction will resurface with additional symptoms.[11] Symptoms, by nature, ultimately point to their source issue. One need only follow the trail—solicited by way of questions, induction, and discernment—to discover what is actually going on.[12]

MAJOR SOURCES OF CONFLICT

When we consider the wide variety of conflicts that plague and even paralyze congregations, we can identify some "major" sources that challenge the perceived peace and foster relational dysfunction.[13] The box below lists some of the sources of conflict that tend to produce stress on congregational covenant and mission.

Several of the sources listed reflect common conflicts associated with transitions within the life of the congregation. For example, anytime a new pastor is added or a tenured pastor is exited or a bold strategic initiative is introduced, the resulting tension in the congregational system predicts conflict.[14] A retiring pastor who decides to remain in attendance at the church where they served twenty years will create the potential for conflict among congregational members as well as with any incoming clergy. Theological differences can be expressed in a pastor's framework clashing with that of the congregation, or even among members of the church council over controversial doctrinal issues: Do we allow same-gender weddings? Do we do baby dedications or only infant baptisms? What if a pastor or church leader gets a divorce?

Conflicts related to leadership style (e.g., the former pastor preached from the pulpit, wore a clergy robe, and gave fifteen-minute messages, and the new pastor wears jeans and an untucked shirt, walks around the "stage," and preaches for thirty-five minutes), unspoken expectations (e.g., in spite of the fact that five people from church came to visit Sally in the hospital, Sally feels that if the senior pastor doesn't visit, "the church really doesn't care"), financial stress (e.g., declining attendance means declining offerings, which means having to make budgetary changes that impact staff jobs), clashes of personalities (e.g., Helen doesn't like the fact that George doesn't organize the kitchen the way she did for the past twenty years when she was in charge), and organizational confusion (e.g., under Pastor Mark, elders and deacons only served as advisors, but under Pastor Ed's leadership, elders and deacons are expected to lead committees, pray during

Major Sources of Church Conflict

addition to or loss of staff

personal family issues

community change

organizational structure ("who's in charge?")

theological differences

expectations (especially unspoken)

performance issues

cultural- or language-based misunderstanding[15]

leadership style

legitimate differences of opinion or style

clashing of values

clashes of personalities

hidden sin (especially sexual)

stress (self, organizational, communal)

attitudes (general or specific)

psychoemotional trauma

fear (of change, failure, etc.)

racism / gender issues / ageism / other "-isms"

desire for power[16]

change/transition

self-esteem (too high, too low)

insecurity/control

clashing goals or methods

closed power systems

personal or family changes

unresolved hurt or pain (projection)

financial stress

anxiety

unmet needs or expectations

grief

betrayal

technology advancements

worship, and attend evangelistic outreach events) are prevalent in congregational life.

Other major sources of conflict can also polarize congregations and derail the divine mission mandate. Hidden sin—especially of a sexual nature—can be devastating to a church. The chronic deceptions connected to a fear of exposure can erode trust, depleting a congregation of its personnel and financial resources. Racism, sexism, ageism, and the like root themselves within the undercurrents of congregational life, causing an impact on how and what decisions are made. Feelings of betrayal can evoke blame, revenge, and animosity—often taking innocent church members hostage into the emotional triangles that form as a result. Closed power systems, controllers, and narcissistic leaders can wreak havoc on the emotional dynamics of a church. The forces that try to preserve the status quo of any organization—for whatever reason—can threaten the creative momentum of missional movement and multiplication.

Quite importantly, grief is an often missed source of congregational discord and missional paralysis. Grief is our normal human reaction to change; the more intense the change, the more intense the grief response. In my professional opinion, grief is the most central emotional, psychological, spiritual, cultural, and social-environmental milieu defining the human experience in the United States in the early twenty-first century. As I write this in mid-2020, the world is in the midst of the COVID-19 pandemic, but our inability to navigate grief—of all kinds, not just coronavirus related—is another sort of pandemic afflicting society. We bring all of that grief into our congregations as well. Unresolved, post-traumatic, all-consuming hurt, pain, fear, brokenness, violations, and loss have colored our views of everyone and everything else, thereby preventing us from seeing beyond our own plight. We therefore act out, react to, and lash out against our interpretation of another's experience. Conflict abounds whenever two or three are gathered. Since every person deals with grief uniquely, and grief is so pervasive, the missional leader must assume that grief is a potential source of the presenting conflict.

Grief also may come from within the pastor. As leaders, many times our losses go unresolved, or they are sidelined in order to help others cope with their crises. Sometimes situations that we as leaders are called upon to mediate touch internal "nerves" that we become aware of only when those situations "push our buttons," causing a reaction.[17] Some losses are so embedded into our own past that they have affected our character development—revealing themselves through boundary crossing.[18] Grief can cause us to forget who we are, why we're here, and where we're going.

Yet not all sources of conflict are as easily observed.

LESS COMMON, OR LESS ACKNOWLEDGED, SOURCES OF CONFLICT

While congregational conflict can emerge in a wide variety of relational connections, there are also conflict sources that typically are not examined as part of the diagnosing of discord. Physical, emotional, or spiritual exhaustion or illness, for example, ranks on my lists as both a symptom and a potential source of conflict, since such exhaustion can be evidence of underlying stress and a reason people act out. A lay leader who has just lost a child may start to project grief onto God, the pastor, or others while trying to come to terms with the loss. A long-tenured volunteer whose spouse is living with progressive dementia may exact a controlling spirit over a ministry team as the only avenue of expressing grief and anger toward God.

Sometimes acts of offense are rooted in unresolved hurt or pain in a person's life, emerging in aggressive expressions of rage or the desire for (or execution of) revenge. At Second Street Baptist Church, a longtime church member sought to get the pastor fired by citing "incompetence." A year earlier, the pastor had challenged this man's daughter's desire to have her father "give her away" at her wedding, explaining that the practice was an invalid expression of love, since she was, in fact, no one's "property." The father saw the pastor's theological framework as a personal infringement on his decades-long dream of escorting his daughter on her wedding day, so he started attacking the pastor's character and credibility.

Another source of conflict is violation of covenants. Congregations typically do not engage in conversations around idolatry, along with the clash of consumeristic values and our respective "gods."[19] We preach about it, certainly, but generally, we do not consider idolatry's implications as a source of church conflict and missional paralysis, as did Paul (2 Cor 6:14–18) or John (1 John 5:21). We approach covenant violations in much the same way. Biblical accounts such as the story of Ananias and Sapphira in Acts 5:1–10 and that of David and Bathsheba in 2 Samuel 11 remind us of the consequences of breaking covenant with God and with one another.[20] Violations of covenant on any level—marital, membership, professional—always have layers of conflict as participants displace emotional tension by projecting shame and guilt onto others. When a pastor has an extramarital affair, for example, it calls into question the premarital counseling they have done for couples and, in parishioners' minds, the integrity of the pastor's overall ministry. Trust has been violated, as multilayered covenants were broken. And missional advancement will be arrested if there is no trust in the pastor.

Unconfessed corporate sin is yet another source of congregational conflict that undermines the divine mission mandate. It often hovers under the radar of both members and leaders within a dense fog of whispered innuendo, abject denial, willful agreement, or complicit silence. The Corinthian church was called out by Paul for this very thing: "It is actually reported that there is sexual immorality among you, and of a kind that is not found even among pagans; for a man is living with his father's wife. And you are arrogant! Should you not rather have mourned, so that he who has done this would have been removed from among you?" (1 Cor 5:1–2). Indeed, I would argue that the Holy Spirit's presence within the corporate life of believers exposes that which is hidden to the light of Christ for the purpose of sanctifying discipleship. Love always demands truth as a price for freedom (John 8:31–32).

Yet another important source of conflict within congregations concerns the outward expressions and behavioral ramifications of mental health issues. Persons who are living with depression, post-traumatic stress, mood disorders (e.g., bipolar disorder), personality disorders (e.g., borderline personality disorder), dementia, and the many faces of emotional and mental health needs are often drawn to the healing, helping, nurturing, and stabilizing facets of faith and grace within community—and rightly so. Unfortunately, sometimes the very environments that nurture may, for some people, become triggers for unhealthy expressions of their struggles. While all people are invited into the grace of the gospel, special care must be brought to those with complex backgrounds and needs, especially when such backgrounds are held within the bounds of sacred trust and confidentiality. I was asked to consult in a conflict situation several years back where a member of the church started a negative letter campaign against the pastor, complaining that every time she preached her sermon, she was using this member's privately shared pastoral conversations. Upon further investigation, the member's mother revealed a long history of her daughter's paranoid schizophrenia as well as the mother's complicit response to it based on her fear of the ramifications of her daughter's emotional health, but the damage was done to the pastor's reputation, trust, and leadership capacity within that church.

Especially challenging are the higher emotional demands of those dealing with narcissism and the spectrum of narcissistic personality disorder. While much can be shared about this mental health category,[21] I have found that at the heart of any narcissist is insecurity. Narcissism is a coping mechanism that, unfortunately, leaves much pain and broken relationships in its wake. When dealing with a narcissist, it is imperative that we get appropriate counsel, surround ourselves with a strong support network, and define our personal boundaries. The best way to interact with a narcissist is to not give them what they want—control over our emotions, attitudes, behavior, time, heart, and life.[22]

Sources Directly Related to Mission

While all of the above sources of conflict may impact the church's mission and ministry, some specific types of conflict emerge *because* the pastor or a parishioner is doing something to advance the church's mission. In that case, it's not helpful to "fix" the conflict because that would mean reverting to the status quo of comfort and ease. Rather, the emerging conflict becomes evidence that a congregation actually is being challenged to grow in discipleship and mission. A pastor-leader may need to allow the conflict's tension to *increase* to foster conversations that can lead the congregation forward in living out its divine mission.

For example, standing up for issues of social justice based on one's faith in Christ may spark resistance or even polarized contention—especially when such issues are controversial. Jesus himself raged at the money changers as he violently cleared the temple courtyard of those violating the sacred domain of worship and prayer (John 2:13–17). Taking such a stand against what had become a prevailing norm of temple life exposed the deeper levels of exclusionary practices of Jews against Gentile converts (for the money changers and animal sellers most likely had set up shop in the Court of the Gentiles) as well as the injustices of inflated exchange rates imposed on those caught at the intersection of ritual obedience and abject poverty.[23] Jesus, indeed, was about the divine mission of setting the captive free, and in this case, allowing tensions to increase for a bit served that purpose.

A few more illustrations: At Second Street Church, it became apparent that the traditional style of worship service, while meaningful to the congregation, was not attracting younger families—a growing demographic within a five-mile radius of the church. So our leadership team made several decisions to move the congregation forward in our mission to "reach the unchurched." First, we added screens and projectors to the front walls of the sanctuary. We also added a new worship service that was contemporary in style and placed that service in the best time slot for reaching the younger demographic. Within one year, the new service became the largest of our three, with quite a few of those who previously had attended the traditional service. On many Sundays, the traditional service's adult choir almost had more members than worshippers in the pews—causing a major reaction of grief, loss, and resentment.

A second example: Early on at one of the congregations I served, I changed the staff performance review process. Specifically, I established one, since up to that point there had been no formal review process. Previously, all staff received annual compensation increases regardless of how well they performed their duties. The review process I introduced was based on outcomes rooted in our newly established missional objectives (e.g., how many people were recruited into ministry areas) as well as alignment to newly taught staff team values (e.g., teachability, shows up to meetings on time). Salary increases would be based on merit resulting from their overall performance review composite score—making one staff person's salary increase a different percentage than another's. One specific staff team member who happened to discover that he had received less of an increase than another staff person complained to my district superintendent about my "unfair leadership practice," explaining that in prior years, all staff had received equal percentage increases. My district superintendent simply told him he had to share his complaints directly with me, which he did. That individual soon resigned and, along with his spouse, began to vote against initiatives leaders were making to begin a new contemporary service.

A third example of how allowing conflict to happen might actually help a congregation move forward in mission: Just prior to my arrival at the congregation I currently serve, the prior pastor and his wife observed a rapidly growing situation of homelessness in the community and a serious lack of housing resources. They felt compelled by their faith to do something about it. With the assistance of a group of individuals, they started a winter shelter—opening up the church facilities to homeless persons for meals and overnight accommodations every night through the winter season. Taking on such a project caused major amounts of stress as theological, methodological, and emotional differences were aired and processed—sometimes in a quite heated fashion. Into that arena of transitional controversy, I was newly appointed as pastor of the congregation. Redefining the conversation around mission, values, and priorities, we made space for that ministry to gain new footing. Now, as the shelter enters its fifth year, it has become part of a larger community outreach movement that not only has served hundreds of people in transitional crisis but has been seen by social service agencies as a reproducible model.

Finally, at both my current and my prior congregational appointments, I introduced the idea of giving away our Christmas Eve offering to community outreach programs. The idea of a church giving money away in a season when it historically counted on Christmas Eve to help reach budgetary goals sounded ludicrous to many of the finance team members. Perhaps out of "honeymoon deference," the leaders in my prior congregation decided to move forward for the sake of our outreach to the community. That year, after we announced that the entire Christmas Eve offering would go to purchase AED units for the local police department's cruisers, nearly double the typical offering was received. In fact, there was enough money to give an additional gift to the local fire department—and, in addition, we ended the year with a budgetary surplus. In subsequent years as we did the same, certain members of specific ministry teams began to complain to the leadership that we were giving away money that could best be used for our own ministries. One year, they lobbied to have the Christmas Eve offering used for several internal projects initiated by those ministry teams; the result was a dramatic decrease in the amount donated that year. At my current appointment, I introduced this concept to some skepticism, given that the church had been in a season of financial challenge, but the lay leaders agreed. That first year was such a "success" in generating excitement for impacting our community that since then, the lay leaders themselves now initiate the conversation about where we will give the Christmas Eve offering.

When a pastor, lay leader, group, or section of a congregation decides to live out the church's mission—taking the word of God beyond the four walls of our comfort zone—the reluctant systems resident in the church will react. Such conflict is essential, as it catalyzes a call to discipleship, and the divine mission elicits a response.

Indeed, conflict will arise anytime someone sets limits or boundaries on boundaryless people, on unhealthy behaviors, or on dysfunctional systems—something leaders must do for the sake of mission. This type of conflict, emerging from within the dysfunction, often reflects those who deceptively try to exert their influence for one main purpose: to get the system to return back to its status quo, no matter how unhealthy. Our behavior tells a story. A conflict may just be a person's or group's reaction to a challenge to move out of its comfort zone.

Going after the sources of our pain rather than simply addressing its symptoms ultimately gives opportunity for God's multiplying mission to be carried out. X—the set of symptoms that first indicates a conflict—rarely marks the spot, the true source of the conflict, but it does tell a story. It's time for us to ask different questions of the symptoms and let those symptoms lead us to their respective sources. The who, what, where, when, how, and why of any conflict have implications for the discipleship of each person involved, as well as of the entire congregation. Addressing these questions and following the trail of symptoms to their sources will enable us to engage or reengage God's mission. There, the good news of freedom and hope awaits to remind us of who we are, why we're here, and where we need to go for the sake of God's global mission.

CHAPTER FIVE

High Control = High Anxiety = High Insecurity

And you, O mortal, do not be afraid of them, and do not be afraid of their words, though briers and thorns surround you and you live among scorpions; do not be afraid of their words, and do not be dismayed at their looks, for they are a rebellious house. You shall speak my words to them, whether they hear or refuse to hear.

—Ezekiel 2:6-7

FOR THE BETTER PART OF MY EARLY YEARS IN MINISTRY, I WAS intimidated by controlling people. Bullies scared me. Something about how they presented themselves—their cocky attitudes, their domineering methods—sparked a Goliath-facing type of fear in me. And, to be honest, something in my personal insecurities gave them more power than they deserved. When I was around them, it felt like I was back in junior high gym class waiting to be picked (or not) by the student captains for their respective basketball teams. (I was the shortest kid in the class.)

Whenever these church bullies would "bark" their gruff attitude at me (their pastor!), my outer self would give the impression of calm (at least, I thought it did), while my inner self would cower under the weight of their overly exaggerated, intimidating stature.

I hated my reaction.

Then one day, Harry, one of the key controlling leaders of the church I served, went into the hospital. Chest pain and a catheterization that showed blockages landed him on the schedule for open-heart surgery. When I visited him the morning of his surgery, what I saw was that my "Goliath" had become vulnerable—scared, anxious, and uncertain of whether he had a future. While even the toughest of people might shrink before the news of heart surgery, Harry's vulnerability created a unique pathway for me. In that hospital room, the Holy Spirit converted my intimidation to sympathy and then converted my sympathy to empathy. God gave me the ability to enter into Harry's intimidation as he faced his own Goliath, and I faced mine—not with five stones and a slingshot but with anointing oil and prayer.

In the intimate connection of that sacramental moment, I learned a life-changing lesson: most of us in life are just trying to cope. The hard shells of our tough exteriors often protect layers of brokenness and vulnerability. Behind every face and every "bark" is a story.

Certainly, there are some mean-spirited, evil people out there. (I'll talk about them in chapter 8.) There are times when genuine sociopaths or psychopaths make their way into our congregations—as they take advantage of gracious people who have been nurtured to be trusting. Mostly, however, in our pews are the broken who, over time, either have chosen to remain in their learned limitations, defending their dysfunctions and bullying those who try to change them, or have remained in denial of their need to be immersed fully into the grace of the only One who can truly set them free. Regardless, the person behind each story is the reason that Jesus died. As followers of Jesus, our challenge within the divine mission is to learn how to love, forgive, share power, and serve in a way that testifies to the fact that we are forever identified by the cross of Christ.

Whether or not he realized it, Harry taught me my second principle of missional leadership: *high control = high anxiety = high insecurity.* I view control as a coping mechanism that we use to protect ourselves from dealing with anxiety—specifically, the anxiety that is associated with having our vulnerabilities exposed.[1] When the anxiety within us begins to intensify, we feel threatened, causing us to become more reactive, so we exert control—or at least, we try to—over our circumstances or other people we feel are causing or contributing to that anxiety. This use of control is a coping mechanism in response to our feelings of anxiety.

But anxiety tells a story. In our contexts, what exactly is it telling us?

Never Underestimate the Power of Anxiety

Within a discipling environment, anxiety is a symptom of something else going on in the anxious person and may also be a symptom of something going on within the systems of the congregation. As such, we pastor-leaders must allow anxiety to *remain* long enough for it to reveal what it's trying to tell us. In fact, we need to let anxiety simmer. When it simmers, it motivates people to keep moving toward a solution. A leader's ability to be fully present, honest but nonreactive, respectfully playful, and willing to move *into* (rather than away from) the emotionally charged arenas of conflict nonanxiously can successfully channel the congregation's reactivity to a level where participants can actually engage or reengage their divine mission. When anxiety is at a simmer, we are able to facilitate positive missional advancement while at the same time providing sufficient pastoral-spiritual direction to the congregation or participants to help them navigate the transition.

We don't want the anxiety to boil, however; when it is at the boiling stage, people can't reason. In that case, we will need to spend concentrated time and effort in processing the emotional needs of those involved until there is enough trust among participants to take the next step forward. Congregations with patterns of chronic anxiety often deal with mission paralysis. They can be just too reactive to engage the mission when it requires them to leave the comforts of what they've been used to. Trust building in those types of situations may take years and the patient, enduring love of a long-tenured shepherd.

Being a leader within a congregation means that we not only have to face into the anxiety of our parishioners; we also need to admit and face into our own. In fact, I contend that anxiety—particularly that of the pastor—plays the largest role in the pastor's overall effectiveness in ministry and, specifically, in their ability to navigate within conflict situations, leading ultimately to missional advancement.[2]

This means, as leaders, that we have to come to terms with our own anxiety *first*. In any organizational system, the only person we can change is ourselves. So, instead of trying to address the anxiety in the congregation, or even trying to resolve the presenting conflict, we first need to address our own anxiety and modify our own behavior within the relational dynamics of the congregation. By adjusting our response to our own anxiety and then moving calmly and nonreactively into the anxiety of the congregational conflict, we will, in effect, shift the trajectory of the conflict—hopefully toward a healthier outcome.[3] Let me explain.

When anxiety is allowed to run amok, it becomes the force that causes pastors to sabotage their ministries, catapult themselves into despair and depression, self-medicate with progressively addictive behaviors, and chronically withdraw from standing up to the destructive and toxic elements that threaten the congregation's mission. Anxiety can also cause normally stable church members to react suddenly to changes introduced into the rhythms and routines of congregational life. As we have seen, anxiety may lead congregations as a whole to sabotage their own growth in order to preserve the status quo.

Anyone who has ever had an anxiety attack or panic attack knows that in the throes of such a moment, our level of vulnerability might compel us to do something we would not normally do, or say something we would not normally say, in an attempt to quell the terror we feel in our body, mind, and spirit. That's why church conflict causes good people to do stupid things.[4]

Anxiety is a challenging emotional response because it involves intense physical, psychological, social, and spiritual components.[5] Often, we refer to it in terms of panic, fear, or phobia, based on what we perceive to be its dominant emotional expressions. Since our emotions are a God-given part of what it means to be human, anxiety must serve a purpose—whether or not, in the moment, we see it as such. Physiologically, it serves our bodies as part of our alarm system, giving us fair warning of potential (or perceived) dangers.[6] Often, it is based on the unknown, which tickles our fear of being out of control.[7] It can be biochemically sourced and often has degrees of post-traumatic elements in its origin and expression.[8] Anxiety, therefore, can be born out of the need to cope in situations that are beyond our control.[9] As such, it is a normal human reaction that, at times, may jump into hyperreactive mode.[10] At other times, it reflects an inner conflict—an ironic interplay between what we desire and a fear of actually getting what we desire.[11] In fact, in family systems theory, anxiety has been defined broadly as a "sense of threat."[12] Even the apostle Paul's encouraging directive in Philippians 4:6— "Do not be anxious about anything" (NIV)—acknowledges the human propensity to allow anxiety to overwhelm us in the midst of circumstances beyond our control.

Anxiety, therefore, actually may be a good thing, although acknowledging its benefits in the moments of panic may be difficult. As a symptom, it points us toward something else that is demanding our attention, if only obliquely. The more intense the anxiety, the more intentionally our body's alert system tries to get us to address whatever is making us feel out of control or vulnerable. At times, our emotions (and perhaps our biochemistry) get out of balance and our anxiety runs haywire.[13] Even so, it serves as a communication tool to get the attention of our brain's "leadership center." We need our anxiety. It's a fundamental part of our survival and coping mechanisms.

The same is true on a congregational level. Congregational anxiety is an important symptom in helping us in our leadership, especially in times of conflict and confusion. For pastors, it can help us discern when we are out of sync with the Holy Spirit, or when we're overtasking ourselves and needing to pull back. It can be a tool that God uses to make us wary about a person's character or motive—even our own. It might help us become aware of how we have been triangled into a conflict that is not ours to bear. In conflicts, anxiety can help us pinpoint relational stress and codependency and whether we are enmeshed.[14] Anxiety can also signal potential or actual boundary violations so that we can protect ourselves. Additionally, it may help us discern dysfunctions within the systems in the church by assessing patterns of overreactions, or determine the readiness of the congregation for change as we present missional strategies, or evaluate where congregation members are in their own spiritual growth as we engage in community outreach.

Yet the concept of moving *toward* anxiety, like running *toward* the battle line of conflict, is not easy. It even pushes the framework of family systems theory a bit out of its comfort zone. Family systems argues, for example, that the best way to define oneself—one's values, one's life goals, one's role within the system, all while staying connected to the relationships that are important to us[15]—is by positioning oneself within the balance between individuality (self-definition) and togetherness (connection).[16] Yet such a posture is difficult to attain within the intensity of relational conflict. If, in fact, anxiety is an emotional response to a real or perceived threat, it does not easily submit to cognitive or logical processing, at least not initially.[17] In other words, it's very hard to reason with anxiety when you're in the midst of a panic attack. Additionally, individuality (self-definition) sounds great from a humanistic perspective, but it seems to challenge the self-denial constructs of discipleship modeled by Jesus (e.g., Matt 6:33; 16:24).[18]

Even so, I find it useful to approach congregational leadership from a family systems perspective because it teaches pastors and leaders the power of self-differentiation. By reframing family systems theory within a discipleship environment, however, pastors and other leaders can define themselves around the divine mission rooted in God's call upon their lives and around which the congregation has formed. Thus anxiety becomes less about a person or people and more about intentional relationships—specifically, a relationship defined by God's mission, a relationship with the God who has called them into new life, and a relationship with the community of believers with whom they are in covenant connection.

We see then that anxiety plays an important role in our individual and corporate spiritual formations within the context of mission and our relationship with others with whom we share God's mission.[19]

How Leaders Process Anxiety

Conflict is always about relationship—two bodies of matter trying to occupy the same space at the same time. When tension rises within conflict situations, anxiety becomes a dominant emotion, although it may be expressed in multiple ways (e.g., anger, withdrawal, accommodation, displacement, sabotage).[20] Conflict, indeed, often may lead to the redefining of self, the redefining of boundaries, and the reorienting of relational dynamics. As such, it prompts a relational *transition* that involves endings, neutral zones, and new beginnings, as previously discussed. As conflict emerges—whether personal or corporate in nature—participants are thrust into scenarios of inner battles of self-definition and what that will mean both for their previous status quo and for the future of the relationships that have been important to them.

Within the New Community of followers of Jesus, leaders must incorporate the values and teachings of Jesus while realizing that not everyone involved in the conflict will have the same interpretations of those values and teachings. We are called into community as diverse people, and the very diversity that creates a beautiful mosaic causes us to push against one another. On our journey of discipleship together, we must recognize the aspects of our individual and corporate lives that are yet to experience transformation and renewal.

Leaders, therefore, must learn and model healthier ways of what pastor and theologian Dietrich Bonhoeffer called "living together in the forgiveness of our sin."[21] Rather than "individuality" and "self-defining," per se, I argue that, as pastors, we need to define ourselves around our communal missional identity *first*; then we need to invite those with the greatest capacity to bring about a healthy shift within the congregation to define themselves around that mission too.[22]

For example, in conflict situations we as leaders can model ways of interacting that demonstrate our communal missional identity by asking different sorts of questions of each other, sharing our stories with honesty and integrity, and filtering our responses through love:

- "Every time I offer ideas at this meeting, I notice that you interrupt me. Can you help me understand what that's about?"
- "It sounds like you have really strong opinions against women serving in ministry. Can you share with us why that perspective is so important to you? . . . May I share with you a different perspective and why it is important to me?"
- "Clearly, contemporary worship is important to you even though it's not my preference. What if we started another service that allows us to reach people for Christ who value that expression of worship? How can I help?"
- "I know that same-gender relationships are important to you, but I've gotta be honest—I'm really struggling with it. I have friends who are gay, and I really love them, but it clashes with what I believe the Bible teaches. Do you mind helping me understand your perspective? Would you listen to me as I talk out mine? I feel really uncomfortable having to choose sides."

Leadership requires at least some degree of confidence. After all, by definition, it is the leader who takes the first step. We must distinguish, however, between confidence and control. Being confident does not negate the presence of anxiety; rather, confidence harnesses anxiety and uses it to spur both self and others toward the missional purpose ahead. Control, by contrast, is an attempt to distract from or displace anxiety.[23] In other words, we seek to control others or our circumstances because we feel out of control or vulnerable, consciously or unconsciously.

So how do we, as leaders, recognize our anxiety and prevent it from negatively influencing our behavior?

SOME WAYS LEADERS AND OTHERS EXPRESS ANXIETY

While I am far from an expert in the psychology of anxiety, I do know from experience in ministry and other areas of life that people respond to anxiety in a variety of ways.

One of the ways we express our anxiety is by our posture—physically, emotionally, or spiritually. Our emotional presence, distance, avoidance, or absence, often expressed physically, is symptomatic of how anxious we are within our present (or perceived) situation. When our anxiety goes up, many times we pull away—from spouse, family, friends, church, God, social gatherings, anything that evokes the emotional discomfort that we're trying to avoid. It is not uncommon even to push away from those who have the greatest capacity to help us. We might express anxiety by working late into the night in an attempt either to earn affirmation or to avoid facing our spouse because we feel like a failure. Or we might absent ourselves mentally or emotionally even though we are present physically—showing our emotional distance in perfunctory sermons or relationally benign visits at the hospital or in symptoms of depression. Chronically calling in sick to work also may be an avoidant or distancing reaction to increasing anxiety.

Among congregational members, we might see this posturing first in changes within attendance patterns. Those who normally attend worship every week suddenly are missing more and more, perhaps even offering excuses of traveling or being busy or sick. Soon, they begin to withdraw their financial support as they slip into inactivity. They may "visit" other churches, or they may not attend any church at all.

Another way that anxiety reveals itself in us is through hyper- or hypofunctioning. When our anxiety goes up, we try to control our environment in order to quell our panic. We may work harder, hoping that by doing so we can "earn points" with God or with the person from whom we want approval. Sometimes we feel overly responsible to "fix" the relational conflict, thinking that if we were a really "good pastor" or a "better leader," we'd know how to do it, or if we really were a "better Christian," we wouldn't have the problems that we have. So we get on the hamster wheel and run faster or work harder, often exhausting ourselves amid increasing disillusionment.[24] Or we do the exact opposite; we stop doing everything, withdraw from all roles, quit ministry, take a "hiatus" in order to "find ourselves." We may avoid coming to work on certain days or avoid certain people (or people in general).

Hyper- or hypofunctioning may also reveal itself physically—with our bodies, our health. Pain, migraines, chronic illnesses, recurrent acute illnesses, panic attacks, a heart attack or stroke: all can be ways that our bodies communicate stress and anxiety to us so that something might be done.[25] Ironically, our hyper- or hypofunctioning may actually reinforce the very anxiety-producing system we are trying to address. In other words, if you, as the pastor, are feeling overwhelmed and alone in bearing responsibility for the health of the congregation, your hyperfunctioning—or "rescuer" role-playing—may actually be promoting the *under*functioning of the rest of the congregation; they don't need to bear responsibility as long as you are doing so to such a great extent.[26]

At times, hyperfunctioning is expressed in overcompensation. In overcompensation, we engage in bargaining behaviors, where we try to "make deals" with God, with culture (e.g., "to get more people in the pews"), and with ourselves or our loved ones. Several years ago, I talked with a pastor who single-handedly went door-to-door within several neighborhoods to invite people to his church because he felt that if he got "more people in the pews, [the congregation's] financial deficit would go away." Panic related to their financial crisis caused him to overcompensate by changing his missional motive for outreach as he transferred the anxiety of the leaders onto himself. Another pastor shared with her husband that she had to "prove to the congregation that a woman pastor can do all that a male pastor can do," so she spent almost every evening in meetings at the church, neglecting her time with her kids, in an effort to preempt the judgment she felt was inevitable from her congregation.

A third way we may express anxiety is through rituals. Not all rituals are expressions of anxiety, of course. Many rituals, such as those associated with seasons of our Christian calendar (e.g., the imposition of ashes on Ash Wednesday, the liturgies of the sacraments of Communion and baptism), are sources of great comfort and spiritual nurture. However, when we begin to believe that certain repetitive actions can influence our present reality, such ritualistic behavior can be symptomatic of larger issues of anxiety.

When what makes us feel out of control is difficult to verbalize or deal with, one of the ways our brains and bodies cope is by unleashing the energy of worry through ritualistic behaviors. Many compulsive habits—and more extreme obsessive-compulsive behaviors—are forged as coping mechanisms for dealing with the unbridled emotions connected with feeling vulnerable. To cope with her fear of causing the death of people whom she loved by passing on "a proximal death curse," one pastor developed a ritual of looking at herself in the rearview mirror every time she passed a funeral home so that she, rather than a loved one, would be the recipient of the curse. This ritual had developed when she was a child and her father died unexpectedly on his way to pick her up from her soccer game. She felt responsible for his accident and internalized this ritual as a coping mechanism for her anxiety. Another pastor would count the number of pews on each side of the sanctuary on his way up the main aisle each Sunday before the service in order to mitigate his fear of people rejecting him based on his sermon. Counting the pews brought a sense of order to his internal, emotional chaos.

Such rituals do not make theological sense; rather, they represent a magical frame of mind that assumes a transactional approach to anxiety—a type of bargaining with God or with self in order to quell the deep-seated feelings of vulnerability. But, in truth, anxiety is not logical; it is emotion based. It must be seen and responded to accordingly.

As mentioned above, in congregations, rituals are often a normal expression of worship. For some, however, those rituals—done exactly the same way, week after week—become important coping mechanisms for feeling out of control in other areas of their lives. Decisions to alter the worship schedule, to add contemporary music, to not use the Apostles' Creed or the Lord's Prayer, even to shift the expected order of worship can cause an anxiety reaction that seems disproportionate to those who are unaware of the reaction's context.

A fourth way that anxiety is often expressed is through projection. Projection is in a category of blaming—where we see in others what we can't see in ourselves. When our anxiety levels rise, our emotions become hypersensitive, causing us to become defensive, wary, suspicious, and less personally reflective. Therefore, we react more to statements made or actions done by others, assuming that they are attacking us in some form. We become paranoid, questioning others' motives, unable to filter through the lens of humility or grace. We view others as "enemies" or "evil" simply because they disagree with us. We feel threatened, blaming the other person for motives that we superimpose onto them. Congregations that are anxious about waning finances, for example, may make the pastor responsible for the decreasing church attendance. They may blame the pastor for the conflicts in the church, saying that bad pastoral leadership is what got people upset. Pastors, in turn, may blame the elders or the congregation or Satan for the church's decline.

Fifth, anxiety often becomes evident through recurrent critical behavior patterns, especially when situations reach a crisis level. Cycles of self-abuse, self-sabotage, other types of abuse, passive or aggressive resistance, addictive patterns, or even illegal risk taking are often the result of coping mechanisms run amok. The pastor having an affair (with a staff member, parishioner, or another), getting arrested with a DUI, or becoming addicted to pornography—all are typical examples of how behavioral patterns expose anxiety, especially anxiety related to stress and a sense of powerlessness.

So how do we interrupt such a cycle?

SET LIMITS ON ANXIETY

As stated above, in contexts of conflict, one of the most effective ways to address systemic anxiety and dysfunction is to modify the behavior of the pastor and other leaders. By facing into our own insecurities, our own anxieties, and choosing to lead toward God's mission, our healthier leadership response has the potential to shift the trajectory of the entire congregation, inviting them to remember who they are, why they're here, and where they're called to go.

Within the framework of discipleship and spiritual formation, control is an illusion. Henri Nouwen puts it best: "Since we are such fearful people, the hardest challenge we face is the reality of our losses and how to let go of the illusion of control, the challenge to go beyond our fears and to trust that one day we will be liberated from the bonds that hold us captive."[27] Discipleship and spiritual formation depend on our willingness to relinquish control to the Holy Spirit. Trying to exert control—over our circumstances, over other people, over God—simply communicates how out of control we are, how vulnerable we are. Whether we are dealing with the reactive systems at work in the congregation, closed power systems within groups or among individuals, or a form of post-traumatic stress within our own personal lives, church conflicts expose our anxiety through the degree of control we exercise.

The environment that we set up in the church for disciple-ship requires, paradoxically, that pastors and other leaders lead differently. Namely, rather than seeking to exert control and to tamp down anxiety and conflict, we walk—or run, as young David before Goliath—into the fray of our own anxiety.

ACKNOWLEDGE OUR OWN ANXIETY

At seven thirty in the morning on September 12, 2001, I was on the air at WJTL radio in Lancaster, Pennsylvania, with my good friend Fred McNaughton, the station manager. We, along with everyone else in the United States, and many around the world, were still coming to terms with the devastating news of the prior day—the terrorist attacks on the World Trade towers and the Pentagon and the deaths of nearly three thousand people. Among the dead were those aboard United Airlines Flight 93, which crashed near Shanksville, Pennsylvania, when several of its passengers courageously countered its hijackers. Fred had invited me to join him on the morning broadcast, and together we interacted with the listeners around both the emotions of grief and the anxiety that resulted from our country having been attacked.

As part of our discussion, I was drawn to the story of King Jehoshaphat in 2 Chronicles 20. In the account, Jehoshaphat had heard that a great army from several surrounding nations was amassing and was planning to do battle against the people of Judah. As soon as he heard the news, Jehoshaphat became scared and called a meeting of the congregation of Judah (v. 3). People from all over the region gathered under Jehoshaphat's leader-ship "to seek help from the Lord" (v. 4). The people looked to Jehoshaphat, their king, for direction, and what they got was an invitation to a prayer meeting!

In response to the news of impending battle, Jehoshaphat led the people in prayer (v. 5). In this amazing callout to God,

Jehoshaphat gave voice to the corporate anxiety of his people: "O our God, will you not execute judgment upon them? For we are powerless against this great multitude that is coming against us. We do not know what to do, but our eyes are on you" (v. 12).

One of the hallmarks of family systems theory is "nonanxious presence." According to both Murray Bowen and Edwin Friedman, nonanxious presence is the capacity of a leader to contain or compartmentalize their own anxiety within a conflict situation, whether or not those issues concern the leader personally, while remaining connected relationally to those involved. By exercising nonanxious presence, the theory posits, the leader will "modify anxiety throughout the entire congregation."[28]

In order to be nonanxiously present with others, we first need to acknowledge our own anxiety. We are, after all, human beings too. Anxiety is as much a part of our lives as it is for those we are called to lead. In truth, our anxiety will reveal itself whether we choose to acknowledge it or not, but if we don't acknowledge it, we will lead from our anxiety rather than from a place of missional integrity and call. As disciples of Jesus, we are to follow a model of vulnerable, servant leadership (e.g., John 13) that admits and accepts the full range of emotional expressions that are part and parcel of our human mosaic.

In acknowledging our anxiety—both to ourselves and to those we are leading—I am not recommending we don the attitude of A. A. Milne's Eeyore, proclaiming the demise of all things good. Nor am I suggesting we use our feelings to manipulate or try to emotionally control our congregation members in order to quell our fears. Rather, I am describing transparent self-regulation that simultaneously establishes personal boundaries and admits vulnerability in order to facilitate communal partnership and mission.[29]

Naming our anxiety does two important things: First, it normalizes the emotions of the transitional season of which the conflict is symptomatic, both for us and for the congregation. The congregation is not looking for two-dimensional, stoic leaders who are devoid of feelings or out of touch with the emotions of the congregation. They are looking for leaders who are emotionally intelligent, able to discern with integrity what they feel, and able to make decisions based on a genuine, empathetic appreciation of the issues and their ramifications on real people, in real time.

Second, naming our anxiety disengages us from the self-protective forces of denial, empowering us to lead from a place of genuine faith. One of my constant reminders of God's grace is found in 2 Corinthians, where Paul, in facing into his "thorn in the flesh," tells us, "And He has said to me, 'My grace is sufficient for you, for power is perfected in weakness.' Most gladly, therefore, I will rather boast about my weaknesses, so that the power of Christ may dwell in me. Therefore, I delight in weaknesses, in insults, in distresses, in persecutions, in difficulties, in behalf of Christ; for when I am weak, then I am strong" (2 Cor 12:9–10 NASB). God is the champion of the weak. It is unmitigated fear that paralyzes. Anxiety mediated by the creative forces of a heart surrendered to God's redemptive, powerful presence motivates not only the leader but the followers as well, through the leader who knows who is on our side.

If we, as pastor-leaders, are doing our job well, there will be some people who don't like us. There always are. There will be people who project onto us all of their reactive emotional angst, blaming us for disrupting "their church" and searching for ways to "crucify" our character, our reputation—or us, personally. One of the most poignant things spoken to me by a mentor years ago, in love, was when, in the midst of a conflict situation at my church, he said to me, "So, Dave, what makes you think you're so special that everyone needs to love you? The fact that you have people who don't may just indicate that what you're doing is exactly what needs to happen for the health of the church." Ouch. But so right. When the biblical David faced Goliath, I'm sure he had some measure of anxiety, in spite of his bravado; after all, he took *five* stones with him rather than just one (1 Sam 17:40). Yet he channeled his anxiety through a filter of faith, reminding himself of the God who had called Israel to a mission greater than his fear.

SING! (OR AT LEAST TAKE VOICE LESSONS)

What happened next in Jehoshaphat's story is powerful to read. The Spirit of the Lord comes upon Jahaziel. Who is Jahaziel? Prior to this moment, he simply was one of the many in the crowd of worship leaders ("a Levite of the sons of Asaph," 2 Chr 20:14) who stood there, afraid. Yet, with God's anointing, his voice would deliver a message of hope and deliverance, telling Jehoshaphat and the crowd, "Do not fear or be dismayed at this great multitude; for the battle is not yours but God's" (vv. 15–17).

In response to Jahaziel's word of encouragement, Jehoshaphat, along with all the people of Judah, bow down and worship God (v. 18). In the morning, the king appoints *worship leaders* (not generals) to walk before the army of Judah (v. 21). And so they sing, praising God with loud voices. It was "as they began to sing and praise" that the Lord "set an ambush" (v. 22) against the invading forces, causing these terrorists to become so confused that they ended up fighting and destroying each other (v. 23).

In the midst of our anxiety, it's important that we remember who we are, why we're here, and where God is calling us to lead God's people. We do that best by singing. Yes, singing! Worshipping God in the midst of our fears gives strength to our faith as we face into the unknowns. Singing gives voice to our trust in the redemptive character and promises of our Lord, reminding us of our identity as children of Almighty God. It also disengages us from the often paralyzing emotional loop that prevents us from taking a stand against the situations that and people who intimidate us. Amid confusion and chaos, singing, along with laughter—especially when we face highly controlling people or our own fears—communicates that we are not defined by the conflict or its pain. The conflict is not the all-consuming focus of our lives that it often threatens to become. Friedman calls this type of response a "paradoxical intervention."[30]

BE AN INTERPRETER OF THE DIVINE MISSION

As pastors amid conflict situations, it is incumbent on us to interpret, illustrate, and model the divine mission in real time. As spiritual leaders, we set the tone. In a recent group mentoring session, one of my mentors, Dr. John C. Maxwell, said, "Problems are what you see when you take your eye off the goal." The unique framework of Jehoshaphat's prayer in 2 Chronicles 20 is that by channeling his own anxiety, and in the presence of the anxiety of the congregation of Judah, he was able to model leadership for us within the New Community: "We do not know what to do, but our eyes are on you" (v. 12), he prayed. Ultimately, Jehoshaphat's vulnerable and faith-oriented leadership empowered Judah's witness within the entire region and brought peace for the remainder of his reign (vv. 29–30).

Keeping our focus on the ultimate divine mission and remembering that the conflict present in the congregation is an opportunity for discipling those involved in the conflict as well as the congregation as a whole can help us mitigate our own anxiety and channel our energy toward equipping our congregation to remember who they are, why they're here, and where they're called to go.

Heading into Advent one year, my church was facing a significant deficit, causing my leaders (and me) to become quite anxious. After I preached a stewardship message in which I shared a story that illustrated how I felt called to give sacrificially in response to the deficit and called on others to tithe along with me, a church member sent me an email chastising me, telling me that I had "mixed motives in asking the church for money" and disparaging my character in no uncertain terms. I replied to the email apologizing that my story had offended her and inviting her to disregard the story if it prevented her from hearing the main part of the message. She then replied, "Now I know that you have mixed motives, since you're telling me to ignore the story!" Admittedly incensed, I wrote a lengthy reply, detailing my motives for preaching the message, giving ample biblical testimony to support my points, and challenging her way of disrespecting her pastor. Before I hit "send," however, the Holy Spirit intervened, whispering into my mind, "She didn't invite you to teach her. She's not ready to hear." In that moment, I realized that my reaction was self-protective and defensive. Her words touched a part of my soul that percolated with my own insecurity. By my reaction, I was giving her control over my emotions. With the click of a button, I deleted my two hours' worth of work and instead wrote the following: "Thank you! Thank you for engaging my sermon! Most weeks, I have no idea who's listening or whether or not my words are impacting them. Clearly, my words impacted you! So thanks for listening!" I hit "send." I received no additional reply. Several months later, she called to ask me to help her family face the very tragic death of a loved one. It was within that context that the Holy Spirit softened hearts—both hers and mine.

As interpreters of divine mission, pastor-leaders can look for opportunities to foster discipleship language for the sake of that mission:

- "Love doesn't mean we always have to agree, but it does mean that we respect each other enough to listen to each other. May we agree to not interrupt while the other is talking?"
- "I can disagree with you and still want the best for you."
- "I'm sorry that I offended you by what I said. That wasn't my intention. I'm trying to tell you how I feel, not hurt you. May I restate what I'm trying to say—and can you help me say it better so that we can at least understand each other's perspective?"
- "I was out of line when I talked about you behind your back. It was inappropriate for me to do so. I was angry at you, and I took it out on you by talking badly about you to someone else. That was very wrong, and I'm sorry. It will not happen again. You're my sister in Christ, and it's my job to protect your reputation. From now on, I'm going to come directly to you when I need to address our relationship. Will you forgive me?"

By keeping our focus on who we are, why we're here, and where we are to lead God's people, we can redirect our own anxiety, channeling its energy into helping us lead.

COUNTER THE DEFAULT

For generations, theologians, psychologists, and sociologists have posited that people, by nature, are generally insecure.[31] The same may be true of congregations. Family systems theory reminds us that the systemic default of any naturally mercy-oriented organization seems to be to defer to the most reactive, most anxious members.[32] Most of us have been trained to believe that doing so is the caring, loving, Christlike thing to do. Usually, however, it is not. If we continue to allow the most reactive, most anxious members to define how the church does ministry, the church will gravitate toward a ministry that solely focuses on healing our *personal* brokenness—becoming a hospital for caring for the sick and dying, literally and metaphorically, and justifying its decision by pointing out how Jesus healed.

Healing brokenness is, indeed, part of what the church is about. However, Jesus did not define his mission and ministry as a healing ministry; rather, he healed as an invitational sign announcing the inauguration of a New Day: "The time is fulfilled, and the kingdom of God has come near; repent, and believe in the good news" (Mark 1:15). As leaders, we need to intentionally counter our overemphasized mercy default in order to move the organization toward the multiplication movement of God's mission. Such confident, mission-driven leadership will cause a reaction, for sure—a reaction that decries the unfairness and callousness of any leader that dares to buck what is perceived to be the caring response.[33]

Organizationally, churches tend to assume that Christlike compassion means we need to cater to those who are reactive. "The squeaky wheel gets the oil" is often the mantra. Without intentionally equipping to do otherwise, we may become convinced that when a person cries, whines, controls, or gives ultimatums, the

Christlike thing to do is to "care for their needs" by delaying or negating decisions that appear to hurt. Our motives may be pure, but by doing so, we inadvertently sabotage the discipleship and growth of both the congregation as a whole and the individual who is reacting.[34] In Friedman's family systems theory, he has made it very clear that it is often the weakest, most dependent members of a system (e.g., family, staff, church, organization) who tend to set the agenda for that system—thereby leveraging power to the most anxious.[35]

People—and organizations—need to mature, and that requires us, as leaders, to increase our tolerance of other people's pain, especially when it comes to ministering alongside chronically reactive people.[36] I have found that this is best accomplished by listening compassionately to those who are reactive while at the same time firmly and assertively setting boundaries on the ramifications of their reactivity as the congregation carries out the divine mission.[37] For example,

- "I can see that our decision to bring contemporary worship into the sanctuary is upsetting you, Gladys. I'm really sad that it's making you reconsider whether you'll keep attending. I know that you said that you don't agree with our desire to reach out to the unchurched people in our neighborhood, but that's what we're going to be doing. I sure hope you'll reconsider, but I certainly understand if you decide that you want to attend elsewhere."
- "Jason, I really want to hear what you have to say, but I find it very difficult to do so while you're yelling at me. If you want me to hear you, you need to stop yelling and talk with me respectfully. If you can't stop yelling, you need to know that you're going to be doing so alone because I'm going to leave the room."

Following this paradigm honors the anxiety of those who feel it while setting limits on how it will define the decisions that ultimately will lead the congregation to "green pastures" (Ps 23:2). That's what good shepherds do.

GET A MENTOR

As leaders, we need to set boundaries on our own anxiety first, as stated above. Our default ways of dealing with conflict and stressful situations may work against our own discipleship and growth, and we can become our own worst enemies. Therefore, it is imperative that we seek the counsel of good mentors and leadership coaches with whom we can navigate the rough waters of our own reactive impulses, and with whom we can establish healthy parameters within which to lead, for the sake of the congregation, our family, and our own health. Genuine discipleship and spiritual growth require that we face the fact that difficulties, too, fall under the sovereignty of God's mission.[38] God is at work at all times, increasing our capacity for leading God's multiplying movement. Sometimes we just need to get out of our own way.

Leaders guide people and organizations through change, conflict, and crisis. The divine mission requires multiplication; therefore, the work of leadership requires that we apply boundaries to our own anxiety in order to facilitate that process. Even though people may rebel against such boundaries, most folks genuinely respond positively to well-defined, well-tempered, love-based leaders. Such leadership makes them feel more secure, which lowers their anxiety, reducing their need to control their environment. We need good mentors and spiritual directors to challenge us to grow in our leadership capacity for the sake of the mission to which God has called us.

That leadership capacity—and our subsequent confidence within conflict situations—starts with getting to know our default styles of conflict response. The emotional nature of conflicts in the church depends on leaders knowing not only who they themselves are but also how to guide people through the stress and back toward the mission to which they have been called.

CHAPTER SIX

Under Stress, We Regress

It is an illusion to think that a person can be led out of the desert
by someone who has never been there.

—Henri Nouwen, *The Wounded Healer*

I'VE MADE MISTAKES OVER MY THIRTY-TWO YEARS OF MINISTRY.
In fact, I've made a lot of them. As a leader in the church, I'm not
alone. Neither are you.

In preparation for a recent workshop I had been asked to lead
for clergy, I surveyed twenty-five long-tenured (at least twenty
years) pastors of mainline churches and asked them to identify
the top one to three "pivotal mistakes" they had made in their
ministries to date. Here are their top answers, in their own words:

- going for the "large church" for the "large salary"
- not seeking counseling in a time of crisis
- thinking that I can "fix" things when I can't
- forgetting this is God's responsibility
- inadvertently allowing someone else to bring me into their
  personal problem
- not doing enough teaching about systems thinking to church
  leadership
- getting swallowed in others' wallows (boundaries!)
- forgetting about taking time to nourish my soul
- becoming alienated from colleagues and others

- procrastinating—especially in dealing with the important stuff
- dealings with staff (both in what I may not have done to support staff and in what I have been reluctant to say to staff because they may not want to hear it or because it might "stir the pot")
- not always meeting conflict head-on
- thinking everything bad is somehow my fault
- thinking everything good is because of me
- lacking prayer
- lacking differentiation
- lacking spiritual direction
- doing everything myself
- trying to please everyone
- becoming the mission instead of leading the mission (in doing so, losing the sense of perspective, sense of humor, and sense of urgency)
- ceasing to grow—or taking on an "oh, well" mentality
- having unhealthy boundaries and lacking interpersonal skills
- not trusting others or having such a strong need to be needed that I am unable to delegate responsibility and authority
- speaking when I should have been listening
- trying to fix people/situations when they did not ask or desire solutions (All they wanted was someone to listen and care.)
- hiring staff primarily for ability rather than character
- not protecting myself against the possibility that people will act out their worst tendencies
- not directly asking people to give generously more often because I was afraid of their response, afraid of what they would think of me

Do you recognize yourself in these comments? I do. So much of what I've become today as a pastor, as a husband, as a person of faith is rooted more firmly in what I've learned from my failures than from my successes. Even when it comes to conflict.

When I started out in ministry, I saw myself as highly competent and clinically trained. Yet when conflict involved me directly, I had an instinctive tendency to retreat into self-protection and relational preservation, accommodating the other person's needs, wants, or demands. When the conflicts involved other people and their issues, I could mediate and moderate like a pro, but when the conflict came at me personally, it would touch my deepest, most soul-wrenching fears of rejection and abandonment, causing me to surrender my own needs for the sake of preserving the facade of intimate connection. When the stakes were high, the emotional and relational tension would cause me to seek the path of least resistance, even when the sacrifices were personally hurtful. That's actually one of the main reasons I began to study conflict, get myself into some serious spiritual direction and mentoring, and make decisions to face into conflicts more directly.

Doing so has taught me a third principle of missional leadership within conflict situations: *under stress, we regress.* And it affects all of us—whether we realize it or not.[1]

I've seen a corporate CEO—someone who makes multimillion-dollar decisions regularly—suddenly retreat under the terroristic outbursts of the seventy-five-year-old woman in charge of a church kitchen. I've seen a bank executive and a corporation's human resources director get into a major shouting match in a church council meeting over seemingly benign agenda items. I've seen highly competent, tremendously gifted pastors sabotage their ministries by having an extramarital affair, or by binge drinking and getting a DUI, or by accessing porn on their church's computer—all because they could no longer face into the stresses of chronic conflicts. I've had my own health problems when, for fear of relational repercussions, I took a year and a half to deal with a staff person who needed to be fired rather than facing directly into the process of termination.

Under stress, we regress. When confronted with situations of emotional tension and conflict, we tend to retreat into the patterns and methods of coping that we have used in the past in order to quell our anxiety. When those past methods were "effective"— whether by engaging the conflict proactively or by succeeding in avoiding it altogether—they became cataloged in our "presets," ready to be set in motion whenever another situation of conflict arose.

I originally became aware of the powerful, reactive impact that stress has on our minds and choices from one of my undergrad psychology professors, Dr. Patricia Snyder at Albright College. The experimental elements of her course on human cognition and learning, which I subsequently facilitated as her lab assistant during my senior year, engaged students in real-time stress-ful memory challenges in order to discover their impact on our mind's capacity to learn and adapt. What I learned was that while our brains have the amazing capacity to adapt to the hormonal changes brought on by stress, we have the tendency, under sig-nificant stress, to revert to what "worked" in the past, however dysfunctional it may have been.

My additional clinical training in family systems and pastoral care in emergency and trauma situations, as well as in critical incident stress management, further clarified the reactive power of post-traumatic stress on our human capacity to cope with con-flict situations. Whether we view it as "trauma" or not, I believe that conflicts in the church connect us to the mosaic of our past experiences of loss, pain, and grief, thereby causing a similar post-traumatic experience of real-time emotional stress. For many of us, church has been a place of safety, a place of spiritual nurture and trust. We have expectations of peace and love, joy and comfort—especially during times of stress, loss, and grief in our own lives. When conflict erupts in the congregation, whether interpersonal or corporate in nature, it disrupts those expec-tations, causing us to become anxious, confused about whom to trust, and suspicious (or even paranoid) about other people's motives. So we react—in body, in mind, in spirit, in attitude, in behavior, sometimes irrationally in ways that betray our normal temperament standards. In the midst of that reaction, we may even allow our personal leadership style to become subject to our anxiety.

All too often the stress of the moment puts us into a fight, flight, or freeze dilemma, triggering our baseline survival reactions and causing us to forget who we are, why we're here, and where we're going. In so many ways, our bodies tell us important information about our leadership—and more specifically, about how we are regulating our own anxiety amid the conflicts within which we are called to lead.[2]

The Challenge of Self-Sabotage

Under such stress, we at times flirt with, or fall for, the temptation to evacuate ourselves from the environment that we perceive to be causing that stress—not always by quitting or retiring or transferring, but sometimes by violating our boundaries, our values, or our vows in order to somehow, ironically, "save face" by not having to admit that we need help. It's a process known as self-sabotage. Sadly, it happens to a lot of great pastors and other leaders.[3]

The challenge of self-sabotage is that while some of us are quite aware of the choices we are making to violate our own personal, marital, or professional boundaries, many of us engage in those behaviors on an unconscious level or, at the very least, within a self-imposed, deeply regressive transactional contract with our shadow side.[4] In other words, we convince ourselves that we're not really doing anything wrong, that we deserve to be happy, that we can stop when we want to, that we don't really have a problem, or that we just don't care in exchange for the "pleasure" of engaging in passive-aggressive rebellion with our call. In simple language, we're angry at God for not rescuing us, or we're angry at the church for treating us disrespectfully, or we're angry at ourselves for—take your pick—failing to be the messiah who saves the day, failing to be the megachurch pastor who gives the impression of having it all together, failing to have the solutions for what's going on in the congregation, failing to have the nerve to stand up to the church bullies, failing to protect our spouse and family from the sinful realities of "church people," or feeling innately afraid or overtly threatened by the conflict and its potential or realistic abusers, or feeling overwhelmingly embarrassed by—or anxious about—any or all of the above. (All of those expressions, by the way, came from actual pastors who had experienced various forms of self-sabotage.)

Rooted deeply in our choices to self-sabotage is anger. And anger is an easier emotion to own than what I believe is most often the real culprit: shame.[5] Erroneously, we believe that because we may not be able to "grow the church" or save our family or save ourselves, we are somehow defective, deficient, rejected, and even unlovable.[6] Under stress, we regress emotionally as the pain touches the deep crevices of our past and exposes the parts of our stories that have been fully redeemed by God, surely, but not fully released by us into the healing light of Christ's love.[7] So we project our pain outward and inward, according to our temperament and timing, according to the level of confusion related to that hidden past.[8] Yet temporary emotions can make for reactionary decisions with permanent aftereffects. Even pastors are human, and the coping mechanism of self-sabotage can easily run amok. I find it is often rooted in how we have been nurtured to deal with conflict—what I refer to as our "default."

Our Default—an Anxiety-Based Reaction to Stress

Over the years, I have seen that when we are faced with stressful moments of high-stakes tension, we gravitate toward the conflict style we learned over the course of our early life—especially from within the constellation of formative experiences shaped by our family of nurture.[9] In other words, we regress to our default. Hopefully, of course, we continue to learn additional, proactive, and healthier ways of addressing conflict, but under stress, we immediately move to our "presets," toward the patterns we learned in our early years.[10]

By the way, I use the term *family of nurture* rather than *family of origin* because, in reality, not everyone grew up in the dynamic of their biological family (e.g., some were adopted into or were placed as foster children in another family). And not everyone was nurtured in conflict dynamics by their biological parents (e.g., some were emotionally raised by grandparents, aunts, uncles, coaches, or others). Regardless, it is within the "family of nurture" that we learn the foundational lessons of how to handle conflict. These lessons influence our character development within the framework of attachment, bonding, love, freedom, and healthy boundaries established from infancy onward.[11]

Discovering our default conflict style is essential to our being effective in leadership within stressful situations.[12] Under stress, our default style will kick into gear automatically unless we are intentional about rerouting our anxiety and choosing a different pathway.[13] It is not that our default style is bad, for as we shall see, each style has its usefulness depending on the nature of the conflict at hand and on our comfort level with the various styles. Our default is the style to which we gravitate automatically, unconsciously, when the stress of conflict rises.[14] Our effectiveness in leadership depends on our ability to acknowledge that default style and to discern whether a different style would work better in any given situation.[15]

Learning our default style of responding to conflict is the starting point for framing our discipleship pathway as well as our ability to lead in the midst of stress.[16] It will help us face our inability to see our fault lines, or blind spots, that mask our pride. Learning our default conflict response style will challenge our unwillingness to admit failure and even expose our false perception of our own greatness. And it will give us hope that we can be better leaders by increasing our capacity to respond in times of crisis.

Five Styles of Conflict Response

While several good resources define styles of conflict response,[17] in my opinion, the best description comes from the Thomas-Kilmann Conflict Mode Instrument, presented by Kenneth Thomas in 1988.[18] Thomas uses a matrix that compares degrees of assertiveness and cooperativeness within five defined modes of conflict temperament: the avoider, the accommodator, the competitor, the compromiser, and the collaborator. I adapt and streamline those styles here to accommodate my framework of missional leadership.[19]

THE AVOIDER

On the Thomas-Kilmann Conflict Mode Instrument, conflict avoiders are "unassertive and uncooperative."[20] When faced with conflict, they retreat from it, seeing it as a threat to the relationship or to their view of self within the context of the relationship (e.g., whether they will be rejected, accepted, loved, affirmed). Valuing the relationship highly, conflict avoiders choose to believe that nothing is wrong rather than risk the potential of rejection. They convince others—and themselves—that the conflict is either not real or "just a misunderstanding" and that "everything will be OK." They may also remove themselves from the arena of conflict—prior to the conflict's eruption or during the conflict as the tension mounts.[21] Avoiders adeptly ply the skill of procrastination to put off dealing with anything too uncomfortable, especially when the presenting issue feels personally threatening. In negative terms, the avoider is the pastor who slips out to go to the bathroom during a heated meeting and then fails to return until the next morning, showing up to work as if nothing happened the night before. Peace in the relationship is not only preferred; it is considered essential, even to the point of denying the reality of personal pain inflicted on the avoider by another—even an abuser. In positive terms, the avoider is the pastor who evaluates a conflict as being insignificant in the grander schema of the congregation's missional objectives and therefore chooses to ignore it rather than applying limited time, energy, and resources toward it.

THE ACCOMMODATOR

Similar to avoiders, conflict accommodators are "unassertive and cooperative."[22] Such individuals place high value on the emotional connection of the relationship and fear both confrontation and the potential for relational trauma, rejection, and abandonment. However, accommodators do not deny the existence of the relational tension. Instead, they acknowledge the conflict while seeking to preserve the relationship at all costs, even to the point of sacrificing their own wants, needs, or health. Fear motivates accommodators to not share honestly with the other party, seeking to placate the other based on their own needs to maintain the perceived relational connection. Accommodators are quick to agree to the terms of the other person, "giving in" even at great personal cost, because the thought of losing the relationship (or levels of connection) is too overwhelming.[23] In negative terms, the accommodator is the pastor who gives in to the demands of the long-tenured church organist who comes into the office and yells to get the pastor to comply with particular styles of worship music and liturgy. In positive terms, the accommodator is the pastor who, when faced with multiple levels of significant conflict, is able to discern which facets are worth taking on and which are best addressed by giving in, especially when seen as part of the larger strategy of systemic leadership.

THE COMPETITOR

Conflict competitors engage relational conflict like a battle or competition. On the Thomas-Kilmann scale, they are "assertive and uncooperative."[24] Within the relational tension, they create a win-lose exchange in which they *must* win. Typically competitive, domineering, or controlling in temperament, they exert influence (power, position, stature, posture, past performance) to get what they want regardless of the real or perceived threat to the

relationship.[25] They apply persuasion and coercion to get others
to comply with their demands. If the relationship is damaged by
their tactics, or if the other person is hurt or demeaned by their
words or actions, they respond with "You're being too sensitive"
or "Don't be such a baby" or "OK, I'm sorry; I take it back." In
negative terms, the competitor is the pastor who either overtly
or passive-aggressively seeks to compel (or "bullies") the church
elders into doing a certain thing or who, when confronted, blames
everyone else for their role in the conflict rather than owning any
personal responsibility in the matter. Competitors see their own
perspective as the right one, listen to the other side only with the
goal of forming counterstrategies, and exert effort at winning
at all costs. In positive terms, the competitor is the pastor who
intervenes in a situation of child abuse and exerts influence to
protect that child at all costs.

THE COMPROMISER

Compromisers also engage conflict from a win-lose perspective,
but unlike with the competitor, they anticipate that both sides will
win some and lose some. On the Thomas-Kilmann scale, compromisers are "moderately assertive and cooperative,"[26] attempting to
satisfy both parties with a middle-ground solution. Compromisers seek a resolution to the relational tension by interacting with
each side's demands based on their perceived values and then
negotiating a "deal" that involves each party sacrificing toward
the greater goal of unity or peace. For some conflict mediators,
compromise is the most common style of conflict response and is
considered the most beneficial for complex conflict scenarios.[27]
The positive side to compromise is that each party both wins and
loses with a perceived intentionality toward equity.[28] The challenge of compromise is that often, true resolution is not obtained
but rather delayed as interests, positions, needs, or wants are
sublimated—later to be projected onto new opportunities for
disagreement. The compromiser is the pastor who, when faced
with conflict, negotiates gains and losses in order to mediate the

tension and moderate the pain required for a genuine deepening of relational connection and resolution. In positive terms, compromisers are able to help participants move beyond communication impasses, empowering them to discover some level of agreement even when complete resolution is yet to be achieved. In negative terms, compromisers can allow the goal of resolving the conflict to overshadow genuine missional advancement.

THE COLLABORATOR

The collaborator literally "colabors" with the other conflicted party toward a mutually agreeable solution. On the Thomas-Kilmann scale, the collaborator is "both assertive and cooperative."[29] Collaboration has been called an "integrative strategy" because it seeks a "win-win" solution within a healthy relational dynamic.[30] Collaboration in congregations works best when both parties are willing to work together toward resolution, redefining the relational boundaries and creating new connectivity within the systems of the organization. In fact, collaboration will not work effectively unless both parties are willing to come to the table of discussion with openness and honesty, sharing all relevant information. The collaborative effort is centered less on how to resolve differences and more on creating a new solution to a mutual problem.[31] Therefore, agreement on the problem becomes essential, as is agreement on the parameters of the collaborative process (e.g., rules of engagement, how discussions will be formatted). In negative terms, the collaborator is the pastor who sees collaboration as the only way to resolve conflict and therefore insists on mediation when either one or both parties are unwilling to come to the table. In positive terms, the collaborator is the pastor who seeks to foster trust and mutuality while focusing on creatively inviting both parties into resolving the relational tension through need-based problem solving.[32]

Which Style Is Right?

While we may assume that the collaborator style is the best conflict response because it involves the ideal of both parties coming together for a mutually agreeable solution (something that sounds natural for those in the Christian faith community), each of the five conflict styles can be an important tool for the missional leader, based on the specific situation. For example, while my default is accommodation and my training is in collaborative mediation, if I encounter someone who is bullying or intimidating another parishioner and perceive that other parishioner as being vulnerable and unable to respond on their own behalf, my normally recessive competitor style will emerge, and I will exert my pastoral influence to eliminate the bullying behavior.

"Which style is right?" is the wrong question to ask. Rather, we need to ask, "Which style is needed for this situation?" Since under stress, we regress, it is imperative that we know our default style of conflict response, lest it prematurely determine our leadership toward the conflict's outcome and thereby leverage power to the most reactive within the conflict.[33] Additionally, it is vital that we gain confidence in each style in order to lead in conflict situations more effectively and more fluidly. It is incumbent upon the pastor, as the congregation's spiritual leader, to develop the necessary interpersonal skills and emotional intelligence to guide people through the conflicts required for spiritual formation and discipleship.[34]

While pastor-leaders who understand their own default style will be able to choose an appropriate response to a given conflict situation, it's important to remember that the other participants in the conflict will be reacting out of their own default styles as well. Since discipleship and disciple making are the main foci of our calling, it also becomes our job as pastor-leaders to coach the participants in how to handle conflict within the framework of the New Community even when we are directly involved with the conflict ourselves. We must be both sufficiently disconnected from the emotional processes of the congregation and fully present within their relational interactions[35] to not lose sight of our role of calling people to new life in Jesus Christ. We are, therefore, utterly dependent on the Holy Spirit to provide discernment, healthy personal boundaries, and emotional maturity sufficient for the task of leading people onward toward mission and multiplication, of helping them remember who we are, why we're here, and where we're going.

Conflicts are inevitable, predictable, and even essential for growth in discipleship. And discipleship is essential for the development of the types of leaders that will carry out God's mission mandate. Facing into relational conflicts as they arise in the congregation with that longer-term perspective will remind us that courage accumulates with character development. The apostle Paul reminds us in Romans 5:3–5 that "suffering produces endurance, and endurance produces character, and character produces hope, and hope does not disappoint us."

Ultimately, it's not the leader in the church but the Lord in the leader that makes the difference. Gaining an understanding of our default conflict response as well as confidence and fluidity in using all five styles will help us facilitate the mission-mandated leadership necessary to reframe church conflicts into contexts for discipleship and growth.

CHAPTER SEVEN

Systems Tend to Self-Preserve

And this is my prayer, that your love may overflow more and more with knowledge and full insight to help you to determine what is best, so that in the day of Christ you may be pure and blameless, having produced the harvest of righteousness that comes through Jesus Christ for the glory and praise of God.

—Philippians 1:9-11

AFTER WORSHIP ON MY FIRST SUNDAY AT SECOND STREET CHURCH, a lone man remained seated in the front pew of the sanctuary, weeping. I did not know him at the time; I was the church's new pastor, and the flow of unfamiliar faces and names was still swirling in my head as I sat on the Communion rail's kneeling pad in front of him. "Was my sermon that bad?" I joked as I tried to create an easy entry point to the conversation with a stranger. He chuckled lightly through his tears. "How can I help?" I asked plainly.

Joe was dressed in casual slacks and a button-down dress shirt, fitting attire for an air-conditioned church on the last Sunday of June. Bunched-up tissues were clenched in his hand, and he looked weary. For the next twenty minutes, he shared a story that had layers of pain and disappointment—his story. He had been born to an unwed mother; in fact, his mother had "several men" in her life, and with each, she had given birth to a child. His mother had long been connected to Second Street Church, and so, when

Joe was born, she requested baptism for her son. In Joe's words, the pastor and the lay leaders had told his mother, "I'm sorry, but we don't baptize bastard children."

On sharing this, Joe's sobs intensified. "Why would they deny me baptism? How could they say that?"

Joe had just turned fifty. So for fifty years, he and his mother had continued to attend Second Street Church, faithfully participating in various ministries, even serving in leadership roles—in spite of the emotional pain of exclusion they bore on their hearts and souls, a pain that his mom had obviously passed on to her son as a legacy of misery. Through waves of tears, Joe poured out the ramifications of his existential alienation—difficult relationships, a struggling marriage, feeling disconnected from God.

"Would you like to be baptized now?" I asked when it seemed like Joe's story had reached its zenith. "There are still enough people here in the back of the church. I can call them up here so we can have a gathering of the congregation and we can baptize you right now."

"You would do that?"

"Let me ask you, Do you confess Jesus as your Lord and acknowledge that he died for your sins?"

"Yes . . . yes, I do."

"Then yes, absolutely I'll baptize you."

Joe went silent for a moment, thinking. "Thank you. Thank you for saying that. I do want to be baptized, but not right now. I want it . . . and I want it at the right time. But thank you."

Over the next several months, I began noticing different patterns in relational dynamics at the church: people who were considered part of the inner circle and those who were not, animosity between different groups of people, veiled comments subtly dropped into conversations about "types" of people. My gut told me something was hiding in the shadows, something that historically blocked this church from living into its freedom in Christ.

That following February, eight months after I had met Joe, I was at home on a Saturday evening. My sermon was written, nothing was on television, and I was looking for something to do while my wife read and my dog napped at her feet. "Why not read something?" Kristine encouraged. So I picked up a small book that had been on my coffee table since my arrival at the church. It was a copy of Second Street Church's history, written and revised by two of our church historians several years prior. I had put off reading it, leaving it for one of those times when I was absolutely bored.

After slowly reading through the opening chapters on various aspects of the history of the congregation, I came upon a paragraph, stuck in the middle of a section concerning the "four pivotal pastorates" of the church, that would seismically alter my burgeoning ministry there. It was so enraging that I memorized it: "In 1923, the administrative board of Second Street Church had the privilege of receiving a gift of the American flag from the local chapter of the Ku Klux Klan. The KKK was subsequently invited to attend worship, unhooded, but they refused."

The history book continued to the next topic without any further explanation. I am not normally a foul person (even though I am an Italian kid from New Jersey!), but reading this caused me to shout out an expletive, making both my wife and my dog jump. I needed to find out more.

It was eight thirty at night, but I decided to call the current church historian, who was the revision author of the book. After reading her the paragraph, I asked her a direct question: "Did this really happen?"

"Yes," she said. "I was very young back then, but I remember my parents talking about it."

"Is that the flag that's in our sanctuary now?" I asked, my stomach tied in knots.

Quintessentially the retired teacher, she said, "There's only one way to tell: count the stars. In 1923, there would only have been forty-eight."

The next morning at church I pulled the American flag by its ends and counted the stars. Fifty. Flag crisis avoided. Yet the floodgate of insight began to open.

At the next meeting of our administrative board, I shared the paragraph and my run-in with the sanctuary flag. I asked the leaders, "How do you feel about what you just heard? This is now part of our shared history." Person after person began sharing actual stories of exclusions, relational tensions, and racism that they had heard or witnessed. Even as recently as two years prior, one person shared, "a Black couple came to visit on a Sunday morning, and the usher at the door informed them that *their* church was up the road." They shared that historically, the geographical area around the church had been a center of racial conflict, bigotry, and even satanic cult worship.

"What you're describing . . . is this the kind of church that you want to be?" I asked. I then shared verses from Nehemiah 1—about how leadership means taking responsibility not only for our own sinful behaviors and attitudes but also for the sinful behaviors and attitudes of those who came before us, our ancestors. Before Nehemiah led a movement to rebuild the walls—and a people—in Jerusalem, he wept and mourned over the sins of his people, sins committed decades before he was even born. Together as leaders, we decided we wanted to be a different church; we wanted to be different leaders. We joined hands around the table, confessed our sins of racism and exclusion, owned what our predecessors had allowed, owned what we had allowed, and asked forgiveness on behalf of the church.

The following Sunday, I shared the same process with the congregation at both of our worship services, concluding with a time of confession and seeking forgiveness, along with a commitment to live differently. Since my first day at Second Street Church, there had been people on one side of the congregation who didn't speak to people on the other. So I had the congregation stand and turn toward the center aisle, facing each other. I asked each person to make eye contact with someone on the opposite side of the room while I led them in a responsive confession and litany of forgiveness. It was a holy moment—one that I know not everyone appreciated, but it was a moment that was critically important for the spiritual life of this congregation.

The stained glass windows did not implode. The roof did not cave in. But something shifted dynamically that day.

As I prepared for worship on Easter Sunday a few weeks later, I felt the nudging of the Holy Spirit to add a baptism and renewal of baptism vows opportunity to the order of worship. It was a last-minute idea added to an already overpacked service, yet in spite of my internal resistance to the time crunch, I set up the baptism bowl and towel and told the worship pastor to be prepared to play some background music during this sacramental moment.

The service was packed that morning. Families were gathered, and there was a heightened energy in the room. We sang, I preached, we shared Communion, and then I gave an invitation for baptism and renewal of baptism vows, sharing that Easter is a time for new life, for connecting with the heart of Jesus, who wants to draw us closer to himself and to each other.

I had barely finished speaking the words of invitation when Joe jumped out of his seat and came forward, tears of joy flowing down his cheeks. He knelt down in front of me at the Communion rail, and I poured the water on his head, laid hands on him, and prayed for him. When I looked up, the entire Communion rail was filled with people kneeling and crying, with a line of others waiting as well. Over forty people came forward. One by one, they came for the life-giving renewal of assurance of the Lord's redemptive love and grace. As I finished, I realized that my face was also baptized—by the overwhelming tears of having been in the healing presence of the Lord.

That's when the church began to grow.

The Best Way to Get Rid of Weeds
Is to Overseed with Grass

I have had an ongoing love-hate relationship with my lawn. For the better part of a decade, it seemed that the only thing I could grow on it was weeds. I tried everything—natural sprays, chemical powders, professional lawn care companies. Each offered their own promises, but weeds continued to thrive. One professional I talked with even said that the only way to "win the war with the weeds" was to use a general herbicide, kill the whole lawn, turn over all the topsoil, and start over from scratch. So I did that too. It was a dirty and muddy mess, especially when it rained, but I persevered. When spring came, I was greeted with a whole new chapter of weeds.

Then one day, I happened to be talking with a friend who works at a local greenhouse. When I shared with him my perennial plight, he said, "Dave, the best way to get rid of weeds is to overseed with grass." It was one of those moments when I knew—beyond the topic of conversation—that God was speaking truth into my life. I literally interrupted the conversation, whipped out my phone, and typed out what he had said. There was wisdom in that statement that went far beyond my high-trafficked turf.

For those of you who are facing into a conflict situation in your church right now, what if that conflict is actually inaugurating a season of essential grace—a time when the Holy Spirit is trying to do a new thing for the sake of advancing God's missional purpose in that community? What if the conflict could be seen as a type of *intervention* meant to interrupt the embedded, controlling factions that have long bullied the congregation, pulling it off course from its inherent purpose? What if the conflict were seen as a means by which the Holy Spirit was exposing unhealthy patterns, deep layers of brokenness, or channels of unrepented sin? Would you treat the conflict differently if you knew it had divine purpose?

In chapter 1, I shared that our job as pastor-leaders is not necessarily to resolve conflict, but rather to equip healthy systems and disciple healthy leaders in order to assist our congregation in living out its divine mission. I have been contending that conflicts are *contexts* within which that equipping and discipling take place. Therefore, conflicts become, in effect, partners with the Holy Spirit in the process of spiritual formation—our own as well as that of the congregation we serve.

The ultimate goal of this process is full transformation into the image of Christ (Phil 1:9–11). For most of us, that involves a lifelong journey of surrendering daily to the lordship of Christ the things we think are important, the frameworks we think define us, and the idols we worship as part of our personal agendas. It seems, however, that within our naturally self-absorbed ways, it takes a lot of coaxing to bring our recalcitrant habits into such submission.[1]

The same is true for congregations. Conflict often exposes areas within our individual and corporate New Community lives that may be in desperate need of God's redemptive grace. In other words, weeds grow where there's vacancy in the turf. So what creates that vacancy? What fosters the growth of weeds (conflicts, dysfunctionality, tense relationships) in our congregations? In addition to what I shared earlier, I believe that three specific environmental factors within congregational life nurture a predisposition toward conflict: a culture of dishonor, a pastor-centered model of ministry, and a legacy of hidden sin.

A CULTURE OF DISHONOR

I am convinced that at the heart of many chronically conflicted congregations is a culture of dishonor. When the apostle Paul wrote his letter to the Romans, he was not necessarily addressing specific issues of contention within the Roman congregation (though there were a few), nor was he addressing invasive heretical influences, as he had done in several of his other letters. Yet this letter does have a context: I'm referring to the context not of the recipients but of the author.

It is believed that Paul wrote Romans while staying in Corinth.[2] As we understand from 1 and 2 Corinthians, the church in Corinth was undergoing significant conflicts—internal division (e.g., 1 Cor 1:10–17; 3:1–23), scandalous ethical behavior (e.g., 1 Cor 5:1–13; 6:1–20), theological contention (e.g., 1 Cor 7–8, 15; 2 Cor 6:14–18; 10:1–11:15), and an early version of what we might call "worship wars" (e.g., 1 Cor 10–14), among other matters. So when Paul writes in Romans 12:9–10, "Let love be genuine; hate what is evil, hold fast to what is good; love one another with mutual affection; outdo one another in showing honor," his words ring out to the growing congregation in Rome from a place of deep understanding regarding the human propensity toward selfish ambition and relational iconoclasm. His word choice—"outdo one another"—is from the Greek compound verb *proegeomai*, which literally means to "lead the way."[3] In other words, Paul is telling his readers that Christians are to act differently than their nonchurched counterparts. Christians are to "lead the way" by example, in how we exalt one another, encourage one another, empower one another, honor one another. Paul says as much again in Philippians 2:3 ESV: "Do nothing from selfish ambition or conceit, but in humility count others more significant than yourselves."

A culture of dishonor is cultivated when we chronically set ourselves as superior to others, when we gossip and therefore disrespect another's reputation, when we disparage another's character, or when we diminish their voice at the table of decision. We cultivate dishonor when we abuse privilege or power, when we dismantle infrastructures of mutual accountability, or when we undermine others who are in positions of authority, whether pastoral or lay. We cultivate dishonor when we violate ethical or relational boundaries that exist to create a safe environment for nurture and growth. We cultivate dishonor when—actively or passively—we fail to protect the characters and hearts of our siblings in Christ who are being disrespected and abused.

Over time, such dishonor robs the soil of the congregation of that which is necessary for healthy spiritual formation and multiplication (e.g., Matt 13:54–58). New leaders rarely emerge, and when they do, they are beaten up by the insecurity of dysfunctional people and systems. Status quo is maintained at all costs, preserving the dysfunctional environment as a breeding ground for control, discontent, animosity, and spiritual hostage taking.[4]

A PASTOR-CENTERED MODEL OF MINISTRY

A second environmental factor—what I call a "pastor-centered model of ministry"—is not as obvious as the first, for it is so mainstream that it seems to have become endemic to Christianity. Yet I would argue that the pastor-centered model of ministry is surreptitiously dismantling the mission of multiplying disciples for the transformation of the world. Now, by no means am I trying to disparage the role of the pastor as shepherd to the congregation. Indeed, I have lived out that calling for over thirty years. Rather, by a pastor-*centered* model of ministry, I am referring to what happens when a congregation assumes that "real" ministry doesn't happen unless the pastor (or senior pastor, in multistaff contexts) is present and participating in the actual ministry function. As such, the pastor must be in the office forty-five to fifty-five hours per week (even if they are part-time) while managing to visit all parishioners in their homes, especially those in nursing homes, as well as being available for all janitorial duties when necessary. The pastor must provide all of the counseling and meet all care needs, single-handedly evangelize the neighborhoods, give great sermons, be an excellent Bible study leader, spend time with the kids in Sunday school, and be involved in the various outreach events of the local ministerium. When a parishioner is in the hospital, they don't feel cared for by the church if the pastor hasn't visited, even if ten other church members showed up with flowers and distribution of Communion.

A pastor-centered model can exist in a church of any size. I saw it in my home church of twenty-five people. It was present in my first church appointment of three hundred people. It was present in my most recent appointment of thirteen hundred people. It has been present—amid much tension—in quite a few of the congregations with which I have consulted. This model of ministry is not about congregational size but about attitude, about legacy, and about a failure to responsibly equip and engage the laity.

The pastor-centered model of ministry is often seen in a long-tenured, dysfunctional, irresponsible misappropriation of a pastor's call to ministry. Since the days of long ago when the role of clergy was institutionalized, many parishioners in such systems have neglected their membership vows and have pushed off their responsibilities onto "professionals," deciding that they would need extra training to do ministry and therefore choosing instead to pay professionals to do it. Additionally, it has been my experience that way too many clergy have supplanted the role of the priesthood of all believers in favor of supporting their own mischaracterization of pastoral identity or a codependent need to be needed or simply bad training. When parishioners genuinely want to engage in ministry, some pastors feel threatened and end up sabotaging the very processes that are designed to empower discipleship and mission. The pastor-centered model of ministry is neither biblically sound nor ecclesiologically healthy—for pastor or congregation.[5] By definition, it has the potential to erode the missionally reproductive nature of discipleship. While an effective discussion of this topic, including the implications of Ephesians 4:11–13, 1 Corinthians 12, and Romans 12, is beyond the scope of this book, suffice it to say that ministry within the framework of a pastor-centered model of ministry inevitably creates an environment conducive to role confusion, misuse of power, codependency, and missional decline—in other words, weeds.

A LEGACY OF HIDDEN SIN

As with Joe's account at the beginning of this chapter, stories need to be told. Even the ones we try to hide. Legacies of hidden sin often reveal themselves within subsequent generations. In my experience, hidden sin is the third environmental factor that creates a predisposition toward missional dysfunction. In the book of Numbers, Moses pleads with God on behalf of the people of Israel in light of their rebellion against God's authority, call, and plan. Reiterating God's own words, Moses says, "The Lord is slow to anger, and abounding in steadfast love, forgiving iniquity and transgression, but by no means clearing the guilty, visiting the iniquity of the parents upon the children to the third and the fourth generation" (Num 14:18). There is a clear picture in this prayer of the longevity of unrepented sin.

The spiritual formation and family systems dynamics reflected in Israel's experience and Moses's prayer are consistent with modern understandings of generational dysfunction and interpersonal-intergenerational conflict. Specifically, addiction, abuse, suicide, broad mental health issues, and even racism—just to name a few examples—are traceable symptomatically within genealogies as families strive to cope with layers of "family secrets."[6] Such family secrets notoriously leave scars on successive generations, as we project onto other issues and people the things that we don't want to see in ourselves. Within those vacuums of personal responsibility, genuine leaders, new ideas, life-giving messages, and even hope begin to disappear—leaving space only for the anxiety that birthed it all.

Developing Environments of Accountability

The goal of missional leadership within conflict situations then is to proactively create healthy systems within which people may be discipled into becoming spiritual leaders who are able, in turn, to reproduce in others the values and culture of the New Community and thus advance God's mission (cf. 2 Tim 2:2). The culture of Christ's New Community defines the integrity of the road upon which the journey of spiritual formation progresses and defines the boundaries of who we choose to be, how we will be known within the community, how we will interact with one another, and for what we would be willing to live or die. The culture of Christ's New Community is the framework that determines our nonnegotiables as well as how we will hold ourselves accountable to one another.[7] When we do it well, the multiplication of leaders who are nurtured in discipleship values and focused on carrying out the mission of Christ eventually crowds out the unhealthy and toxic elements. "Weeds," therefore, cannot gain a foothold.

Specifically, conflicts in the church expose three primary opportunities for discipleship: accountability to our divine mission, accountability to our covenant, and the creation of healthier systems.

ACCOUNTABILITY TO OUR DIVINE MISSION

In Matthew 9:35–38, we read, "Then Jesus went about all the cities and villages, teaching in their synagogues, and proclaiming the good news of the kingdom, and curing every disease and every sickness. When he saw the crowds, he had compassion for them, because they were harassed and helpless, like sheep without a shepherd. Then he said to his disciples, 'The harvest is plentiful, but the laborers are few; therefore ask the Lord of the harvest to send out laborers into his harvest.'"

While a lot can be said about this passage, notice two specific things: First, "the Lord of the harvest" is responsible for both the harvest itself ("his harvest," v. 38) and the deployment of laborers ("ask the Lord of the harvest to send out laborers," v. 38). The harvest is a given. Fruit is ready to be picked. When we "ask the Lord of the harvest to send out laborers," God raises up the church. It's the church's job to go reap a harvest that they themselves did not plant.

Second, notice the phrase "to send out." The Greek verb used is *ekballo*—which literally means "to cast out" (the same word, by the way, used to describe the casting out of demons[8]). What Jesus is saying, in effect, is "the harvest is so huge, ask God to throw out as many workers into the fields as possible to disciple the abundance of transformed lives coming our way."

Do our congregations see the abundance of transformed lives needing to be discipled?

The mission and values of the New Community must become a part of the DNA of the congregation. Accountability to this mission and these values must be foundational to everything that happens within and through the church. Through the teaching from the pulpit, the equipping in small groups, the warmth of hospitality, the hiring of staff (both clergy and nonclergy), and everything else the congregation does, God's mission must be learned and modeled as the primary reason the church exists. The New Community mission and values also must be defined by the leadership in advance of and reiterated in the midst of conflict. It is very difficult to tell someone they are rebelling against the direction in which the church is headed if, in fact, the church doesn't know where it is going.

In conflict, the mission and values of the kingdom of God, the New Community in Christ, provide the objective plumb lines by which behavior is either accepted or not tolerated.[9] They create a self-defining anchor that both invites new people to align with the congregation and sets boundaries for those who will not. When pastors and lay leaders are approached by those who stand apart from the leadership, clear values and mission give leaders the ability to say calmly, firmly, and with integrity, "I'm sorry that you don't agree with what we're doing, but this is how we do things here in order to live out our mission. We really hope that you will come with us on this journey, but we respect your right to choose not to." Every individual must have the freedom to choose to align or not.

Leaders must be resolved in their quest to honor God above all else: "Strive *first* for the kingdom of God," says Jesus (Matt 6:33; my emphasis). God's mission is our job description. The self-definition required to align ourselves to that mission equips us to move beyond peacemaking as our primary goal. Making disciples of Jesus Christ for the transformation of the world is our primary goal. Jesus did not die an excruciating death in order to make us feel good about ourselves. For the congregation to get this, the leaders must get it first.

So how do we develop an environment of accountability to the divine mission? Defining our call, leading from that call, and equipping those in the congregation who have the greatest capacity to join us in scrupulously living out that call can ultimately cause the entire congregation to shift toward health and growth.[10] Once this mission is defined, leaders must choose to remain committed to it—even to the point of inviting people to adapt to the new way of living in that mission if they want to remain or become a part of the congregation.[11]

Unless we are in a brand-new church plant that has been organized around a centralized mission, as we move into congregational self-definition, conflict will surely erupt. While it may feel troublesome and raise the anxiety of those involved, it is important to realize that such conflict is actually an indication that we are pushing against long-embedded forces of homeostasis (status quo). By design, *systems tend to self-preserve.* Even in our dysfunctions, we protect what we're used to.[12] In other words, we may actually defend our dysfunctions. Any venture that asks us to challenge—or leave—our comfort zone can bring suspicion or even sabotage.[13]

In such instances, it is important for the leaders first to unite themselves around the unified mission and values that define who they are, why they're here, and where they're called to lead the congregation. Pastors and lay leaders must work together through this process of discernment—for the communication and presence of a visually unified partnership among the leaders of the congregation will be vitally important for the transition to healthier systems. Even if anxiety initially arises because of the transition, my experience is that, over time, it will decrease as trust in the leadership grows.

Additionally, it will be important for the leaders to increase their tolerance of emotional pain—their own as well as others'.[14] Seeing and hearing other people's anxiety related to change may make us want to alter our course. However, mission must trump our pain. We must place boundaries around our own propensity to be reactive to other people's anxiety. And we must learn how to be nonanxious and nonreactive around the reactions of others.[15]

I have found that it is possible to be fully compassionate and present with people during these seasons of transition yet not be caught up in their reactivity. In fact, significant discipleship can occur when mentor-leaders see the best in those they are called to serve, love them enough to lead them where they do not yet know they need to go, help them navigate the grief related to transition, and equip them to grow along the journey. "Leading" people into maintaining their status quo in their relationship with God is not discipleship. It's codependency.[16] Indeed, no actual leading is called for if people are just staying where they've been. This is not to say we can make people change; only the Holy Spirit can. Yet when we engage in intentional prayer, study, and discernment, seeking God's direction for the greater witness and ministry of the church, I believe the Holy Spirit takes us seriously.[17]

The harvest is ready, and God is sending us. It's time to step up. So who in our congregation is actually seeking God's direction? What will we as leaders do with God's answer? And who will hold us accountable for how we lead the congregation in carrying out its divine mission?

ACCOUNTABILITY TO OUR COVENANT

Conflicts in the church also expose dysfunctions within our discipleship processes. When someone chooses to align with the congregation, do they understand the expectations of what life in the New Community looks like? Have those expectations been taught to them, modeled for them, and agreed to by them? Many congregations have the equivalent of baptism or membership vows. We use those vows to elevate publicly the covenantal nature of the church.[18] We may ask new members to renounce sin and resist evil, to confess Jesus Christ as Lord and promise to trust in his grace and serve him, to commit to learning the Scriptures, to serve in and outside the congregation, to attend worship regularly, and to tithe—all as outward signs of our membership covenant.[19]

So here's a key question: How are we doing at holding members accountable to these vows once they've joined? Some churches seem to have their version of "rule police," enforcing judgmental policies as an act of pious control.[20] Others have almost a laissez-faire flippancy about covenantal connections, allowing parishioners to engage in first-century Corinthian-like abuse of Christian freedom.[21] Still other congregations, however, seem to have learned the value of equipping their members to live out explicitly taught expectations set within boundaries of love such that members are held accountable by leaders who model mutual submission and servant hearts.[22]

How do we establish such a system of covenantal accountability? A fundamental principle that I have used in ministry for the last fifteen years is this: the best way to change the culture of the church is at the front door. By this I mean that it's easier to create something new than to reform the old. Of course, not everything old is bad, and not everything new is good. My point is that when it's time to introduce shifts to the culture of a congregation, it's best to begin with those who are already moving toward the mission you're promoting—namely, prospective new members. If there are no prospective new members yet, we can start with those who seem to be gravitating toward what we are preaching and teaching. In other words, we move to the places where God seems to be opening a door.

Developing accountability from a point of entrance gives clarity, fosters unity in mission, engages commitment, and increases the likelihood of maturity within the process of spiritual formation.[23] Therefore, it is essential that pastors and leaders develop a discipleship "pipeline"—a clear pathway for moving people progressively along their faith journey.[24] Accountability is built into the pathway, facilitating a process of mentored growth. Partnership within the mission and values of the New

Community, as well as in how to navigate through conflict, is, in this framework, apprenticed from the point of entry.

Another way to establish accountability is through membership covenants. Former senior consultant and director of consulting for the Alban Institute (and my former pastor) Gilbert Rendle suggests that behavioral covenants may be the best way to frame our relational connections, especially in times of conflict and transition.[25] I agree. Taking it one step further, I have found that it is good practice to equip congregations with a clear picture of what New Community life is meant to be. We cannot hold anyone accountable for what they have not been taught. Engaging the membership as a whole on those expectations, as well as the accountability process related to them, equips the church proactively for times of transition and conflict.[26]

To begin, Rendle recommends involving leaders and congregation in developing covenantal expectations. Once these covenantal boundaries are agreed upon, the congregation is invited to align with them, ideally agreeing to a process of mutual accountability for the sake of doing life together. Adjustments are made periodically, and members are asked to recovenant annually or as needed within seasons of conflict and transition.

Membership covenants can vary in detail, based on the congregation's context, denominational culture, and governance style. Yet they all hold certain characteristics in common: they give leaders and congregation an opportunity to engage in a process of self-definition regarding what life in that community of faith looks like, how members can expect to be treated, how they are expected to treat others, and how accountability—especially amid disagreements—will be accomplished.[27]

New members are oriented to the church's covenant at the outset. Invitations to existing members are rolled out within the process of the covenant's development. Covenants help objectify the expectations, establishing trust in both the leadership and the congregational environment.[28] When tested, the covenant becomes the tool used for accountability. Appendix A shows, by way of example, the membership covenant in use at my present congregation.

Ultimately, of course, accountability starts with leadership. It's important to ask questions like these:

Are there job descriptions for both paid and volunteer positions?

What are the matrices by which staff and volunteers are held accountable?

How and by whom will they be supervised?

How are performance reviews done?

What is asked of the staff and volunteers who enforce the priorities and values of the mission?

What qualities do we look for in hiring people for pastoral and staff team roles?

What about for training of volunteers?

Is there a structure of church discipline that is taught before it is enforced?

How is the effect of a staff person's or a volunteer's underperformance communicated to the team?

How are power and responsibility shared?

What would it look like if we created a culture of accountability within our congregations for how we live together in the discipling culture of the New Community and then taught that culture within the fabric of the congregation?

Working through questions such as these illustrates a congregation's intentionality toward healthy accountability and commitment to discipleship and mission. Leaders model that accountability by initiating learning goals, submitting to mutual review processes, and engaging in mentorship relationships that encourage spiritual formation and growth. Rather than happening linearly—as in a traditional "chain of command"—accountability is a team process, as members engage one another in a 360-degree feedback loop.

Accountability to the covenant is a rhythmic reminder that our individual behaviors—including how we engage one another during seasons of disagreement—have ramifications that impact the congregation's witness within the community and beyond.

So how can we proactively create that healthy, overseeded "turf"?

CREATING HEALTHIER SYSTEMS

As discussed in chapter 2, every conflict has its roots in violation of some sort. Two bodies of matter are trying to occupy the same space at the same time. Someone steps into our proverbial space, or challenges our sense of normal, or threatens to push us out of our comfort zone, or abuses us with overweighted power, or vandalizes our reputation, or dishonors our identity, or desecrates our connection to our faith. Sadly, that describes a typical week in the life of a highly conflicted congregation—as well as in some congregations going through seasons of transition in leadership. Systemic "violations" are incredibly common as new leaders and new ideologies begin to introduce change and the existing systems react.

While Jesus was occasionally invitational with the Pharisees (e.g., Nicodemus, in John 3), he didn't spend much time trying to reform the religious constructs of Judaism. He simply gathered a ragtag group of twelve—enhanced by an amazing following of women and other men—and created something new. He did it by pouring his teaching into them for three years, apprenticing them in how to lead the movement he had begun, and empowering them with the Holy Spirit so the movement had a chance to multiply. Jesus has been using that same process within God's mission ever since.

And he wants to do it again with us.

So let's ask the question more specifically. Instead of trying to reform or "heal" dysfunctional systems at work in the church, what would happen if we created new ones, simpler ones—with new boundaries, new accountability, new matrices for growth, and a new purpose?[29] The current systems may have been designed with great intentions. They may have worked well for their particular season of congregational life, but somehow over time they have become less useful for subsequent generations. After three weeks at my new church appointment in 2003, I called a special meeting of the usher team after worship to share a new model of hospitality ministry. For twenty minutes I poured out a passionate plan, accompanied by several stories of lives changed by warm greetings provided by ushers who saw their role as frontline ministers of hospitality. After I finished, one longtime member of the church raised his hand and said, "We've been doing ushering the same way for decades. It works. Why change it? I make a motion that we keep doing things the same way." It was seconded. All others joined in, and within moments the sanctuary was cleared, leaving me standing alone at the Communion rail.

We're dealing with a method or practice that has become a deeply rooted weed if, when change is suggested, we hear, "We've been doing it this way for the past ten years, so why change it?"

Methods, however, are not meant to become the source of our personal or congregational identity.[30] The church is called to be a people whose identity is rooted in God, not in what style of music they sing, how the trustees handle the use of the building by outside groups, or whether coffee is allowed in the sanctuary. Often, people of good intent get put into leadership positions in order to fill required vacancies. Then they lead out of their level of ability without direction, training, or accountability. When their activity has some degree of success, releasing the rest of the congregation from responsibility for that aspect of doing life together, their behavior is reinforced, often solidifying their longevity within their position. Over time, they *become* their role. As a result, any new leader, idea, value, or opportunity that threatens to change the status of "that person's ministry" is met with sabotage, aggressive or passive-aggressive power plays, and victimization, thereby leveraging power to the most anxious in the congregation.[31]

We can certainly celebrate that everything we have right now in our congregations is the fruit of the efforts of those who have gone before us. There is no waste in God's economy. God uses all things—the good, the bad, and the ugly—to create a pathway for discipleship. Trust me—the systems at work in our churches predate us. Some will postdate us too. The ones that are God-honoring will continue to bear fruit as the Holy Spirit inspires and equips them. The ones that are selfish, controlling, life sucking, idolatrous, or long past their expiration date, however, need to be pruned. And we need to allow that pruning to occur for the sake of the divine mission (John 15:1–6).

Depending on the change tolerance of the congregation, we may need to adjust our course strategically over time. In my experience, it takes anywhere from seven to ten years for a turnaround toward mission focus and discipleship to take effect within an established congregation. Some will take longer, some shorter, depending on the time it takes to build a discipleship culture with those who will be your leaders. Our leaders will need to be trained in how to navigate through transition, how to apply boundaries to their own anxiety, how to listen genuinely to the reactivity of the congregation without it swaying their commitment to the mission, and how to "release" those from the membership covenant who choose not to align. This is difficult emotional work, but it is the work of missional leadership—especially in times of conflict.

In reality, conflict always leaves traces. As leaders, we will be able to discern those with the greatest capacity to effect a sustainable shift in the discipleship environment of the congregation.[32] We can begin there to build our team by inviting them to join us in a "huddle"—a small group that will engage them in Bible study, leadership development, and mission casting—for one to three years (depending on how conflicted the congregation has been).[33] During that time, we intentionally equip them with leadership skills and faith development, following a model similar to what Jesus used. While the details of how to do such leadership skills and faith development are beyond the scope of this book, I have listed in appendix B resources I have used with my own huddles and congregational leaders to help you get started. In the meantime, as pastor-leaders, we must commit to praying for these teams daily and equip them to pray for each other and the congregation, as well as for signs of the Holy Spirit's presence in their lives. We need to invite them into our homes and allow them to invite us into theirs. We need to let them see us pray (beyond weekend worship). We need to let them see us hopeful. We need to let them see us cry for those in the community who are disconnected from the heart of God. We need to let them see us interact nonanxiously with others in the congregation, listening to their stories, engaging them with questions, learning from them the values they find important. Over the course of our time together, we must then equip them with an understanding of how to multiply the huddle experience by identifying others in whom we see spiritual curiosity—the initial attraction of persons toward the idea of spiritual growth.

When the one- to three-year period is up, we must help them multiply, nurturing their courage to launch. As vacancies emerge among the church's leadership positions, we can begin to nominate into those positions individuals who have been going through—or who have been through—this discipleship process. Please note: as this process continues, we will be accused of playing favorites, especially by those who have long held positions of influence. That is a sign that we are shifting the status quo. Keep doing it.

When I began at my present church appointment, the congregation had been through a long season of difficult conflict. While I did need to address some systemic issues rather quickly, from day one, I focused on identifying individuals with an internal God-oriented capacity to effect sustainable shifts in the discipleship environment of the congregation. I gathered a group of six people and invited them to join me in my first huddle. Over the course of my first year there, it became clear that God was working in ways that far outpaced my own strategies. While we didn't always agree, we bonded—with God and with each other. Three and a half years later, that original group has multiplied to involve over one hundred people in discipleship groups. That's about one-quarter of the worship attendance of the church. Today, just about everyone in leadership positions is connected to one of those groups, intentionally growing in their faith and leadership within the mission of the church.

As a congregation, do we now agree on everything? Absolutely not. We still have conflict, but our conflicts are processed through a different sieve of love and humility, of engaging one another with a commitment to the overall mission of the church and to growing in discipleship. I am humbled and amazed by what the Holy Spirit has accomplished in this congregation in such a short time—taking a group of embattled people and restoring them to a place of hope and partnership in the gospel, where they are now leading the missional charge within our broader community.

My intuition tells me that because this turnaround happened more quickly than expected, there will be a significant testing that will occur. At the time of the editing of this book, we are dealing with the global COVID-19 pandemic, the emotions connected to multiple months of social distancing and quarantine, and the tensions of endemic racism surging in response to substantiated injustice. There is no question in my mind that all of these issues are creating the parameters for such a time of testing. When such testings do occur, it is so important for us to remember that they are often used by God to shore up the foundations that have been laid, to sharpen the character and integrity of the movement God began (Matt 7:24–27; 1 Cor 3:13–16), and to expose areas that need additional support and nurture. The trickle-down nature of what is coming within our global community will be seismic, for sure. Yet it will be an opportunity for each person, leader, pastor, congregation, and denomination—nationally and internationally—to define themselves, remembering who they are, why they're here, and where they're going.

It seems God often operates through conflict to expose holes in the integrity of the vessels God is preparing to use to carry forth the divine mission. As such, it is important for us to lean into conflict for what we are called to learn about ourselves—indeed, to run *toward* it—in faith that the God who calls us is the God who equips us.

How vulnerable is your congregation to the invasive weeds of dysfunction? How vulnerable are you? It's important to remember that weeds sometimes look like flowers. There may be people in your church who appear spiritually minded but who have such a need to keep the church from changing that they will sabotage your leadership efforts overtly or passive-aggressively. Some will seek to undermine your leadership; others will attack your character. Still, others will challenge the well-being of your family, a particularly vulnerable spot for many pastors.

It is to people whose dysfunctionality is like weeds among grass who we now turn our attention.

CHAPTER EIGHT

Closed Power Systems Exist by Permission of the Congregation

Every team member is important to the whole, yet the team can move on without any individual.

—Tony Dungy, *The Mentor Leader*

But the Pharisees went out and conspired against [Jesus], how to destroy him.

—Matthew 12:14

IN THE CHURCH, BULLIES CAN LOOK SPIRITUAL. THEY ALSO MAY be serving a very unique function in the life of the congregation.

In many churches, there are individuals or groups who pose a rather unique challenge to the multiplying movement of God's mission. While some of those persons are simply reacting with anxiety to changes implemented by leaders, others may have a more defined plan to sabotage any idea that does not originate with them. Still, others may have an even more sinister plot in mind to undermine anything that is holy and mission focused.[1] At any given time, but especially during seasons of transition, those persons or groups will exert their influence in order to challenge or thwart what God is birthing in the congregation. And they will use any tactics necessary to accomplish their goals.

Three Distinct Expressions

In my experience, these persons or groups can be categorized broadly into three distinct expressions, each with their own unique behavior and motivations. I classify them as Anxious Annie and Andy, Entitled Edward and Edith, and Noxious Nellie and Norman.

ANXIOUS ANNIE AND ANDY

In 1988, pastor and clinical psychologist Kenneth Haugk debuted a book that would forever shift the trajectory of my career. *Antagonists in the Church: How to Identify and Deal with Destructive Conflict* opened the church to much-needed dialogue on the destructive nature of certain types of people and specific toxic behaviors that, when left unchecked, would leave a wake of destruction both in churches and in individual lives.[2] After over thirty years of ministry, my experience has shown that the vast majority of negatively reactive people are not genuine antagonists, by Haugk's definition. Rather, most of them are what I have labeled "Anxious Annie and Andy"—people who, in order to cope with their own anxiety related to change, exert their influence as best they can to quell the changes that pose a threat to their status quo. As a general rule, the more anxious Annie and Andy are, and the more influence they have within the systems of the church, the more potent their attempts will be at squelching the activities of catalytic pastors and other leaders.

The progressive anxiety of Anxious Annie and Andy, if left unchecked, can provoke destructive behavior—including toxic gossip, false accusations, explosive diatribes in congregational meetings, and even melodramatic mood swings within worship settings.[3] When in positions of power or influence, Anxious Annie and Andy will use their resources—personal (friends and allies) along with the emotional forces of collusion (victimization and triangulation)—to plow a trail of intentional sabotage to gain advantage of the situation.[4] They see their agenda as "righteous" and "for the good of the church," often denying any sense of culpability when their behaviors cause conflict, dissension, or division within the congregation.

Anxious Annie and Andy are usually either well loved or long tolerated within the congregation—perhaps not by everyone, but over their tenure, they have engendered relational connections with other parishioners. When their anxious behaviors escalate, Annie and Andy gather those relational connections into a collusive force, often causing some of their friends to become confused by the cognitive dissonance of challenged loyalties: Do they align with their friends, Annie and Andy, or do they support the pastor, with whom they might actually agree? Do they remain neutral on the issues, or do they look for (or make up) reasons to distrust the leaders? Depending on the power and influence disparities, a decision to remain neutral or to not align with Annie and Andy will bring relational consequences. Therefore, this invitation to collude will either bolster polarization or silence those who are noncompliant.[5]

ENTITLED EDWARD AND EDITH

Similar to Annie and Andy, Entitled Edward and Edith may be motivated by anxiety, but if so, they hide it under the auspices of long-tenured and powerful influence. By virtue of their self-proclaimed entitlement, their behavior borders on that of antagonists. Edward and Edith have endured the tests of time. Whether united by family dynamics, tenure of membership, longevity of leadership, or layers of historic (or histrionic) dominant behavior, Edward and Edith succeed in obtaining and retaining deferential authority over the direction and operation of the church, virtually holding God's mission hostage.[6]

In effect, Entitled Edward and Edith are bullies—whether beneficent in temperament (at least, until challenged) or terroristic. Very little in the church happens without their approval. Many are "matriarchs" and "patriarchs" and may be experienced as individual powerhouses or strongly fortified groups. Often, they exert strong influence on congregational life, viewing their role as "parental," guarding the community of faith with the effect of turf boss–like control. When "benevolent" in nature, they appear to be nurturing, care taking, and spiritually mature, yet by virtue of the fact that they are the ones who dispense blessings—or chastisements—to their "offspring," in reality they are benevolent *dictators*, still controlling the others in the congregation and, therefore, oppressive in nature.[7] When tyrannical, they wield control of resources and opinions, often both within the congregation and beyond it, in the broader community. They have the influence to empower your network as a pastor within the community, and they have the ability to blacklist you, sabotaging your voice within neighborhoods around your church.[8]

At times, Anxious Annie and Andy look like Entitled Edward and Edith because they are long tenured in the congregation. The difference, however, is in how much deferential power is bestowed and in how reactive they are.[9] Annie and Andy wield power through collusion—harnessing other peoples' emotional pain or anxiety to support their cause. For them, misery loves company, and they succeed in harvesting and cataloging other people's anxiety and pain and using it to serve their agenda—whether or not it makes logical sense to do so. Edward and Edith, on the other hand, wield power through fear and deference—meaning that people defer, or yield, to their influence either because they are intimidated by them or because they assume that longevity of tenure entitles Edward and Edith to their influence.[10] Often, you can tell the difference by how people respond to their behavior either verbally or in body language. Church people may genuinely love Anxious Annie and Andy—or they may tolerate them with eye rolls, sighs, or comments like "That's just Betty." As for Edward and Edith, church people tend to react with "You don't know what you're up against" or "I wonder how Sam will respond to that change" or "I'll support this if you can get Terry on board."

Also, Edward and Edith are less likely to react emotionally or be outwardly defensive initially when challenged or confronted. Instead, they will simply retaliate by exerting greater control or by working to "eliminate the problem." When confronted, Annie and Andy, however, tend to make a scene. Their reactions—often emotional and melodramatic—will draw attention to how they are being victimized or how they are "just doing what's best for the church." Annie and Andy will not hesitate to yell, cry, whine, or throw tantrums—in whatever context—to gain the attention of those who have the influence to alter their source of anxiety.

NOXIOUS NELLIE AND NORMAN

On the scale of genuine bullies within the church, there is a category much more vicious than Entitled Edward and Edith. I call them Noxious Nellie and Norman to describe particularly caustic personalities that may be part of the trouble in deeply conflicted congregations. Others have called them "demagogues,"[11] "evil people,"[12] "antagonists,"[13] "nth-degree jerks,"[14] or "Ahabs and Jezebels."[15] Regardless of how we refer to them, I find they are best understood by describing specific personality, character, and behavioral traits—traits that follow predictable patterns within congregational life.

A Foothold in Mental Illness

Noxious Nellie and Norman are "people whose desire it is to hurt others and do destructive things."[16] Quite often they have a serious mental illness—perhaps borderline personality disorder or narcissistic personality disorder or sociopathic personality disorder, although as pastor-leaders we may not be privy to a formal diagnosis.[17] While persons dealing with any of these personality disorders can wreak havoc on congregational community life and mission, the sociopath, by far, is most challenging. When present in churches, true sociopaths are distinguished by what psychiatrist Dr. Paul Meier refers to as their "ability to abuse others selfishly and feel no real guilt in doing so . . . they manipulate, control, dominate, abuse, and even kill with no feelings of guilt."[18] As sociopaths, narcissists, or other people with untreated significant personality disorders engage us, our leaders, and our ministries, they consume large amounts of time, energy, and resources and progressively undermine the pastoral and leadership base of trust within the congregation.

An Attitude of Superiority and a Plot to Gain Authority

Regardless of their actual mental health diagnosis, Nellie and Norman tend to have a superiority attitude and often become retaliatory if they are confronted or crossed. Ultimately, they have a disregard for anyone in authority, often assuming that they deserve the role more than those in such positions.[19] They may, however, initially align with people in authority positions, using flattery to gain emotional access and trust, only to turn on them when they have identified areas of vulnerability. They often will use various tactics freely, including sex and sensuality, and show no remorse or guilt when boundaries are crossed or covenants are violated. They easily can create division within congregations by the use of gossip, slander, and intimidation.[20]

While Noxious Nellie and Norman certainly may be classified theologically as children of God, able to be changed by the gospel, they themselves do not acknowledge their need for God's grace, nor do they care.[21] At best, they may tolerate religious rituals and faith-based conversations or give the impression that they are "deeply spiritual" and "into their faith," but they do so to serve their own agenda. They are not open to reason, do not see themselves as offensive (unless it suits their ego), and are hoping we will approach them with a caring spirit so they can, in turn, take advantage of our vulnerability in whatever selfish way they are able—with an ultimate goal of destroying our reputations, ministries, or churches.[22]

They Foster Discontent and Division

Unlike Anxious Annie and Andy and Entitled Edward and Edith, whose behaviors—however damaging—are rooted in anxiety and control, Noxious Nellie and Norman infiltrate the congregation deceptively, with slow and purposeful strategies not only to undermine the spiritual authority of its leaders—specifically, the pastor—but also to lure parishioners away from established biblical foundations of discipleship (e.g., prayer, Bible study, acts of service) and to invalidate the church's witness for Christ by challenging the reputations of its leaders.[23] Clearly, these are wolves "in sheep's clothing" (Matt 7:15) whose agenda is to breed discontent and division and to steal, kill, or dismantle movements that advance God's mission (John 10:10).[24]

Through deception, Nellie and Norman increasingly attain a level of spiritual authority or influence, positioning themselves within the congregation so that others defer to them—either due to a perceived sense of Nellie and Norman's spiritual superiority or through their fear-based manipulative tactics that undermine others' personal security.[25]

Bait-and-Switch Tactics

It is often the case that Noxious Nellie and Norman will initially align themselves with the pastor, gradually luring the pastor into deeper levels of trust. If the pastor shares vulnerabilities—especially revealing anything challenging about personal matters such as marriage, family, or other struggles—Nellie and Norman become comforters and confidantes to give the impression of support. In initial low-level conflicts, they stand by the pastor, using their influence to communicate alliance and to create pathways for peace.[26] Their motive in doing so, however, is to gain influence and emotional control, to discover vulnerabilities that will aid in their dismantling of the pastor's reputation, and to begin a subtle and progressive campaign to overthrow the pastor's character and spiritual authority.[27] Their destructive strategies generally do not begin overtly but progress from a place of perceived spiritual care laced with innuendo and manipulatively placed doubt: "Hey, Gladys, we need to pray for our pastor. She wouldn't say this publicly, of course, but she told me confidentially that she's in some major conflict with our choir director, Mandy. Mandy's been here forever. I can't imagine what the pastor's problem is. We don't want any divisiveness in our church, of course, so will you join me in praying for the pastor?" Or, "Hey, Pete, have you noticed that the pastor has been seeming tenser and more distracted lately? I sure hope he's not headed for an emotional breakdown like the last one they put in our pulpit." They are masters at manipulation, deceptive in wooing trust, and seemingly emotionally detached from the hurt and pain they inflict with their behavior.[28]

Whether understood from a mainstream theological perspective or a charismatic one, whether rooted in mental illness or a demonic influence, whether seductive and increasingly deceptive or blatantly antagonistic in their disregard of pastoral authority and bold in their accusations (especially once they have garnered influence and power within the congregation), Noxious Nellie and Norman require us to exert great care and discernment in dealing with their deceitfulness.[29] Whatever their modus operandi, the effect is to intentionally sabotage the nurturing, discipling environment of the congregation and its leadership. Our response to them, according to experts, must include self-protection, strong boundaries, and avoidance.[30]

Yet one of the roles of the shepherd is to protect the sheep. Noxious Nellie and Norman's destructive behavior may need to be confronted for the sake of others in the congregation. Such a confrontation must be handled with much prayer and within a team approach as outlined in this chapter. Trust me, "This kind can come out only through prayer" (Mark 9:29).

While Annie and Andy use their ploys to mediate their anxiety, and Edward and Edith seek to remain in power and control, Nellie and Norman are ambassadors of evil. In their own ways, all three types seek to delay, dismantle, or destroy the congregation's formative movement within God's mission. Each forms a potentially collusive base known as a closed power system.

Closed Power Systems

In most of our relational, or "family," systems, such as congregations, boundaries set parameters for what influences we allow to define us. When the dynamic is healthy, certain boundaries establish the perimeters of what are deemed acceptable beliefs, behaviors, and frames of interaction while allowing expression and exchange of ideas and constructs. People are free to dialogue, debate, disagree, and decide within mature interactions of self-definition. Conflicts are seen as normal interchanges as ideas are tested and refined and identities are integrated or challenged within an environment of warmth and love.

When the dynamic is stressed by rigid boundaries and high demands for conformity without the freedom of self-expression, however, the system becomes closed: in other words, members become isolated within belief systems, behavior expectations, and emotional enslavement.[31]

In Mark 8:11–13, Jesus encounters such a closed power group—the Pharisees: "The Pharisees came and began to argue with him, asking him for a sign from heaven, to test him. And he sighed deeply in his spirit and said, 'Why does this generation ask for a sign? Truly I tell you, no sign will be given to this generation.' And he left them, and getting into the boat again, he went across to the other side." Notice a few hermeneutical points that Mark's account raises: First, the religious leaders came with an agenda—namely, to "test" Jesus. It's really important to realize that when a leader comes into an established church and begins to make changes to the status quo—including anything that advances the missional objectives of the New Community—the greatest initial threat to their work is likely to come from longtime church members. In the Gospels, the religious leaders—those who are "looking after" the spiritual matters of the people of

Israel—are most threatened by Jesus. When you begin to build an intentional discipleship-oriented, mission-minded culture, there will always be those who argue with you and "test" you. If they did it to Jesus, they will do it to you. Some will be genuinely trying to understand and adjust to appropriate changes that are introduced. Others, however, will have more divisive plans. It will be up to the leaders to determine the motive behind the testing.

Some of these individuals will "look" spiritual: They will seem to behave like followers of Jesus, come to church like followers of Jesus, and talk like followers of Jesus. They may be high-capacity servers—always at the church, involved in many programs, serving on many committees. Congregation members might often remark positively on how Jane is always giving her time or how Bob has been serving the church for twenty years without fail. Some are second- or third-generation members of families with high stakes in the history and legacy of the congregation. They may be well established in the community—and the lines of differentiation between church and community are often blurred. Initially, they may be the first to greet the new pastor with hospitality, yet embedded in that hospitality can be a not-yet-verbalized "understanding" of how things are to play out with church matters.

Second, notice in this episode from Mark that Jesus defined himself in response to the Pharisees' verbal baiting. He said to them, "Truly I tell you, no sign will be given to this generation" (v. 12). And then he "left them" (v. 13). In fact, he went to the other side of the lake! Arguing with those whose purpose is solely to disrupt God's mission is a waste of time, energy, and resources. The Pharisees here remind us that there are times when people argue not to understand but to control, not to grow but to maintain, not to lead judiciously the people under their care but to guard their own power and position. There are times when we must take them on, and there are times to wait for a better context (Eccl 3:1–8).

What we learn from this exchange between Jesus and the Pharisees is that we should never get into a power play with those who disagree with us. It actually tells your "opponent" that they are winning. Power plays occur when we try to respond to someone's aggression with aggression.[32] It is conflict's "baiting game." The other person is using a strategy—consciously or unconsciously—to draw you into reacting, thereby distracting your focus and exposing your vulnerability. If you "take the bait" and react, your reaction then becomes what the other person will use as a weapon against you.[33]

A closed power system is an anxious system. It may look the opposite because closed power groups give the impression of being strong, being in control, while dominating others within the congregation. But in my experience, most are made up of insecure and anxious people who have been allowed by the rest of the congregation to gain and maintain power and influence.[34]

Let me state that again: *closed power systems exist by permission of the rest of the congregation*. That is the fifth principle in missional leadership. In other words, a closed power system serves a purpose within the congregation, and that purpose has been reinforced over time. Sometimes the permission is active—a volitional choice made by the congregation to affirm their (benevolent) dictators. More often, the permission is given passively—through a process of plausible deniability (e.g., "Pastor, we had no idea that you were having such difficulties dealing with Jason. I wish we had known before you decided to resign").

How Congregations Nurture Bullies

In fact, churches actually raise up their own bullies. This is so vitally important: church bullies get their power from the people they bully.

Why do congregations empower closed power groups? In my experience, there are at least four possible reasons.

THE CONGREGATION GAINS SOME APPRECIABLE BENEFIT

Whether or not we like to admit it, many closed power groups in congregations are made up of those who do most of the work in the church. They mow the lawn, take care of the finances, clean the boiler, wash down the pews, shovel the snow, champion the trustee workdays, and do the majority of the rhythmic work of the congregation—and the rest of the congregation enjoys not having to rise to that level of responsibility. A closed power group may gain its power from the fact that they are invested as doers, and they use that fact judiciously to wield influence.

THE CONGREGATION DEFERS TO TENURED INFLUENCERS

Some closed power groups are modeled on family dynamics: "Betty is the matriarch of the congregation—nothing happens without her approval." Or, "Grandpa George has been a trustee for thirty years; no one knows this church better than him." What looks like respect is better understood as deference: People defer to those whom they perceive to have more power, influence, or knowledge. People also defer to those whom they want to keep active in their volunteer roles so that they themselves don't have to worry about volunteering.

THE CONGREGATION IS HELD HOSTAGE

Some closed power groups gain their power through access to historical information—whereby they may hold others in the church accountable for shameful deeds, family secrets, or other forms of emotional or spiritual blackmail.[35] Those in power use such knowledge to subjugate others to their control, effectively silencing any voices of challenge and enslaving them to their own fears of exposure. In effect, these bullies have been given permission, explicitly or implicitly, to continue their behavior by those who are too scared to counter them, who perceive themselves to be too weak to stand up to them, or who have become passive in their responsibilities as members of the church, thereby making the bullies (ironically) responsible for the discipleship activities of the church.

THE CONGREGATION HAD BAD LEADERS

Another reason congregations inadvertently raise up bullies is that they have created a vacuum of discipled, spiritual leaders. When spiritual leaders fail to mentor the next generation of leaders, they passively subject the congregation to a cadre of "false prophets" or "false teachers" who rise to the level of their incompetence.[36] As such, the congregation has allowed into the fold identity thieves and terrorists who take advantage of the vulnerability of "sheep without a shepherd" (Matt 9:36).

Reasons to Dismantle a Closed Power Group

So, if closed power groups exist by permission of the rest of the congregation, should we, as pastor-leaders, do anything to disturb the congregation's choice?

The challenge of being purveyors of hope is that God calls us into territories of darkness to bring light, into expressions of slavery to announce freedom, and into circumstances of despair to implant life. Regardless of whether we are dealing with Anxious Annie and Andy, Entitled Edward and Edith, or Noxious Nellie and Norman, God has placed us into our congregational context for a reason. With Elijah as precedent, God's unique call on our lives involves casting down idols, challenging patterns of destructive behavior, and realigning God's people to the divine mission to which we have all been called. The message and mandate of the cross of Christ may require a realignment of power—even at the risk of the loss of our ministry role.

Whether the congregation is fractured, out of alignment, rebellious, or in collusion with evil, the divine *hesed* (lovingkindness, penetrating grace) reaches out to all of God's children, inviting them to repent. The image of the prodigal son coming to self-awareness within the muck of a pigsty, embracing responsibility for his actions, and returning to his father's house only to be embraced by unmerited grace applies not only to the people of Jesus's day but to every congregation caught up in collusion with unmitigated denial and in complicity with anything that robs them of the freedom Jesus died to provide. By virtue of our call, we have been given the role of God's agents of reconciliation (2 Cor 5:17–20) and are thereby compelled by the love of God to engage any force that threatens the safety, freedom, and integrity of the body of Christ.

Reasons to Not Try to Dismantle a Closed Power Group

On the other hand, there are times when it is prudent for us to delay or forgo the dismantling of a closed power group.

One reason to not dismantle a closed power group might be that the congregation is functioning in a relatively healthy way given its limited resources. Some churches—small ones, in particular—depend on such a power group for survival. What may look like a justice issue for those of us who are so theologically inclined may be a lifeline for that particular congregation, the only thread by which it continues to exist. As such, the congregation may not only tolerate but even embrace a reasonably beneficent power group if that group is their key to keeping their church doors open. In fact, actions to confront the power group may even be sabotaged by the parishioners under the influence of those in power because they fear the loss of identity that would come with the closure of their church. Indeed, they may support those in power even if it means sacrificing their sense of freedom—and the pastor-leader who would dare lead them to it.

Also, we may not want to dismantle a closed power group if we do not have a cohesive team of leaders to address the wave of issues that will surely result from our coup. Addressing a power group in the congregation takes an enormous amount of energy and personal resources. We cannot—indeed we must not—try to do so on our own. While we may succeed in evacuating the power person or group from positions of control or influence, if we don't have the support to establish healthy systems to fill the vacancy, our overall efforts at discipling the congregation for missional purposes will fail.

Similarly, we do not want to dismantle a closed power group if we're not able—or not willing—to step into the void of responsibility created by their exit. As stated above, in many churches, closed power groups have their power because they're invested in doing the work of the congregation. If we exit them, who will do the work they have done? It is best not to assume that other members will pick up the slack. Moving people out of their comfort zones and on toward discipleship is significantly difficult. Even if we have highly responsible people willing to take up the mantle, unless we develop healthier systems and processes, those volunteers will either burn out or embed themselves into the very roles that caused the collusion in the first place.

A fourth reason to delay or forgo the dismantling of a closed power group is quite personal for pastors: we may not be willing—or are not planning—to engage in long-term ministry as that church's pastor. In my experience, it takes seven to ten years to turn a congregation around, and the leadership of a pastor is key. Unless we're willing to remain with the congregation for at least that amount of time, most likely our role will be to develop some strategies that lay the groundwork for our successor to move in and dismantle the power system (provided, of course, that the new pastor and their appropriate denominational or supervisory authorities are made aware of such strategies and are part of the process of transition).

A case might be made, on the other hand, for us to see ourselves as interim pastors with the specific task of taking on the closed power group so that the next pastor would not need to. Ideally, to maximize the momentum within a pastoral transition, such an "interim pastor's" exit would overlap with the incoming pastor's inaugural year. Admittedly, in many cases this would be financially difficult or is simply not how things are "done" in the denomination. However, to do so could reap a harvest of benefits, especially in terms of mitigating the influence of a closed power group.

Dealing with a Closed Power Group

Since closed power groups exist by permission of the rest of the congregation, addressing them can be complicated. Assuming that the conditions are right for a process of dismantling (based on the information presented above), you will want to employ some very specific strategies.

ESTABLISH A DISCIPLESHIP CULTURE

First, you need to begin crafting a discipleship environment by embracing, modeling, and inculcating into the congregation's culture the principles of the divine mission outlined earlier in this book. Developing such a congregational culture takes time, so obviously, this is not a "quick fix" to your closed power group situation. Remember—the best way to get rid of weeds is to overseed with grass. We must begin by developing the healthier systems and discipling the healthier leaders needed so that the congregation can engage or reengage God's multiplying mission mandate.

To do so, we must begin by establishing a foundation of covenantal values that will define the parameters of the congregational culture. Clinical psychologist and author John Townsend defines a value as "something that you determine has a great deal of worth . . . those realities you believe in at the deepest level, so much so that they dictate your decisions and your leadership, even at your own risk."[37]

In other words, values express the character of our covenant community. In our congregations, values describe the environment within which we choose to gather, worship, fellowship, serve, play, grow, relate . . . and fight. They are the boundaries that define who we choose to be, how we will be known within our community, how we will interact with one another, and for what we are willing to live or die. They determine our nonnegotiables as well as the positive frameworks by which we will hold ourselves accountable to one another and to the mission to which we are called. And they define the ways in which we will engage the mission that has brought us together.

In fact, Pastor Tim Keel, in his insightful book *Intuitive Leadership*, argues that leaders are to become "environmentalists" in order to "create and shape cultures of trust that respond and adapt creatively to their location and what is going on there."

Following are examples of values that might define a church's environment for mission:

- *excellence*—where everything we do is governed by a striving to glorify God with our best, inviting us into consistent evaluation and improvement of our outreach and witness
- *innovation*—where new ideas and risk taking are rewarded rather than feared and fully engaging the mission has become normalized
- *compassionate outreach*—where we care more about the needs of those who don't know Jesus than we do about our own
- *unity*—where we strive to bring everyone together around the mission, even if individually we disagree about method
- *honor*—where we will assume an intent of love rather than offense in dealing with one another's differences, choosing to limit our assumptions concerning one another's motives[38]

Based on such values, we can shift the way we respond when conflict situations threaten to pull us away from living out our divine mission. For example, we might ask, "Can you help me understand why you said . . . ?" in order to clarify motives rather than stating, "How dare you say that! What kind of Christian are you?!"

Defining our missional values in advance of conflict is critically important, for doing so frames the covenant to which we will hold ourselves accountable amid conflict. Teaching, modeling, and reinforcing those values are even more important, for we become what we allow. Involving the community of faith, especially our leaders, in the formation of those values not only helps shape the culture of our congregation but also builds into the value system a participatory desire to hold one another accountable. We are much more likely to abide by the rules that we help define.

It's also important to recognize that unless we are initiating a church plant, our congregation already has a corporate culture shaped by the values of prior leaders. Where do we see these covenant values in the environment of a congregation? Where do we see them in the interactions of our people, in leadership meetings, in fellowship events, in how they process differences of opinion? Why have these values been important to this congregation? What was it that made them set up protocols twenty years ago and still has them defending those protocols now? Understanding a congregation's values can help us reframe them as needed, bringing them into alignment with God's global mission. Existing values reflect who we are, what we believe about ourselves, and how we interact with one another. *Proactive* values—those that we craft intentionally together—create the environment within which we choose to live while moving forward in covenant for the sake of living life together on mission within the New Community.

My dear friend and colleague Dan Gulnac is doing just this process with his new congregation. After reflecting with his leaders on the results of "listening sessions" they held with members of the congregation, a list of values began to emerge. With Pastor Dan's creative research and reframing, the leaders were able to articulate these under the umbrella of a discipleship-mission perspective. As leaders help the congregation recognize these values, and together they make a point to model them, they lovingly reshape the character of the congregation within a discipleship culture. Pastor Dan and the lay leaders' goal is to form a covenanting community for doing life together engaged in the mission of Christ. Here's a sampling of their church's newly articulated values to illustrate the point:

- We believe everyone was created in the image of God.
- We see disciple making as the call of every believer.
- We intentionally move people from rows to circles.
- We strive to balance grace and truth.
- We value and protect unity within the congregation.
- We intentionally organize our ministry with margin (healthy boundaries) in mind.

Taking the time to develop a discipleship culture is critically important. The closed power group in your church is a long-tenured, deeply rooted weed. Even if you were to succeed in tearing off the plant, the root tendrils most assuredly would spawn new growth somewhere else in the systems of the congregation. There is a reason Jesus taught, in parable form, to allow the wheat and thistle to grow together until the time of the harvest (Matt 13:24–30). Cultivating an environment of discipleship over time produces the healthiest results when addressing invasive, freedom-stealing groups.

DEVELOP A TEAM

To assist with the development of a discipleship culture, you need to equip a leadership base—a team—that will help navigate the congregation toward its mission. Elijah succeeded in wounding Jezebel, but it was Elisha and Jehu who were God's instruments to ultimately bring her to her necessary end (2 Kgs 9:35–36). It is incredibly difficult, and often quite painful, to face into a closed power group by yourself. It's not impossible, of course; Jesus did it. But he was crucified for doing so. If you choose to do it alone, you might be crucified too. Jesus, however, had a larger plan. To take on a closed power group in your church you need one too. And it's best to do so with a team.

The goal of this team of leaders is to engage or reengage a heart for the divine mission. Mostly, this begins by establishing a mission statement and a statement of values. More important than the actual statement is the process of coming together to craft it. Doing so has the effect of uniting people around a common identity and purpose. Specifically, what eventually will evacuate a closed power group is a team of people united around who they are, why they're here, and where they're going. Closed power groups exist—and thrive—within the soil of uncertainty. Cohesion and purpose and community and collective energy change the environment within which closed power groups can exist.

RENOUNCE THE PERMISSION

Once your mission and values are defined and embraced by your leaders, it is critically important that you lead them confidently (but not arrogantly, nor reactively) to where they are able to renounce the congregational permission given to the closed power group. This is done most effectively by helping your leaders systematically make decisions based on the new mission and values. If the closed power group was on the benevolent side, your leaders—in united, calm, and assertive voices—can say something like "Harriet, we want to say thank you for all that you did for this congregation while we were in a significant season of transition—trying to figure out what God was calling us toward. You helped us not only survive but get to a point where we now have that mission and direction figured out. Thank you for the sacrifices you've made to keep us going. Because of you, we now have the confidence to lead this church forward from here."

If the closed power group is not so benevolent, it becomes critically important for your leaders to maintain a calm yet assertive, nonreactionary stance that sides with the mission and values that were just created. You might say, "Fred and Ethel, we understand you're angry that we are now allowing nonchurch groups to use our gym. Reaching out to the community is part of our mission, and we're committed to doing whatever it takes to make them feel welcome here. We would love for you to be a part of this journey with us, but we understand if you decide not to." As Fred and Ethel begin to lose effective control over the congregation, they will become more reactionary. They may try to use their influence to undermine the leaders, attacking their character, spreading gossip, drawing others into their collusion, and even blacklisting the leaders in broader community circles. The leaders must remain united, calm, and assertive, repeating the same message: "This is what our mission is. I'm sad that you're upset. Is there any way that we may help you cope with this change?"[39] Over time, the closed power group will go silent, align (however passively), or leave. They may, in fact, exit with a group of like-minded people. Even though such an exit can be painful, at least on some levels, their evacuation will create a shift in the environment, enabling the congregation to engage God's mission.

DISCOVER A "YES"

While taking the time to develop a discipleship culture, you need to find a way to harness the energy of the closed power group. You do that by looking for and engaging a "Yes." This particular step is so important and has such larger contextual implications that I address it as its own principle in chapter 9. For closed power groups, however, this step needs to be pastorally framed.

As difficult as it may seem, in working within the current context of our call, our leadership role involves inviting people to move from where they are now to where God is calling them in mission. That includes those within the closed power group. We must constantly remind ourselves that they are people made in the image of God who also need to be offered the invitation to New Life. What helps me personally with this important mandate is remembering that Jesus's message impacted at least two Pharisees—Nicodemus and Joseph of Arimathea—even though the majority of that religious sect sought to overthrow his influence. In fact, the apostle Paul consistently went to the Jews first in each town he visited and then to the Gentiles, producing an influx of birthed churches for the New Community movement. We go into actual or potential conflict with the expectation that the Holy Spirit will create a pathway that may not make logical sense.

Jonah rebelled against bringing an invitation of repentance to the people of Nineveh because he had a preconceived conclusion about their worthiness of forgiveness (Jonah 2; 4:1–2). Ananias initially resisted the Holy Spirit's directive to go find the man Saul, the terrorist of Christians, out of fear for his life (Acts 9:10–18). We serve a God who does what we think is impossible.

Looking for and engaging a "Yes" means looking for opportunities to discern and clarify the motives of those we are called to serve, as well as to offer them an invitational attitude of grace regardless of their readiness or unreadiness to hear it (Ezek 2:7). Is there something—anything—redemptive in the ideas, values, or behaviors of the closed power group (especially of the leader)? Is there a cause they embrace that might be reframed and harnessed in order to invite their involvement in the congregation's new work? As purveyors of hope, we must always assume that God works in ways we cannot see.

Please hear me: I am not advocating that we collude with or condone evil, oppression, or sinful behavior. Building alliances with the enemy of love (regardless of what that enemy looks like) never produces the "fruit of righteousness" consistent with being followers of Jesus (Phil 1:9–11 NASB). Rather, I'm talking about looking for opportunities to be light amid darkness, to be invitational, to be an ambassador of reconciliation (2 Cor 5:17–20) in order to witness to the freedom that Jesus died to inaugurate. We are, after all, called to "overcome evil with good" (Rom 12:21). Invitation must always precede challenge or discipline.

EMBRACE THE MISSION

Once the new mission and values are established and the leaders have renounced the congregational permission that allowed for the closed power group, the new leadership and missional direction must be embraced publicly with loyalty and accountability. Commissioning those new leaders, with the laying on of hands during worship, along with teaching the mission and values through sermons and small-group discussions, becomes an avenue for shifting the cultural norms of the congregation. Doing so will cause some degree of reactivity from the members of the closed power group as well as from the congregation as a whole. Of course, you're changing the status quo, so this is quite normal and expected.[40] In view of such reactivity, it's important to maintain your course. The connection of your congregation to God's mission must drive the momentum to where the Holy Spirit is leading it. As the pastor-leader, you will need to endure the inevitably increasing and often painful resistance of the exited power group as well as to equip the other leaders—and the congregation—to set limits on the old regime's emotional influence. It is important to remember that it is quite possible to love someone in Christ by saying no to their behavior.

BRING IN A CONSULTANT

Finally, when you're dealing with a Noxious Nellie and Norman type of closed power group—or even a challenging Annie and Andy or Edward and Edith—it may be important for the sake of your sanity, as well as for the well-being of your leadership team, to bring in a consultant to address the long-embedded cultural issues that have created the present conflict environment. A consultant can add a measure of objectivity to your leadership voice by asking the tougher systemic questions while preserving your relational trust with the congregation. You are not meant to do this alone.

The presence of closed power groups in a congregation is, in itself, symptomatic of the deeper layers and lengths of missional and discipleship vacuums. When we treat them as such, we change the questions we ask. As discussed throughout this book, instead of looking at the conflict's content, we focus on the conflict's context: What are the unhealthy relational systems that are creating a breeding ground for dysfunction? In what ways has this congregation been neglecting its mission mandate and "consuming itself"? What does this conflict reveal about the vacuum of discipled leadership here? What do the patterns of repeated conflicts tell us about unresolved grief or unrepented sin? To gain confidence in asking these questions, we must believe that the cost of doing nothing is greater than the cost of doing something.

Closed power groups can actually serve an important function in the congregation: they point to ways in which this local body of believers has become stagnant; is living in a vacuum of leadership, mission, and discipleship; or has been held in bondage and is crying out for freedom. God is listening to their cries.

So perhaps what's needed is a response that disengages us from the emotional constraints of the bullies and the unhealthy systems that created them.

CHAPTER NINE

"Yes, and . . ." Is Better Than "No, But . . ."

> You are 100 percent in control of your side of the relationship.
> —Henry Cloud, *The Power of the Other*

> For no matter how many promises God has made, they are "Yes" in Christ.
> —2 Corinthians 1:20 NIV

WAY TOO MANY CONFLICTS START WITH "NO, BUT . . ."—ESPECIALLY in the church. And way too many "No, buts . . ." come out of the mouths of pastors and other leaders who, in spite of how earnest they are in wanting to carry out their mission and ministry, are yet insecure in their call, defensive about their pastoral identity or role, or missing the fact that most people, in most circumstances within the congregational context, are disciples in formation, an invitation waiting to happen.

I know because I was one such pastor.

For way too many of my early ministry years, I lived out my call defensively. I was insecure, focusing too much on pleasing everyone, assuming that every part of my role as a pastor defined who I was as a person. Annual performance reviews were especially painful. I would wait outside the room of the pastor-parish relations meeting with palpitations, a clenched stomach, and sweaty palms as the committee talked about my work—or, as I believed, evaluated *me*. When they finally called me in, I felt like I was being called to the principal's office, and I immediately became defensive toward any challenges, even when their challenges (which were few) were legitimate. "No, but you don't understand!" I would protest. "That was not what I was trying to do . . ."

As time progressed and I matured a bit in ministry, I became less concerned with the annual reviews. (In fact, I redefined those annual reviews as 360-degree feedback sessions rather than pastoral, or staff, evaluations.) Yet my defensiveness still showed up when a member of the congregation was angry about something I had said, done, or not done. My immediate response was to justify myself: "No, but you obviously didn't hear what I was trying to say . . ."

As I pursued doctoral studies and leadership coaching, I began to see and address my defensiveness. I learned healthier responses to conflict and confrontation that helped increase my leadership and ministry capacities. As with any person in recovery, my self-awareness has also helped me see similar patterns in others: "No, but I'm the pastor—it's my job to do all the preaching (counseling, pastoral care, visitation, youth ministry . . .). If the lay leader does it, what will *I* do?" Or, "I know what you're telling me is true, but I just can't imagine changing what I've done for the past twenty years."

Now years later, I see "No, but . . ." in many congregational conflicts, from worship wars to risk-taking strategic planning, from annual budget debates to neighborhood revitalization programs. I see it most frequently, however, within seasons of missional transition—when any shift in the status quo forces the congregation to move outside its comfort zone. For example, as this book is being edited, the COVID-19 pandemic has been creating tension for several months now within congregations all over the United States (perhaps even globally). In my own congregation, we have people with strong opinions about when we should begin to regather for in-person worship services, whether we should require masks, and whether we should have congregational singing. Each of the various groups has a "No, but . . ." approach to their respective opinions—each also classifying their opinions as "the Christian thing to do."

When two bodies of matter try to occupy the same space at the same time, at some point, one or both parties are going to utter their rendition of "No, but . . ." It's inevitable, since, after all, conflict is the clash of wants, needs, ideologies, theologies, and the like. Anything that stretches us beyond the arena of our desired outcome is bound to receive pushback—the action-reaction of our earlier physics lesson.

What if, in facing into the conflict in front of us, instead of a "No, but . . . ," we assumed a "Yes, and . . ." mindset? What if we approached conflict situations as opportunities to mature in our relationship with God, our relationships with one another, and our ministry as a community of faith? And what if we took this tack regardless of the tenor of the emotions involved, the intensity of the disagreement, the specifics of the offense, or even whether we are involved directly in the conflict ourselves? What if we assumed that every conflict involving Jesus-followers was a context for sanctification—where the Holy Spirit would be present and at work, redemptively shaping the character of those involved for the sake of the greater witness and mission of the congregation (Rom 5:1–5)?

In order to lead amid conflict in today's congregations, we need to accommodate an increasingly complex and unpredictable church culture.[1] While the mainline Christian culture has matured in terms of engaging with scientific and technological advancements, we seem to have become hypersensitive to offense, riddled with anxiety, and often regressive in our emotional and missional development.[2]

What we need is a new framework for leading people in the arenas of discipleship and mission—where formative growth is dependent on the leaders' ability to respond rather than react, to lead rather than manage, and to improvise rather than prescribe solutions.[3]

Improvisational Leadership

In the opening scenes of Jesus's ministry, as recorded in Mark 1, we are introduced to the divine mission: "The time is fulfilled," Jesus says, "and the kingdom of God has come near; repent, and believe in the good news" (v. 15). Immediately following the healing of a demon-possessed man in the Capernaum synagogue (vv. 21–28), word spreads about this fascinating man who has supernatural abilities and who teaches with a new sense of authority (vv. 27–28). By evening of that day, he has added the healing of Simon Peter's mother-in-law to his reputation (vv. 29–31), and we read that "the whole city was gathered around the door" (v. 33), engaging Jesus in various dimensions of conflict intervention.

Yes, conflict *intervention*. According to Mark's Gospel, Jesus begins his ministry by confronting the forces that kept people in bondage physically, emotionally, and spiritually, giving them a renewing dose of the love of God. Notice in verse 34 that Jesus "cast out many demons; and he would not permit the demons to speak, because they knew him." With rapid-fire illustrations, the writer of Mark designs a mosaic of sorts that, progressing throughout the account, depicts how Jesus's catalytic presence and power created conflict wherever he went: with the old religious paradigms (e.g., Mark 2:6–7, 16, 18, 24; 3:2, 22; 7:1–23; 8:11, 31; 9:31; 10:2–9, 33; 11:15–18, 27–33; 12:18–27, 38–40; 14:1–2, 43–49, 53–65), the current political regimes (e.g., Mark 3:6; 10:33–34; 11:1–11; 12:13–17; 15:1–20), and the seemingly ubiquitous spiritual forces of the enemy of love (e.g., Mark 5:1–20; 6:12–13; 9:14–29; 13:5–37).

Before dawn on the morning after these emancipating miracles of Mark 1, Jesus goes off by himself to pray, causing the disciples to go on a search for him (vv. 35–36). When they find him, they admonish him: "Everyone is searching for you" (v. 37). It's early yet in their experience of Jesus's ministry. Perhaps the disciples saw the crowds, saw Jesus's healings, heard his life-giving teaching, saw demons surrendering to his authority, and thought, "Now, *this* is what I signed on for!" It seems Jesus's popularity is registering high among the common people in the public opinion polls. Perhaps the religious leaders are getting nervous. Certainly, this was the plan.

So why would Jesus up and leave?

"Let us go on to the neighboring towns, so that I may proclaim the message there also; for that is what I came out to do," says Jesus (v. 38). His response must have startled Simon and his cohort of friends. A true understanding of Jesus's mission was yet to be shaped in their hearts and minds. From Jesus's perspective, much remained to be done in a brief amount of time.

So Jesus begins to teach them the profound importance of improvisational leadership.

In fact, later, according to John's Gospel, Jesus would invite the Pharisee Nicodemus into that same improvisational leadership: "The wind blows where it chooses, and you hear the sound of it, but you do not know where it comes from or where it goes. So it is with everyone who is born of the Spirit" (John 3:8). Nicodemus at that moment, of course, did not quite understand this oblique invitation to be "born from above" (v. 3). Yet, for the reader of John's Gospel—and the other three Gospels, as well—that invitation would portray the rhythm of Jesus's agenda for his disciples' three-year apprenticeship: "Come and see" (John 1:39).

My own journey with improvisation began my junior year of high school under the tutelage of my school's music director. In preparation for the spring musical, *You're a Good Man, Charlie Brown*, an ensemble cast with minimal staging, our teacher exposed us to the fundamentals of improvisational theater. His hope was that we would become so comfortable with each other that we would be able to respond fluidly to whatever happened on stage—no matter *what* happened (we were teenagers, after all). I still remember his very first lesson: "The first rule of improv is 'Yes, and . . .' rather than 'No, but . . .'" The premise was simple: it's easier to ride the wave of energy coming at you and then reframe it in the direction you want to go than it is to stop it and start something new. (Remember our physics lesson about a body in motion tending to stay in motion?) To help us learn this lesson, he created acting "prompts" that put us into situations where we had to think on our feet, look for the "yes" in our scene or in our fellow actor's words, and respond accordingly for the sake of the team and the scene.

Since then, I have applied those early lessons on improvisation to many different facets of life and ministry—from navigating conflicts to working with teenagers to responding to the varied emotional reactions people have to change. In fact, it is one of the key reasons I enjoy speaking extemporaneously, facilitating discussions in groups, and leading workshops. There is something exciting about stepping into the chaos of the moment and discovering creative possibilities.

Stepping into the chaos of church conflict situations with a mindset of engaging the creative edge of improvisation can actually produce an environment of substantive hope for both participants and congregations.[4] So, for our purposes here, I have reframed some dynamic principles of improvisation for missional leadership within conflict. Before describing those principles, allow me to share some essential parameters to set the stage.

The Parameters of Improvisation

First, in order to engage improvisational leadership within conflict contexts, we have to deconstruct our mindset that the chaos of conflict is a negative thing.[5] Obviously, chaos can raise our anxiety, and when our anxiety goes up, we seek to control our environment in order to return to a place of relative peace. But here's the thing: control is an illusion.[6] In reality, peace does not bring resolution to chaos; boundaries do.[7] Applying healthy boundaries to our anxiety will enable us to stand in the midst of the storms of conflict and lead people to the transformation that our redeeming God ultimately promises.

Improv asks us to suspend our old way of thinking that sees chaos as bad and order as good.[8] In fact, chaos is often the birthplace of creativity. In his book *Managing Transitions*, Bridges reminds us that "innovation will take place automatically in the neutral zone if you provide people with the temporary structures [to do so] . . . and if you encourage them to find new ways to do things."[9] It is within the chaos of conflict that a genuine leader can influence the systems at work—often by way of nonreactive, creative presence, even employing a bit of humor—and thereby shift the outcomes toward a transformative end.[10] In improvisational leadership, control is an illusion, leadership is influence, and boundaries are freeing.

Second, while improv within the context of comedy and acting depends on in-the-moment reactions and real-time communication among team members (like we see on *Whose Line Is It, Anyway?*), improvisational missional leadership lives out an alternate axiom: *don't react; maybe respond.*[11] Within our overreactive culture, the best way to interrupt the cycle of insanity is to not join in on the reactivity. In congregational contexts, every time we react to someone's anxiety amid conflict, we perpetuate the momentum toward missional degradation and succeed in triangling ourselves into someone else's agenda. What's more, our reactions always say more about us than they do about the participants in the conflict—or even about the conflict itself. For example, every time we react defensively, we are telling the other participants we are insecure. Every time we react in a controlling fashion, we are telling the others we are anxious. Reactions simply show our hand before we're ready to play it.

Rather than reacting, we need to discover our personal grounding—that internal security out of which we may respond to the chaos around us. For pastors and other leaders, I argue that internal security is rooted in our call. We must remember who we are, why we're here, and where we are to lead God's people. It is out of our mission mandate—and God's—that we find the courage to stand in chaos and assert nonanxious, self-defining direction for the sake of the overall missional objectives of the New Community.

Notice, though, that the axiom says to "maybe respond." As leaders, our response to chaos and conflict does not have to be one that fixes that chaos and conflict, nor one that follows an expected pathway. Improv, after all, is not based on predictability. Often, it marches into chaos with nothing more than five smooth stones and a slingshot—what Friedman might call a "paradoxical intervention."[12] Not all conflicts require us to respond. In fact, as conflict expert Mark Gerzon writes in *Leading through Conflict*, sometimes our best response is to *not* respond.[13] By our choice to not respond (provided that we are not simply being conflict avoidant), we actually may catalyze a systemic reaction—uncovering dysfunctions in the systems of the church or evoking a response from previously silent voices at the table of decision or forging a new pathway for creative thinking. Sometimes, by choosing to not respond to a conflict, we discover that the participants will actually figure out a solution on their own, especially if we have worked to equip those persons with the discipleship framework described earlier and in the formative principles of the priesthood of all believers (where every follower of Jesus has a unique role to play in the New Community). The overall principle here is that as leaders, we need to be fluid with our abilities to respond regardless of the circumstances before us.[14] We need—and have—the freedom to choose our response, or nonresponse, to any specific situation.

Third, in this improvisational mission-leadership framework, I have discovered that it is better to approach life with a proverbial open hand than with a closed fist. In conflict situations, as tension and anxiety rise, our fear of loss increases, causing us to hold on more tightly to our positions, our demands, our needs, our side of the issue.[15] Yet covenant life within the New Community demands that we love, forgive, share power, and live generously. To be consistent within that framework, we as leaders need to model, assert, and reinforce an *openhanded* approach. Jesus's teachings are quite often paradoxical: You find love by giving it away; you discover who you are by seeking God; if you love your life, you lose it. Holding tightly to our side of a matter amid conflict reveals not only how important our positions are to us but also where we are in our journey of spiritual formation, individually and corporately. What we will discover, also quite paradoxically, is that an openhanded approach is actually a posture of deep, inner strength. Detachment from positions, demands, wants, and the like frees us to focus on what's really most important—the relationships of love that embody the message of the gospel of Jesus Christ for the transformation of the world.[16]

Finally, improv leadership for the sake of mission within the New Community looks for the "yes" by engaging the Holy Spirit, whose work is always redemptive, revelatory, and ready to engage the divine mission (John 14:26; 16:7–15). The beauty and the spontaneity of improvisation are rooted in the hard work of preparation that occurs well before we are called to step into the chaos of conflict. In improvisational leadership, we assume that the active agent of change is the Holy Spirit. Therefore, as pastor-leaders, we need to submit ourselves before the Lord on a regular, rhythmic basis, prayerfully seeking the direction of the "wind" of God (John 3:5 MSG) and engaging the Spirit's fruit (Gal 5:22–23) and gifts (1 Cor 12; Rom 12) for building up the body of Christ (Eph 4:11–13).

For example, for years, I took what I called "a week of Sabbath prayer" three times each year (once per trimester) to spend time in listening retreats. This was not vacation time, but eight-hour days of worship, journaled discernment, listening for the Holy Spirit's direction within my personal devotions, and broad-based congregational planning. Often, I spent additional days in silence at a local Jesuit retreat center in heartfelt communing with the Lord. In more recent years, I have engaged in formal spiritual direction and seasons of leadership coaching—specifically, to remember who I am, why I'm here, and where I need to be going with my life and ministry.

We discover the common ground of "Yes, and . . ." when our hearts are prepared, our eyes are open, and our ears are listening to the voice of the One who knows what we don't and sees what we cannot. Improvisational leadership is not something that just happens in a vacuum; it is nurtured in the crucible of surrender—where we submit ourselves to being vessels through which the Lord will bring healing and hope to the church and through the church to the world.[17]

Within the rhythms of our daily and seasonal devotional times with the Lord, the Holy Spirit develops our intuitive capacity, preparing us for the practiced spontaneity of listening for the Spirit's direction amid conflict situations. Chaos does not scare God. It is from within chaos that God creates (Gen 1:2).

Let's recap the parameters I've outlined: First, the chaos of conflict is not necessarily bad; chaos is often the birthplace of creativity. Second, as leaders, we should follow the axiom "Don't react; maybe respond." Third, it's better to approach life with an open hand than with a closed fist. And fourth, look for the "yes" by engaging the Holy Spirit. With these four parameters in place, the principles of improvisation can nurture missional leadership.

The Principles of Improvisational Missional Leadership

Dramatic improvisation abides by specific principles that govern how it can be done effectively.[18] I've reframed those principles here within the context of missional leadership.

LISTEN ACTIVELY

The first—and most important—principle is that for improvisation to be a valid tool, the missional leader must listen actively.[19] Communication is the key to any effective improvisation—especially in conflict situations.[20] In conflict, we tend to move toward polarization and away from dialogue.[21] Improv teaches us that everything—spoken, shown (in body language), acted out (in behavior)—is part of the information loop that keeps the narrative of the conflict flowing and participants interacting.

As pastors, many of us received training in pastoral care conversations. We were taught the basics of active listening. Other leaders may have received similar training within their managerial or leadership development. I suggest we apply all that we learned in those pastoral care and communications classes to the larger context of the congregation, especially in times of listening amid conflict. Generally, people want their stories, their hurts, their perspectives, and their values heard; they want to know that their lives matter to the other person or people. By listening deeply and nondefensively and paying attention to everything within the context of the conflict, we help people feel that their metastory has been heard.

In improvisational leadership we recognize that communication involves both a sender and a receiver. At any time, the flow of the narrative may become blocked, internally or externally, by the variables of a chaotic context. Missional leaders pay attention to what is being communicated on all levels within the environment so that their response is one of integrity, consistent with the honor due to all people as a witness to the gracious, redemptive love of Christ.[22] In fact, the act of genuinely listening to another is one of the most profoundly intimate expressions of Christ-centered love that we can offer within the New Community (1 Cor 13:4–7). While communication is two-way, it is incumbent on the leader, whenever possible, to ensure that the flow of information is safe, open, and fluid.[23]

As a general formula for engaging that communication, I apply the following paradigm: listen—look—acknowledge—reframe. *Listening* and *looking* are tools for gathering information about our environment, the conflict, the participants, and their stories.[24] Words, body language, emotional undertones, position in the room, the feel of the room (e.g., whether there is good heating or

air-conditioning), who else is in the room, the historical framework of the conflict and its participants, the platform on which
the conflict is being addressed (e.g., email, in a team meeting,
through gossip), and your intuitive sense of where the participants are in processing the conflict—all of these are elements to
be "listened" to in discerning a "Yes, and . . ." response.

As part of the listening process, it's important to let the participants know that you've heard them. It's important to *acknowledge* with the group—out loud—what you've heard. Obviously, not
every observation is critical to the present conversation, so to
discern what to share, I ask myself the following three questions:

1. Is it something that group members have repeated—a *pattern*?
   (e.g., "Several of you have said the same thing, that you don't
   feel you can trust the denominational leadership. Can you
   say more about that?")
2. Is it information the group *needs to know* in order to process the conflict? (e.g., "You may not have realized this, but
   there have been about two dozen emails being circulated
   among the congregation about this situation, but none of
   them has the facts as to what actually happened. May I walk
   through the details with you so we're all on the same page?")
3. Might it be a *stumbling block* to the group's process if it were
   ignored? (e.g., "Everyone seems to be sweating and fanning
   themselves. It doesn't seem like the air conditioner is working. Perhaps we should move to a different room.")

Such an acknowledgment is an important step in the improvisational response because it lets the participants know that they
were taken seriously and that they are considered part of the team
invested in the creative relational interchange.[25] In working this
process within groups, I often use a whiteboard or newsprint
to write down in front of the group what I've heard them sharing, especially as feelings, thoughts, or ideas are generated. This
is a tangible way to show that their perspective matters. After

acknowledging observations, the conflict leader can gauge reactions to those observations on the part of the participants, looking for common-ground opportunities, potential "yes" markers that may be *reframed* in order to enable the flow of communication to continue (or restart).

DISCOVER A "YES, AND . . ."

Such reframing leads to my second principle of improvisational missional leadership—discovering a "Yes, and . . ." A "Yes, and . . . ," by the way, does not imply a resolution to the conflict. Rather, it is the process of seeking and finding something—anything— within the perspectives of the conflicting parties that has the potential to advance the relationship, project, mission, values, or the like and on which we might further engage the relational dialogue.[26] By discovering this "Yes, and . . . ," the missional leader validates—indeed, honors—the participants and their respective frameworks, acknowledging their present perspective and establishing an expectation of hope within an environment of conferring together respectfully.[27]

SPEAK THE "YES, AND . . ."

Third, it is critically important within improvisational leadership in conflict situations to actually *say*, "Yes, and . . ." rather than "No, but . . ."—and to say it out loud and frequently throughout the process. Doing so increases the likelihood of generating a positive momentum and establishes an environment of creativity and innovation (and, occasionally, humor). It also affirms the partnership of the different participants, cultivating a trust that they will be seen as valued contributors to potential solutions that will emerge—especially within the covenantal environment of the New Community.[28] Generally, people are more likely to abide by resolutions that they themselves participate in crafting.

COLLABORATE TO INNOVATE

Fourth, improvisational missional leadership invites the participants to collaborate in order to innovate.[29] Conflict tends to cause people to move away from each other. Improv seeks to draw them back toward each other—to partner with each other in creatively innovating new ways to view the "problem" and the relationship. The focus here is on being a "team sport," where, ultimately, we work together to bring out the best in one another as well as to bring about a brand-new way to look at solutions to the disagreement. Once participants discover their common ground, they are encouraged to reframe their original conflict toward that which unites them—the team goal, the church's mission, the organization's values, and so on. Within the context of the congregation, the goal is to reengage the relational strengths in order to move toward each other as a reflection of their discipleship and then move toward the church's overall mission and witness. "Yes, and . . ." is less concerned with the presenting problem and more concerned with the overall witness for Christ that keeps us talking and walking together even in the midst of our dialectical tension.[30]

EXPERIMENT

Finally, since improvisational leadership involves innovation and collaboration within the arenas of tension, conflict, and chaos, and since tension, conflict, and chaos evoke anxiety even within a positively crafted environment, creative interactions and solutions can be engaged as "experimental." Often, I use the following statement as I wind down a collaborative process: "Let's commit to trying this for six months and see what happens." Doing so gives all participants an opportunity to move forward while still negotiating the newly emerging relational boundaries. Navigational adjustments can still be made en route to the next leg of the relational or missional journey. Missional leadership can advance incrementally in the context of discipleship rather than being seen as simply "resolving a problem." It also avoids the inevitable stalling caused by the myth that we need to resolve conflict before moving forward in mission. In truth, the more time people take to resolve conflict, the more time the conflict will take to resolve. Discipleship can continue, even within conflict situations, by engaging God's mission mandate within the value structures of the New Community.

But what does improvisational conflict leadership look like?

How It All Plays Out

Let's illustrate improvisational missional leadership using a few tangible examples, along with a variety of responses, to demonstrate the range of both reaction and improvisation.

After worship one Sunday, a woman comes through the greeting line, shakes Pastor Earl's hand, and says, "Pastor, I didn't like your sermon today. I just can't agree with what you said."

An insecure response: "I'm so sorry, Ethel! I didn't mean to offend you." (Internal conversation: "I hope no one is listening to her say this to me. Does this mean she doesn't like *me*? What if this is a sign that they're going to get rid of me?")

A defensive response: "Well, Ethel, that doesn't surprise me. You haven't liked any of my messages. In fact, you've been downright nasty to me since I came here!"

A patronizing response: "Well, Ethel, I'd be delighted to meet with you for a few more minutes so that I can elaborate on my theological reasons for preaching what I did. When would you like me to come by?"

An improvisational response: "I'm so glad that you engaged my message today, Ethel! What specifically did you not like?"

The insecure, defensive, and patronizing responses above focus on the pastor's issues and miss the opportunity to pursue the internal conflict that the Holy Spirit may have initiated in Ethel. The improvisational response focuses on Ethel while opening up the flow of communication that has the potential to expose an opportunity for Ethel to grow in discipleship. Remember, in improvisational leadership, we assume that the active agent of change is the Holy Spirit. Therefore, our attention is toward what may be going on in the other person, the group, or the congregation to set the stage for deliverance, conviction, comfort, healing, and transformation on the way toward living out God's mission.

Let's look at another example. Pastor Janice has spent the better part of the past year outlining with her elders a discipleship pathway that involves small groups. She's detailed how those small groups will engage the teaching of the Sunday message by using specifically crafted group questions. After a meeting, one of Pastor Janice's leaders comes to her and says, "Pastor, I have a great idea for one of the small groups you've been telling us about. What if we get a group of guys together to play poker on Friday nights? It's great outreach! And [*laughter*] a lot can be discussed when beer is involved!"

An insecure response: "Uhh . . . I—I—don't know, Henry. What do you think the women's prayer group will think about that idea?"

A defensive response: "Henry, I just spent a year describing what these groups are going to be doing. Have you not been listening to me?"

A patronizing response: "Henry, it sounds like I need to go over the details of my small-group plan again . . . perhaps a little slower so that I don't lose you."

An improvisational response: [*laughing*] "Henry, I love the fact that you captured the larger reason of why we're doing our small-group ministry—to equip us to engage the community! While the poker and beer may push some people out of their comfort zone a bit, I'm intrigued by your creative thinking! Do you think we can talk some more? I'd like to pick your brain on how else we can do outreach with these small groups."

Let's do one more. At a meeting of your church council, two of your ministry leaders start to argue over whether to hire a full-time custodian to do the groundskeeping and general maintenance of the church facilities or to keep asking for volunteers from a rapidly diminishing pool of trustees. As they argue, the tension in the room begins to rise, and some of the council members start taking sides. Finally, one of the leaders looks at you and says, "Pastor, we don't seem to know what to do. What do you think we should do?"

An insecure response: "Uhh . . . I think I need to use the restroom first." (Internal conversation: "Why are they asking me? No matter what I say, I'm going to offend someone. Why do I keep getting put into churches like this?")

A defensive response: "Wow! You're putting me into an awful bind! How'd this become *my* problem?"

A patronizing response: "Clearly, you guys don't know how to handle conflict. Perhaps I'm going to need to do a four-week sermon series on how to handle our differences so that you all can learn how to model it for the congregation. We're leaders, after all."

An improvisational response: "George, you said, 'We don't seem to know what to do.' I'm curious, What would we all say if we *did* know what to do?"

Exposed "Buts"

In Matthew 19:16, a young man comes to Jesus and asks him what "good deed" he must do to have eternal life.

Jesus responds, "If you wish to be perfect, go, sell your possessions, and give the money to the poor, and you will have treasure in heaven; then come, follow me" (v. 21). As the young man walks away sheepishly, Jesus says to his disciples, "Truly I tell you, it will be hard for a rich person to enter the kingdom of heaven. Again I tell you, it is easier for a camel to go through the eye of a needle than for someone who is rich to enter the kingdom of God" (vv. 23–24).

I have often wondered what led the young man to approach Jesus in the first place. We may never know. Yet I would speculate that something about Jesus—his teaching, healing, casting out of demons, presence, or persona—caused an internal conflict for that young man that drew him to ask what he did. Jesus's response is nothing short of radical in terms of its invitation to discipleship.

Before we pull out our cell phones and video the young man's embarrassing exit to post on Instagram, we must ask ourselves, What would we have done in that moment? I contend that Jesus engaged the young man's internal angst with improvisational leadership. Jesus's focus was less on the destination aspect of the man's question ("eternal life") brought about by obedience to the law but more on the discipleship aspect of the fact that Jesus himself was the way to get there.

Conflict is often the best way to ford the deep rivers that separate us from God's best, from God's purpose for God's people, individually and corporately. Jesus does not resolve the young man's conflict; in fact, he brings it out in the open, acknowledges it, reframes it, and invites the young man to join him on a creative and innovative journey to see God do a new thing. Camels, however, don't go through the eyes of needles (v. 24). "Who then can be saved?" the disciples ask Jesus (v. 25 NIV).

Jesus's invitation was for the young man; his sardonic humor was for the sake of training his disciples. Both invitation and humor caused conflict for the young man and the disciples, respectively—the good kind of conflict that invites light into darkness and brings freedom to those who have been held in bondage.

This account causes conflict in us too. In the mirror of Jesus's invitation to discipleship, alongside the rich young man who said, in effect, "But I can't give up so much" and the disciples who protested, "But then no one can be saved," our own "buts" get exposed: "But I'm not good enough at this." "But what if they don't like me?" "But I don't know how to . . ." "But the seminary didn't train me for conflict management!" "But this will require too much of me." "But if I let you preach, what role will *I* have?"

Whether we are facing a Jezebel or our own anxieties, whether we feel isolated in our Ezekiel-like petition to present God's word to a community where no one seems to care, or whether we feel up to the task of being an agent of subversive hope, God has called us for such a time as this, for such a place as the one where we are. It is that call that compels us to stand in the rift of conflict—where our greatest fears and fiercest foes come face-to-face with the divine mission and the Messiah, who bids us to "come and see" what God is up to. It is in that moment of testing that we must choose the mantle of our apprenticeship. In so doing, we will discover that only one stone is needed to defeat Goliath—when slung by a shepherd chosen and led by God.

Conclusion

Now to [God] who by the power at work within us is able to
accomplish abundantly far more than all we can ask or imagine, to him be glory in the church and in Christ Jesus to all
generations, forever and ever. Amen.

—Ephesians 3:20-21

Reframing the Aftermath

THE CONFLICT WAS BRUTAL. THE BLOOD THAT WAS SHED, GRAPHI-
cally presented, paled in comparison to the gut-wrenching wails
of grief from David's chambers. Even though Saul and David had
become enemies, news of Saul's death—and of the death of Saul's
son Jonathan, David's best friend—plunged David into deep lam-
entation (2 Sam 1).

Victory has a price tag, and the cost is very dear.

It is one thing for us to focus on the battles of personalities,
the clashing of desires, and the two bodies of matter trying to
occupy the same space at the same time. It's quite another thing
to live into the ramifications of conflict's resolution.

With the death of Saul, David, the onetime shepherd boy who
had taken on Goliath and was now war scarred and grieving, had
to rebuild a nation and unite a people. His very first act in this
moment is telling: "After this David inquired of the Lord" (2 Sam

2:1). Rebuilding would not be easy. Reuniting a people scattered among torn legacies and loyalties would be even harder. Yet his first act was one of submission to God—a millennium prior to the time when God's plan became incarnate within a Bethlehem feeding trough.

Bethlehem. The "house of bread." David's hometown. The birthplace of royalty—then and a thousand years later.

In Hebron, the people of Judah anoint David as their king. In that act of commissioning, David hears of the fate of his predecessor, the one whose armor not long ago David himself had borne. Saul's body was buried graciously by loyalists in Jabesh-Gilead.

In conflict, people take sides. In conflict resolution, whether the outcome is perceived as positive or negative, those loyalties often persist.

Yet a leader has to reunite the people. God's divine mission must advance. The mosaic of God's larger salvation story is still being created. So King David sends a messenger to the people of Jabesh-Gilead and, through the messenger, does two very important things: First, he thanks the people for their loyalty to Saul (2 Sam 2:5–6). Don't miss this: he thanks them for showing loyalty to his enemy! Why? The clue is found in 2 Samuel 1:14–16 in how David responds to the one who ultimately took Saul's life—"Were you not afraid to lift your hand to destroy *the Lord's anointed*?" (my emphasis). Despite the fact that they were opponents, David never really saw Saul as his enemy. In spite of it all, David maintained a holy respect for Saul, the "Lord's anointed."

The second thing David did in his message to the people of Jabesh-Gilead was to let them know that *he* was now their new king (2 Sam 2:7). He invited them to apply their same loyalty now to him. Invitation and challenge become important partners in the aftermath of conflict. The renegotiation of boundaries, the clarifying of roles and identities, and the reengaging of the divine mission must reshape the priorities of the people. The movement must advance. God's agenda must trump everything else.

Remembering Who We Are, Why We're Here, and Where We're Going

For David, it would take time. A lot of time. Saul's sons are installed as kings over opposing factions. More battles ensue. One victory often inspires next-generation conflicts.

Both grace and strategy are essential within church conflict and its aftermath. We must become adept at living out the Great Commandment and the Great Commission as the expression of who we are, why we're here, and where we're going. Not all conflict resolutions are ones we desire. But then again, within the mandate of God's mission, the very presence of conflict can be a sign that new life is on the horizon. As we surrender our anxiety to our call, as we change how we respond to the others' reactivity, as we dare to equip teams to pursue passionately those who do not as yet know that they are dearly loved children of God, as we trust the improvisational wind of the Holy Spirit, we may discover that we are part of God's subversive plan to transform the world. Thus our life together, founded in God's love made known in Christ, will testify to the fact that we are people of the New Community of Christ.

There is no church conflict, great or small, that ought not be filtered through the sieve of love and humility, of grace and accountability, of personal mercy and corporate witness. For the Artist behind the grand mosaic of creation, redemption, and sanctification, nothing is wasted—no fight or word of forgiveness, no conflict or collaboration, no gossip or act of goodwill, no trauma or transition. God uses all things in a wonderful stewardship of grace to spread the word that nothing—*nothing*—will be able to separate us from the love of God in Christ Jesus (Rom 8:31–39). God's mission moves onward.

Conflict is not a surprise to God. It's been going on since the beginning of time. How does God want to use the conflict we face—now or in the future—as a tool to increase the leadership capacity of God's people under our charge? How does God want to use the conflict to increase our own leadership capacity in preparation for what is next on God's agenda for us? How does God want to use the conflict to awaken the evangelical fervor of our congregation to be about God's plan?

When we remember who we are, why we're here, and where God is calling us to go, we find the courage to move into the rift, into the deeper challenges of living out the divine mission.

Benediction

My longtime dear mentor, friend, and seminary professor, the late Dr. Cullen I K Story, said the following blessing over me as I faced into my new appointment at a highly conflicted church. His words have been prophetically accurate through the years . . . and deeply treasured. So I offer them as a blessing for you: "May you be sufficiently overwhelmed in ministry as to always find yourself on your knees in utter dependence on the Lord Jesus Christ. Amen."

Acknowledgments

IT IS VIRTUALLY IMPOSSIBLE TO ACKNOWLEDGE EVERY PERSON who has contributed to making this book a reality. Since I am, first and foremost, a follower of Jesus Christ, I must thank God for preparing me for this endeavor by taking me through some of the most significant, defining moments of my life—the good, the bad, and the ugly. Especially the ugly. For this book was incubated in the nursery of the difficulties of life and ministry. For all of that, I am truly thankful . . . now.

I must also acknowledge the personal sacrifices that my parents, Paul and Rita Woolverton, made to provide me with an excellent education, as well as the foundation of values that has shaped my life from day one. Without their solid nurturing, as well as their vision for my life that was often larger than what I had for myself, I would not be where I am today. Similarly, my wife, Kristine, provided such persevering encouragement to me—especially in seasons when I just wanted to give up. Her daily prayers to God, laboring on my behalf, and unrivaled belief in me truly make her my spiritual hero and my inspiration.

While I have been "writing" this book for nearly two decades (in my head) and teaching many of these principles in workshops since 2009, I must offer my appreciation to Dr. Johnathan Pritchett, the professor for my doctoral research and writing course at Trinity Seminary. He may not realize this, but while teaching that course, Dr. Pritchett made the offhanded comment, "None of us likes to read dissertations. Students write about what other people have said, and then their work sits on a shelf somewhere collecting dust. Give me something unique to read—a project that will actually advance the kingdom!" When I heard that, my spirit stirred, and I knew I had to write this book instead of a traditional dissertation. I didn't want to waste my professors' time or my own. Therefore, I also thank the late Dr. Ingrid Buch-Wagler, my advisor, who allowed me to trailblaze outside of the norm and who, throughout my coursework with her, affirmed my abilities, my writing, and my learnings. This project would conclude a twenty-four-year doctoral student career that Dr. Pritchett and Dr. Buch-Wagler helped shape, in spite of my numerous interruptions over the years.

Then to convert a doctoral project into a publishable book—switching audiences, formats, and in some respects, research—became an unimaginable feat requiring many late nights. I am humbled by and indebted to the incredible staff at Fortress Press / 1517 Media for taking a chance on a first-time writer like me. One of the first leadership lessons I learned from the esteemed Dr. John C. Maxwell was that leaders surround themselves with people who are better than they are. Clearly, I have done just that with the editing team of Heidi Mann, Elvis Ramirez, and Beth Ann Gaede. Heidi, with the skill of a finely tuned artist, had an uncanny, insightful way of elevating the integrity of what I was trying to communicate. In so many ways, she made my words sing. Elvis, the book's project manager and developer, then, picked up the baton and humbled me by his attention to detail. He wielded a proverbial scalpel in ways that brought deeper levels of integrity to the material—and to me—all while making the formatting of my manuscript suddenly look like a book worth reading. And Beth inspired me from day one with her tremendous coaching and her consistent pursuit of the great over the good in my work. For each of them, and the many on the Fortress Press team, I am forever grateful.

This book also would not have been possible without the many cheerleaders who have had my back—mentors, dear friends, family, colleagues, members of my "huddles"—too numerous to name, but each held dearly in my heart. You, along with the congregations I have served, have been the crucible within which God has shaped my call and refined my character. I am deeply blessed. You are dearly loved.

To God be the glory.

Appendix A
Sample Membership Covenant

St. Paul's United Methodist Church
Elizabethtown, Pennsylvania
Our Membership Covenant

IN JOINING ST. PAUL'S CHURCH, YOU ARE JOINING A SPIRITUAL *movement* of the Holy Spirit. We are a people on a *mission* who unite together as a *community* of believers in Jesus Christ in order to impact Elizabethtown, the region, and the world. It is not like any other organizational membership. Membership in the church is a "covenant." A covenant is a promise or agreement that we make with God as we commit ourselves to God's greater plan and purpose. When you join the church, you actually give up your rights and privileges for the sake of the greater cause of advancing God's mission; you begin to live out the teachings and values of Jesus in how you treat others rather than anticipating how you expect to be treated. Your partnership on this journey is a partnership that we all count on. God works through us most powerfully when we work together in this covenant. We build our covenant membership at St. Paul's Church around these foundational expectations:

I make a commitment to

1. **love God**—with all my heart, mind, soul, and strength. **I will...**
   - **gather regularly to worship with fellow believers**—I realize that in my complex world, I must choose how I

want to spend my time. I want to tune my heart and life to honor God by worshipping the Lord daily in my personal life (as an expression of my love for God) and regularly as part of my local faith community (as an expression of the unity I share as part of God's family). As a believer, worship reminds me that my submission to Jesus's lordship is always my first priority;

- **uphold my covenants**—with God, in my marriage, for my family, with my fellow believers—as a reflection of how Jesus has changed my life from the inside out. **I will pray** earnestly—for my spouse, my family, my pastors, the St. Paul's staff and leaders, my fellow believers, and my congregation and our witness. I will also pray for God to stir up a movement of the Holy Spirit here at St. Paul's and that the Spirit would begin it with me. I will honor my covenant vows and seek to build positive relationships that honor the Lord. I will seek to be a spiritual leader in my home by how I model for my family what it means to have a personal relationship with Jesus Christ. I will not blame others for my behavior, my brokenness, or my weaknesses; and

- **seek God, not my preferences**—I will not make worship or church or my spiritual growth all about my preferences, my style of music, my expectations . . . but will seek to honor the Lord by loving God, loving others, and doing what's best for the church's mission and witness.

2. **love and encourage other believers**—treating them the way I would want them to treat my loved ones. **I will . . .**
   - **become involved in a "huddle," GROW group, or other type of nurturing ministry group**—a small group of fellow believers for the purpose of growing in our relationship with Jesus, sharing life together, and supporting one another as we seek to live out our faith in Jesus. Growing in my faith and in my relationships with other believers is important to me;
   - **avoid gossip**—Gossip is one of the most destructive forces in a local church. I choose in advance not to be a

part of it, no matter what. I commit to guarding the reputations of my pastors, St. Paul's staff and leaders, and my fellow congregation members. I will interrupt and stop conversations that are gossip oriented. Gossipers are people who are hurting (whether they realize it or not). I lovingly will redirect them to the people with whom they have issue, and I will refuse to participate in conversations that hurt the reputations of others; and

* **handle conflicts and disagreements from a biblical perspective**—I will not always agree with my fellow believers, but I do need to love and respect them. When disagreements arise, I will follow the teaching of Matthew 18:15–20 and go directly to the person with whom I am in conflict in order to work out our relationship. When that proves difficult, I will involve one of the pastors or leaders as part of a mediation process. I will resist triangling others into our disagreement—in order to live out my faith with integrity and to make reconciliation a priority. I will honor confidentiality. I will believe that God can overcome all obstacles.

3. **love and serve others within my arenas of influence**—in order to live out Jesus's commandment to love sacrificially and intentionally. **I will . . .**

   * **engage in volunteer service**—within the ministries of the congregation or in the community, or both. This could be serving as an usher, a greeter, a huddle group leader for children or for youth; assisting with vacation Bible school; serving on a short-term mission trip; assisting at a local food bank; or participating in one of the many opportunities of service offered through St. Paul's or the community of Elizabethtown, the region, or the world. I will serve others in Jesus's name;

   * **live in mission to my community**—praying for my neighbors and neighborhood, looking for ways that I may be of help to those in need, offering acts of kindness when I'm

able . . . so that my life can be a witness to what I believe about Jesus and so the light of Christ through me can bring hope to those in need; and

- **give in proportion to how God has blessed me**—The Bible teaches that the "minimum standard" of giving is the "tithe" (giving 10 percent of our income to the general operations fund of the local church). I will believe and trust that God is my provider—and that giving generously enables me to partner with God in impacting individual lives, my community, and my world for Jesus Christ. I believe generosity is the heart of God.

4. **invite, connect with, and grow**—in order to share with others the life-changing good news of Jesus Christ. **I will** . . .
- **invite others to join me on the faith journey**—It may start as an invitation to a meal, to my community group, to an event, or to join me in worshipping the Lord on Sunday morning, but my goal is to be invitational with people so that they too one day might have a personal relationship with Jesus;
- **connect people and connect with people**—I want to create an environment with my attitude, in my home, at St. Paul's Church, and in my community that is warm, welcoming, and engaging. I commit to looking for people I do not know yet, introducing myself to them, and then introducing them to others I do know. I will take relationship connections very seriously; and
- **build the house of God**—I will join my fellow believers in "building the house of God"—which means that I will take seriously my role in witnessing to those who don't yet know Jesus Christ. I will not make anyone else the scapegoat for my evangelistic weakness.

My Signature: _____

Date: _____

Appendix B
Leadership Development Resources for Huddles and Teams

THE FOLLOWING IS A LIST OF RESOURCES I HAVE USED IN THE establishment and spiritual development of leaders and potential leaders, as described in chapter 7. Some of these books (under "Design Resources") were for me—to equip me to design and engage the specific model that works in my context. The other books (under "Curriculum Resources") have been used to equip the group participants.

Design Resources

Breen, Mike. *Building a Discipling Culture: How to Release a Missional Movement by Discipling People like Jesus Did*. 2nd ed. Pawleys Island, SC: 3DM, 2011.

———. *Leading Kingdom Movements: The "Everyman" Notebook on How to Change the World*. Pawleys Island, SC: 3DM, 2013.

———. *Multiplying Missional Leaders: From Halfhearted Volunteers to a Mobilized Kingdom Force*. Pawleys Island, SC: 3DM, 2012.

Breen, Mike, and Alex Absalom. *Launching Missional Communities: A Field Guide*. Pawleys Island, SC: 3DM, 2010.

Hagberg, Janet O., and Robert A. Guelich. *The Critical Journey: Stages in the Life of Faith*. 2nd ed. Salem, WI: Sheffield, 2005.

Im, Daniel, and Todd Adkins. "Episode 211: Leadership Pipeline & Discipleship Pathway." *New Churches Q&A Podcast on Church Planting, Multisite, and Leadership*. Accessed September 25, 2019. https://tinyurl.com/yythvxaw.

Maxwell, John C. *The 21 Irrefutable Laws of Leadership: Follow Them and People Will Follow You*. 10th anniversary ed. Nashville: Thomas Nelson, 2007.

Mulholland, M. Robert Jr. *Invitation to a Journey: A Road Map for Spiritual Formation*. Downers Grove, IL: InterVarsity Press, 2016.

Patterson, Kerry, Joseph Grenny, Ron McMillan, and Al Switzler. *Crucial Conversations: Tools for Talking When Stakes Are High*. 2nd ed. New York: McGraw-Hill, 2012. Kindle.

Stanley, Andy, and Bill Willits. *Creating Community: 5 Keys to Building a Small Group Culture*. Sisters, OR: Multnomah, 2004.

Stetzer, Ed, and Eric Geiger. *Transformational Groups: Creating a New Scorecard for Groups*. Nashville: B&H, 2014.

Curriculum Resources

Bonhoeffer, Dietrich. *Life Together: A Discussion of Christian Fellowship*. San Francisco: Harper & Row, 1954.

Breen, Mike. *Huddle Leader Guide: How to Release a Missional Movement by Discipling People like Jesus Did*. 2nd ed. Pawleys Island, SC: 3DM, 2017.

———. *Huddle Participant Guide*. 2nd ed. Pawleys Island, SC: 3DM, 2017.

Cloud, Henry. *Boundaries for Leaders: Results, Relationships, and Being Ridiculously in Charge*. New York: HarperCollins, 2013.

———. *Necessary Endings: The Employees, Businesses, and Relationships That All of Us Have to Give Up in Order to Move Forward*. New York: HarperCollins, 2010.

Dungy, Tony. *The Mentor Leader: Secrets to Building People and Teams That Win Consistently*. Carol Stream, IL: Tyndale House, 2010.

Easum, Bill, and Bill Tenny-Brittian. *Dinosaurs to Rabbits: Turning Mainline Decline to a Multiplication Movement*. Scotts Valley, CA: CreateSpace, 2018.

Friedman, Edwin. *A Failure of Nerve: Leadership in the Age of the Quick Fix*. New York: Seabury, 2007.

Garvey-Berger, Jennifer. *Unlocking Leadership Mind Traps: How to Thrive in Complexity*. Palo Alto: Stanford University Press, 2019. Kindle.

McNeal, Reggie. *Kingdom Collaborators: Eight Signature Practices of Leaders Who Turn the World Upside Down*. Downers Grove, IL: InterVarsity Press, 2018. Kindle.

Osborne, Larry. *Sticky Teams: Keeping Your Leadership Team and Staff on the Same Page*. Grand Rapids, MI: Zondervan, 2010.

Notes

Preface

1 Peter T. Coleman and Robert Ferguson, *Making Conflict Work: Harnessing the Power of Disagreement* (Boston: Mariner, 2015), introduction, Kindle, differentiate between "constructive" and "destructive" conflict and build a case for "constructive conflict management" and positive power dynamics. I'm reframing their perspective and applying it to congregational leadership.

2 Edwin H. Friedman, *Generation to Generation: Family Process in Church and Synagogue* (New York: Guilford, 1985).

3 Edwin H. Friedman, *A Failure of Nerve: Leadership in the Age of the Quick Fix* (New York: Seabury, 2007).

4 Friedman, 59.

Chapter 1

1 Friedman, *Failure of Nerve*, 14.

2 Friedman, 64, 203.

3 Friedman, 221.

Chapter 2

1 The stories used in this book are true. The names of churches and people have been changed and a few of the details altered to honor and respect those involved.

2 There are obvious exceptions to this, as detailed in the United Methodist *Book of Discipline*.

3 Leonard Sweet and Frank Viola, *Jesus Manifesto: Restoring the Supremacy and Sovereignty of Jesus Christ* (Nashville: Thomas Nelson, 2010), 39.

4 Bridget Illian, "Church Discipline and Forgiveness in Matthew 18:15–35," *Currents in Theology and Mission* 37, no. 6 (December 2010): 448, https://tinyurl.com/y6hy7gho.

5 Elaine Ramshaw, "Power and Forgiveness in Matthew 18," *Word & World* 18, no. 4 (Fall 1998): 403, https://tinyurl.com/y5eqs4qh.

6 Donald A. Carson, "On Abusing Matthew 18," *Themelios* 36, no. 1 (May 2011): 2, https://tinyurl.com/yxhf4x7d.

7 Don B. Garlington, "'Who Is the Greatest?,'" *Journal of the Evangelical Theological Society* 53, no. 2 (June 2010): 287–88, https://tinyurl.com/y3xg995e.

8 While the Greek uses the term "whoever" rather than the NRSV's "any of you," the context supports that Jesus is referring to his disciples (Matt 18:6). I would argue the entire chapter here in Matthew is about the equipping of Jesus's disciples.

9 Tim Kuepfer, "Matthew 18 Revisited," *Vision: A Journal for Church and Theology* 8, no. 1 (2007): 38, https://tinyurl.com/yybppeqz, argues that "obedience to the words of Jesus in this text will mean pursuing exclusively the well-being, restoration, and wholeness of the person who has committed the wrong."

10 For an insightful perspective on forgiveness as a "discovery," see John Patton, *Is Human Forgiveness Possible? A Pastoral Care Perspective* (Lima, OH: Academic Renewal Press, 2003).

11 A parallel to v. 15.

12 Susan E. Hylen, "Forgiveness and Life in Community," *Interpretation: A Journal of Bible & Theology* 54, no. 2 (April 2000): 155–57, https://tinyurl.com/yxn8apvn.

13 Darrell Puls, *The Road Home: A Guided Journey to Church Forgiveness and Reconciliation* (Eugene, OR: Cascade, 2013), 11, writes, "More than two-thirds of church conflicts end with damaged relationships and a general sense of melancholy, followed by leaders leaving and declines in attendance and revenue." The impact of this on the church's witness within the community is exponential.

14 Coleman and Ferguson, *Making Conflict Work*, chap. 1.

15 K. Brynolf Lyon and Dan P. Moseley, *How to Lead in Church Conflict: Healing Ungrieved Loss* (Nashville: Abingdon, 2012), chap. 1, Kindle.

16 W. W. Wilmot and J. Hocker, *Interpersonal Conflict*, 8th ed. (New York: McGraw-Hill, 2011), 11, quoted in Peter G. Northouse, *Introduction to Leadership: Concepts and Practice* (Thousand Oaks, CA: Sage, 2012), 174.

17 "Newton's Third Law," Physics Classroom, 1996–2018, accessed September 26, 2018, https://tinyurl.com/ycaguhqs.

18 Speed Leas and Paul Kittlaus, *Church Fights: Managing Conflict in the Local Church* (Philadelphia: Westminster John Knox, 1973), 28.

19 For example, see Sherry Anderson, "Women as Stewards of Social Change: The Narratives of American Baptist Women Who Held Senior Leadership Positions as Pastors, Deacons, and Teachers" (DA diss., Franklin Pierce University, 2014), 9, 15, 103, https://tinyurl.com/y6fz46kj; and Otto D. Harris III, "Transforming Race, Class, and Gender Relationships within the United Methodist Church through Wesleyan Theology and Black Church Interpretive Traditions" (PhD diss., University of North Carolina at Greensboro, 2014), 14–16, 256–57, https://tinyurl.com/y27z8858.

20 Patty Lane, *A Beginner's Guide to Crossing Cultures: Making Friends in a Multi-cultural World* (Downers Grove, IL: InterVarsity Press, 2002), 169.

21 Mark Gerzon, *Leading through Conflict: How Successful Leaders Transform Differences into Opportunities* (Boston: Harvard Business School Press, 2006), chap. 3, Kindle.

22 Charles H. Cosgrove and Dennis D. Hatfield, *Church Conflict: The Hidden Systems behind the Fights* (Nashville: Abingdon, 1994), 89–90, for example.

23 Friedman, *Failure of Nerve*, 2, 12, 69.

24 See Bill Easum and Bill Tenny-Brittian, *Dinosaurs to Rabbits: Turning Mainline Decline to a Multiplication Movement* (Scotts Valley, CA: CreateSpace, 2018), for a challenging perspective on this topic.

25 Friedman, *Failure of Nerve*, 12.

26 Friedman, 12–13.

27 Friedman, 19.

28 Friedman, 19.

29 Norman L. Shawchuck, *How to Manage Conflict in the Church: Understanding and Managing Conflict*, vol. 1. (Leith, ND: Spiritual Growth Resources, 1983); Coleman and Ferguson, *Making Conflict Work*; Speed Leas, *Moving Your Church through Conflict* (Bethesda, MD: Alban Institute, 1985), Kindle; and Christopher W. Moore, *The Mediation Process: Practical Strategies for Resolving Conflict* (San Francisco: Jossey-Bass, 2014), for example. Leas, *Moving Your Church*, in fact, discusses conflict in terms of five "levels" and astutely posits characteristic behaviors for each level.

30 Friedman, *Failure of Nerve*, 12, 53. See also "Public Highly Critical of State of Political Discourse in the U.S.: 6. The Challenge of Knowing What's Offensive," Pew Research Center, June 19, 2019, https://tinyurl.com/y4a685vo; Marty Nemko, "Taking Offense," *Psychology Today*, October 11, 2014, https://tinyurl.com/y4yuy44c; Mobeen Azhar, "Offence, Power and Progress," produced by Tim Mansel, *Analysis*, BBC Radio, November 20, 2017, accessed February 21, 2020, https://www.bbc.co.uk/programmes/b09fy1qp; and Daniel Burke, "The Four Reasons People Commit Hate Crimes," CNN, June 12, 2017, https://tinyurl.com/ybqr8y5l.

31 Christian Smith and Melinda Lundquist Denton, *Soul Searching: The Religious and Spiritual Lives of American Teenagers* (New York: Oxford University Press, 2005), quoted in R. Albert Mohler Jr., "Moralistic Therapeutic Deism—the New American Religion," *Christian Post*, April 18, 2005, https://tinyurl.com/y7h4p0gq.

32 See Gary T. Waldecker, "Organizational Learning from Cross-Cultural Experiences: An Ethnomethodological Case Study Examining the Relative Importance of Social Structure and Cultural Values during Dynamic Interaction" (EdD diss., George Washington University, 2011), 213–15, https://tinyurl.com/ybnhzn40.

33 B. W. Tuckman and M. A. Jensen, "Stages of Small-Group Development Revisited," *Group & Organization Management* 2 (1977): 419–27, https://tinyurl.com/y8r7vhff.

34 B. W. Tuckman, "Developmental Sequence in Small Groups," *Psychological Bulletin* 63, no. 6 (1965): 384–99, https://doi.org/10.1037/h0022100.

35 Tuckman and Jensen, "Small-Group Development," 3.

36 Peggy Reynoso, "Formed through Suffering," in *The Kingdom Life: A Practical Theology of Discipleship and Spiritual Formation*, ed. Alan Andrews (Colorado Springs: NavPress, 2010), 165–66.

Chapter 3

1 "Newton's First Law," Physics Classroom, 1996–2018, accessed February 25, 2019, https://tinyurl.com/ycfb5fyg.

2 "Newton's First Law."

3 Gerzon, *Leading through Conflict*, introduction, suggests that we need "a new model of leadership that puts conflict at the center, as an essential test of leadership."

4 For an interesting perspective on this, see Reggie McNeal, *Kingdom Come: Why We Must Give Up Our Obsession with Fixing the Church—and What We Should Do Instead* (Carol Stream, IL: Tyndale Momentum, 2015), Kindle.

5 As illustration within relationship dynamics, see Valerie A. Handley et al., "Exploring Similarity and Stability of Differentiation in Relationships: A Dyadic Study of Bowen's Theory," *Journal of Marital & Family Therapy* 45, no. 4 (October 2019): 592–605, https://doi.org/10.1111/jmft .12370.

6 See Nadine Pierre-Louis, "Theory of Conflict Resolution Behavior: Dimensions of Individualism and Collectivism and Perception of Legitimacy of Power and Ideology; a Hermeneutic Comparative Analysis" (PhD diss., Nova Southeastern University, 2016), 7, https://tinyurl .com/yxrggufg. Global history is replete with examples. For a different slant, see Robert Ovetz, "Turning Resistance into Rebellion: Student Movements and the Entrepreneurialization of the Universities," *Capital & Class* 17, no. 58 (Spring 1996): 113–52, https://tinyurl.com/y6rafcb7; and Sarah Barringer Gordon, "The First Wall of Separation between Church and State: Slavery and Disestablishment in Late-Eighteenth-Century Virginia," *Journal of Southern History* 85, no. 1 (February 2019): 61–104, https://doi.org/10.1353/soh.2019.0002.

7 Pierre-Louis, "Theory of Conflict Resolution," 115.

8 William Bridges, *Managing Transitions: Making the Most of Change* (Reading, MA: Addison-Wesley, 1991); Deborah van Deusen Hunsinger and Theresa F. Latini, *Transforming Church Conflict: Compassionate Leadership in Action* (Louisville, KY: Westminster John Knox, 2013), Kindle; McNeal, *Kingdom Come*; and Pierre-Louis, "Theory of Conflict Resolution," 14.

9 Gerzon, *Leading through Conflict*, chap. 11, writes, "Innovations, not just demonstrations, are needed to create change."

10 Reggie McNeal, *Kingdom Collaborators: Eight Signature Practices of Leaders Who Turn the World Upside Down* (Downers Grove, IL: InterVarsity Press, 2018), chap. 2, Kindle.

11 Gerzon, *Leading through Conflict*, chap. 11. In describing the leader's role in engendering an environment of innovation, he writes, "To become an innovation, something must change the way people in a conflict situation think or act. It must make a difference in their lives. In order for this to occur, the innovative idea, plan, or process must be adopted by those who are driving the conflict." Within the faith context, I would

reframe that language around hope. It is the leader's job to engender hope.

12 For an interesting perspective, see Leas, *Moving Your Church*, chap. 1.

13 For a beautiful explication of this "new age," see Walter Brueggeman, *The Land: Place as Gift, Promise, and Challenge in Biblical Faith*, 2nd ed. (Minneapolis: Fortress, 2002), 157–72.

14 Henri Nouwen, *The Wounded Healer: Ministry in Contemporary Society* (New York: Image Doubleday, 1972), 80.

15 For example, see Katalina Tahaafe-Williams, "Churches in Ecumenical Transition: Toward Multicultural Ministry and Mission," *International Review of Mission* 101, no. 1 (April 2012): 170–94, https://doi.org/10.1111/j.1758-6631.2012.00093.x.

16 McNeal, *Kingdom Come*, chap. 1.

17 McNeal, chap. 2. McNeal writes, "Any action or dynamic that undermines what is good and pure and right is sin, whether it originates with and is controlled by immediate agents or reverberates from some long-ago action that continues to affect God's good purposes."

18 McNeal, chap. 7. McNeal correctly argues that "moving from a church-centered approach to a Kingdom-centered narrative will demand a complete change of principles, priorities, and practices—in other words, a culture shift. To transform a culture, you must be willing to change your vocabulary, reconfigure your scorecard, and alter your leadership behavior."

19 Bridges, *Managing Transitions*, 19. My axiom is adapted from his overall principles. I have reframed his perspective that "change causes transition, and transition starts with an ending" to accommodate both an ecclesiological framework and a discipleship platform.

20 I am reframing the post-traumatic stress principles of Bessel van der Kolk's *The Body Keeps the Score: Brain, Mind, and Body in the Healing of Trauma* (New York: Penguin, 2014), Kindle, to accommodate this context of church conflict. The emotions and framework of post-traumatic stress fit easily into this context.

21 Bridges, *Managing Transitions*, 20.

22 Bridges, 4.

23 Bridges, 3.

24 Bridges, 4–6.

25 Bridges, 3.

26 An additional resource to use here is Henry Cloud, *Necessary Endings: The Employees, Businesses, and Relationships That All of Us Have to Give Up*

in Order to Move Forward (New York: HarperCollins, 2010). Dr. Cloud utilizes similar principles related to transitions and endings.

27 Bridges, *Managing Transitions*, 37.

28 Bridges, 37.

29 Leas, *Moving Your Church*, chap. 2.

30 Bridges, *Managing Transitions*, 34–49.

31 Bridges, 35.

32 McNeal, *Kingdom Come*, chap. 7, reminds the church to expect resistance when an effort is begun to renarrate toward a "Kingdom-centered" story.

33 As illustration, see Gaspar F. Colón, "Incarnational Community-Based Ministry: A Leadership Model for Community Transformation," *Journal of Applied Christian Leadership* 6, no. 2 (Fall 2012): 10–17, https://tinyurl .com/y2vc9730.

Chapter 4

1 See Friedman, *Generation to Generation*, 19–20; and Friedman, *Failure of Nerve*, 59, 223.

2 Apple Inc., *Dictionary*, version 2.3.0 (2018), s.v. "symptom."

3 For example, see Friedman, *Generation to Generation*, 20.

4 Friedman, 23.

5 As illustration, see Jennifer Garvey-Berger, *Unlocking Leadership Mind Traps: How to Thrive in Complexity* (Palo Alto: Stanford University Press, 2019), chap. 6, Kindle. See also Leas, *Moving Your Church*, chap. 2.

6 Leas, *Moving Your Church*, chap. 2, writes that "because local churches are voluntary religious organizations, sometimes led by marginally skilled leaders, have heterogeneous belief systems, and are less and less admired and bolstered by society at large (factors which make their very existence an early warning sign of conflict) they are rife with the potential for conflict."

7 Terry S. Wise, *Conflict in the Church: Practical Help for Understanding and Dealing with Conflict* (Newburgh, IN: Avalon, 1994)

8 Charles A. Dailey, "The Management of Conflict," *Chicago Theological Seminary Register* 59 (May 1969): 3, similarly provides an early illustration of what he calls "indices of tension change."

9 Leas, *Moving Your Church*, chap. 2.

10 Leas, chap. 2.

11 Friedman, *Failure of Nerve*, 60.

12 See also Kerry Patterson et al., *Crucial Conversations: Tools for Talking When Stakes Are High*, 2nd ed. (New York: McGraw-Hill, 2012), chap. 5, Kindle; and Gerzon, *Leading through Conflict*, chap. 3.

13 Leas, *Moving Your Church*, chap. 5, states that "local church leaders should assume that conflicts are multiply caused."

14 Leas, chap. 2.

15 Sherwood G. Lingenfelter, *Leading Cross-Culturally: Covenant Relationships for Effective Christian Leadership* (Grand Rapids, MI: Baker Academic, 2008). Lingenfelter's perspectives are quite helpful in discerning cultural nuances related to conflict.

16 See Coleman and Ferguson, *Making Conflict Work*; and Eric H. E. Law, *The Wolf Shall Dwell with the Lamb: A Spirituality for Leadership in a Multicultural Community* (St. Louis: Chalice, 1993).

17 For example, see Robert W. Gauger, "Understanding the Internal, External, and Spiritual Factors of Stress and Depression in Clergy Serving the Southside of Jacksonville, Florida" (DMin diss., Regent University, 2012), 24–50, https://tinyurl.com/y5yyrr5m.

18 Gauger, 57–65.

19 Tara Klena Barthel and Judy Dabler, *Peacemaking Women: Biblical Hope for Resolving Conflict* (Grand Rapids, MI: Baker, 2005), offer an insightful perspective on this.

20 See also Mark D. Maxwell, "God in the Marital System: A Theory of Covenant Attachment" (PsyD diss., Alliant International University, 2013), 5, 53–61, https://tinyurl.com/y2hcos23.

21 David Orrison, *Narcissism in the Church: A Heart of Stone in Christian Relationships* (independently published, 2019); R. Glenn Ball and Darrell Puls, *Let Us Prey: The Plague of Narcissist Pastors and What We Can Do about It* (Eugene, OR: Cascade, 2017); and Tony Sayers, *Narcissistic Personality Disorder: How to Spot the Subtle Signs of a Narcissist and Continue to Thrive after an Encounter* (independently published, 2019), are all good resources.

22 For this topic, see Orrison, *Narcissism in the Church*; Ball and Puls, *Let Us Prey*; and Sayers, *Narcissistic Personality*.

23 Matthew 21:12; John 2:13–22. See also Stan Duncan, "Jesus and the International Currency Exchange Traders in the Temple," Huffpost, March 3, 2015, https://tinyurl.com/yym8etqk; and Gayle Somers, "Jesus and the Moneychangers," CatholicExchange, March 7, 2012, https://tinyurl.com/yxw7ym8z.

Chapter 5

1 Les Parrott III, *The Control Freak: Coping with Those around You, Taming the One Within* (Wheaton, IL: Tyndale, 2000), 47.

2 For a solid rationale on this, see Friedman, *Generation to Generation*, 29, 208.

3 See Friedman, 18.

4 van der Kolk, *Body Keeps the Score*, chap. 6, says that "we now know that panic symptoms are maintained largely because the individual develops a fear of the bodily sensations associated with panic attacks." That means that in both pastors or parishioners who have trauma in their background, the triggers experienced within and surrounding the issues related to church conflict—both conscious and unconscious—may instigate reactionary behavior that may have very little to do with the overt relational tension.

5 Peter L. Steinke, *Congregational Leadership in Anxious Times: Being Calm and Courageous No Matter What* (Herndon, VA: Alban Institute, 2006), 3.

6 van der Kolk, *Body Keeps the Score*, chap. 4 and 5. See also Steinke, *Congregational Leadership*, 3.

7 Christopher G. Ellison et al., "Prayer, Attachment to God, and Symptoms of Anxiety-Related Disorders among U.S. Adults," *Sociology of Religion* 75, no. 2 (Summer 2014): 208–33, https://doi.org/10.1093/socrel/srt079; and Yolanda Dreyer, "Transcending Fear and Anxiety: The Great Cleanup," *Pastoral Psychology* 67, no. 5 (October 2018): 475–91, https://doi.org/10.1007/s11089-018-0819-z.

8 van der Kolk, *Body Keeps the Score*, prologue and chap. 4.

9 Karen Horney, *Neurosis and Human Growth: The Struggle toward Self-realization* (New York: W. W. Norton, 1970), 18–19.

10 For example, see van der Kolk, *Body Keeps the Score*, prologue and chap. 1 and 3.

11 Rollo May, *The Meaning of Anxiety* (New York: W. W. Norton, 1977); and Horney, *Neurosis and Human Growth*, 19.

12 Ronald W. Richardson, *Creating a Healthier Church: Family Systems Theory, Leadership, and Congregational Life* (Minneapolis: Fortress, 1996), 42.

13 van der Kolk, *Body Keeps the Score*, chap. 5.

14 See Ellison et al., "Prayer, Attachment," 2; and Jessica A. Lara, "The God of Anxiety," *Journal of Psychology & Theology* 46, no. 2 (Summer 2018): 113, https://doi.org/10.1177/0091647118767984.

15 See Murray Bowen, *Family Therapy in Clinical Practice*, 3rd ed. (New York: Jason Aronson, 1985); Friedman, *Generation to Generation*, 27; and Friedman, *Failure of Nerve*. This principle is threaded throughout their works.

16 Friedman, *Generation to Generation*, 27.

17 Henry Cloud, *Boundaries for Leaders: Results, Relationships, and Being Ridiculously in Charge* (New York: HarperCollins, 2013), 72, 212, asserts that our brains are "wired to avoid pain and anxiety."

18 Friedman, as a rabbi, had a special affinity for faith communities.

19 Peter Scazerro, *Emotionally Healthy Spirituality: It's Impossible to Be Spiritually Mature While Remaining Emotionally Immature* (Grand Rapids, MI: Zondervan, 2017), 103–4.

20 Bryan P. McCusker, "A New Consultative Tool Measuring Conflict and Climate: A Study Utilizing NILT Survey Data to Assess Conflict Dealing with the Current Climate of Northern Ireland since the Brexit Referendum" (PhD diss., Benedictine University, 2018), 23, https://tinyurl.com/y2uk7ans.

21 Dietrich Bonhoeffer, *Letters and Papers from Prison* (New York: Macmillan, 1972), 46.

22 Friedman, *Generation to Generation*, 22.

23 Ellison et al., "Prayer, Attachment," 213–14.

24 Lara, "God of Anxiety," 114.

25 Friedman, *Failure of Nerve*, 221.

26 Friedman, *Generation to Generation*, 30, 211.

27 Henri Nouwen, Michael J. Christiansen, and Rebecca J. Laird, *Spiritual Formation: Following the Movements of the Spirit* (New York: HarperOne, 2010), 43.

28 Friedman, *Generation to Generation*, 208.

29 Friedman, *Failure of Nerve*, 188.

30 Friedman, *Generation to Generation*, 50–51.

31 See, for example, May, *Meaning of Anxiety*; Horney, *Neurosis and Human Growth*; and Soren Kierkegaard, *The Concept of Anxiety: A Simple Psychologically Oriented Deliberation in View of the Dogmatic Problem of Hereditary Sin*, trans. Alistair Hannay (New York: Liveright, 2014).

32 Friedman, *Generation to Generation*, 24.

33 Friedman, 210, explores this dynamic of homeostatic self-preservation. I'm applying the family systems principle to the congregation.

34 This concept is consistent with the principles posited by Friedman, 208–9.

35 Friedman, *Failure of Nerve*, 12.

36 Friedman, 201; also Friedman, *Generation to Generation*, 47.

37 Friedman, *Failure of Nerve*, 12, writes, "There is a widespread misunderstanding of relational destructive processes (among leaders) which leads leaders to assume that toxic forces can be regulated through reasonableness, love, insight, role-modeling, giving of values, and striving for consensus, rather than setting limits to the invasiveness of those who lack self-regulation."

38 M. Robert Mulholland Jr., *Invitation to a Journey: A Road Map for Spiritual Formation* (Downers Grove, IL: InterVarsity Press, 2016), 45.

Chapter 6

1 For example, Patterson et al., *Crucial Conversations*, chap. 3, argues that "when under attack, our heart can take a similarly sudden and unconscious turn. When faced with pressure and strong opinions, we often stop worrying about the goal of adding to the pool of meaning and start looking for ways to win, punish, or keep the peace."

2 van der Kolk, *Body Keeps the Score*, chap. 3. See also Cloud, *Boundaries for Leaders*, 54; and Friedman, *Failure of Nerve*, 59, for a good discussion on how fight-or-flight/stress impacts leaders.

3 R. S. Beebe, "Predicting Burnout, Conflict Management Style, and Turnover among Clergy," *Journal of Career Assessment* 15 (2007): 257–76, https://doi.org/10.1177/1069072706298157.

4 Gauger, "Internal, External, and Spiritual," 157–58.

5 See the broader conclusions in Gauger, 108–58, as illustration.

6 Hunsinger and Latini, *Transforming Church Conflict*, chap. 3. For a broader treatment of shame, see Varda Konstam et al., "Toward Forgiveness: The Role of Shame, Guilt, Anger, and Empathy," *Counseling & Values* 46, no. 1 (October 2001): 26, https://doi.org/10.1002/j.2161-007X.2001.tb00204 .x; Michael Lewis's exceptional book *Shame: The Exposed Self* (New York: Free Press, 1992); and Lewis Smedes, *Shame and Grace: Healing the Shame We Don't Deserve* (New York: HarperCollins, 1993).

7 Gauger, "Internal, External, and Spiritual," 156–57.

8 We become triangled with our past, present, or perceived pain or by becoming overresponsible for facets of ministry or even for the church itself.

9 Coleman and Ferguson, *Making Conflict Work*, chap. 3, argue that "our dominant conflict-response tendencies are the product of many

personal influences: our personality and temperament, habits, cultural upbringing, gender, social intelligence, formal training, education level, socioeconomic status, parental and peer influences, popular media, and so on." To simplify the point, I posit that we learn our default style within the domains of our primary influencers—from those who are our nurturers within our formative years.

10 Handley et al., "Exploring Similarity and Stability," 594, argue that "emotional reactivity is a reactive response that is heavily triggered and influenced by the emotionality and behavior of others."

11 van der Kolk, *Body Keeps the Score*; Friedman, *Failure of Nerve*; Cloud, *Boundaries for Leaders*; Jesse Gill, *Face to Face: Seven Keys to a Secure Marriage* (Bloomington, IN: WestBow, 2015); and Susan Johnson, *Attachment Theory in Practice: Emotionally Focused Therapy (EFT) with Individuals, Couples, and Families* (New York: Guilford, 2019), are all great resources for this discussion.

12 Olivier Doucet et al., "The Impacts of Leadership on Workplace Conflicts," *International Journal of Conflict Management* 20, no. 4 (September 2009): 340–54, https://doi.org/10.1108/10444060910991057.

13 Patterson et al., *Crucial Conversations*, chap. 4, offer a survey to assess your self-awareness while under stress.

14 Tara Klena Barthel and David V. Edling, *Redeeming Church Conflicts: Turning Crisis into Compassion and Care* (Grand Rapids, MI: Baker, 2012), loc. 148 of 3758, Kindle.

15 Hunsinger and Latini, *Transforming Church Conflict*, introduction.

16 Barthel and Edling, *Redeeming Church Conflicts*, loc. 149 of 3758, argue that "every church has a corporate pattern of response to conflict" as well.

17 David Augsburger, *Caring Enough to Confront: How to Understand and Express Your Deepest Feelings toward Others* (Scottdale, PA: Herald, 1973); Norma Cook Everist, *Church Conflict: From Contention to Collaboration* (Nashville: Abingdon, 2004); Gerzon, *Leading through Conflict*; Hugh Halverstadt, *Managing Church Conflict* (Louisville, KY: Westminster John Knox, 1991); Keith Huttenlocker, *Conflict and Caring: Preventing, Managing and Resolving Conflict in the Church* (Newburgh, IN: Trinity, 1988); and, perhaps the most definitive resource, Speed Leas, *Discover Your Conflict Management Style*, rev. ed. (Lanham, MD: Rowman & Littlefield, 2014), as examples.

18 Kenneth W. Thomas, "The Conflict-Handling Modes: Toward More Precise Theory," *Management Communication Quarterly* 1, no. 3 (February 1988): 430–36, https://doi.org/10.1177/0893318988001003009.

19 In focusing on Thomas's five styles, I must pause to give salute to Leas's *Discover Your Conflict Management Style*. Leas uses six different styles—persuading, compelling, avoiding/accommodating, collaborating, negotiating, and supporting. Thomas's five (and my current reframing of those five) capture the essence of Leas's material while also streamlining it for the average pastor.

20 McCusker, "New Consultative Tool," 40.

21 McCusker, 37–38.

22 McCusker, 40.

23 McCusker, 38.

24 McCusker, 40.

25 Coleman and Ferguson, *Making Conflict Work*, chap. 3.

26 McCusker, "New Consultative Tool," 40.

27 Arnold Kurtz, "The Pastor as a Manager of Conflict in the Church," *Andrews University Seminary Studies* 20, no. 2 (Summer 1982): 119, https://tinyurl.com/y4lp6t2y.

28 McCusker, "New Consultative Tool," 38.

29 McCusker, 40.

30 Kurtz, "Pastor as Manager," 119.

31 Gerzon, *Leading through Conflict*, chap. 3.

32 For exploring how to do this, see Roger Fisher and William Ury, *Getting to Yes: Negotiating Agreement without Giving In* (New York: Penguin, 1991).

33 Friedman, *Failure of Nerve*, 12.

34 For a good discussion on this, see Kurtz, "Pastor as Manager," 121, as well as Lloyd Edwards, *How We Belong, Fight, and Pray: The MBTI as a Key to Congregational Dynamics* (Bethesda, MD: Alban Institute, 1993).

35 Friedman, *Failure of Nerve*, 14.

Chapter 7

1 Eugene Peterson, *A Long Obedience in the Same Direction: Discipleship in an Instant Society*, 2nd ed. (Downers Grove, IL: InterVarsity Press, 2000), chap. 1, Kindle.

2 Paul J. Achtemeier, *Romans*. Interpretation: A Bible Commentary for Teaching and Preaching, ed. James L. Mays (Louisville, KY: Westminster John Knox, 1985), 19.

3 Walter Bauer et al., *Greek-English Lexicon of the New Testament and Other Early Christian Literature*, 2nd ed. (Chicago: University of Chicago Press, 1979), s.v. "proegeomai."

4 Cloud, *Boundaries for Leaders*, 14, reminds us that "you always get what you create and what you allow." Additionally, Janet O. Hagberg and Robert A. Guelich, *The Critical Journey: Stages in the Life of Faith*, 2nd ed. (Salem, WI: Sheffield, 2005), 10, state that "sometimes people get stuck early in life and simply stay there. They can be difficult to be around because, unaware of their condition, they have become very defensive about where they are."

5 Greg Ogden, *Transforming Discipleship: Making Disciples a Few at a Time* (Downers Grove, IL: InterVarsity Press, 2003), 24. Also, Ephesians 4:11–12 NIV, for example, clearly reminds us that "some" are called to be pastors, but all who are called are to "equip [God's] people for works of service." Even the role of "shepherd" (e.g., Ezek 34:1–10; Jer 3:15; 1 Pet 5:1–4), in my opinion, is a contextually misunderstood metaphor in today's congregations.

6 "Patterns of Use: From Initiation to Treatment," Substance Abuse Treatment: Addressing the Specific Needs of Women, Treatment Improvement Protocol (TIP) Series (Rockville, MD: Substance Abuse and Mental Health Services Administration [US], 2009), accessed September 28, 2019, https://www.ncbi.nlm.nih.gov/books/NBK83243/, for example.

7 Jonathan Leeman, *The Church and the Surprising Offense of God's Love: Reintroducing the Doctrines of Church Membership and Discipline* (Wheaton, IL: Crossway, 2009), chap. 4, Kindle, believes that "the loving rule of Christ creates and holds a people together."

8 See Matthew 8:31 and Mark 6:13, for example.

9 As illustration, see Leas, *Moving Your Church*, chap. 4.

10 For a great discussion on this process, see Friedman, *Failure of Nerve*, 18–22.

11 Leeman, *Surprising Offense*, chap. 3.

12 Friedman, *Failure of Nerve*, 67.

13 Garvey-Berger, *Unlocking Leadership Mind Traps*, chap. 6, calls this a "mindtrap" when she states that "we protect and defend the identity we have rather than be open to new possibilities."

14 Friedman, *Failure of Nerve*, 135, 201.

15 Friedman, 81.

16 Friedman, 133–35.

17 This is a better environment for church "discipline." The term *discipline* needs to be reframed out of its misunderstood and often abusive

background and into a renewed covenantal accountability for the sake of the congregation's mission and values.

18 Leeman, *Surprising Offense*, chap. 4.

19 The wording of these membership vow samples is based on those within the liturgy of the United Methodist Church. See Mark W. Stamm, "Our Membership Vows in the United Methodist Church," *Discipleship Ministries: The United Methodist Church*, June 23, 2014, https://tinyurl.com/y4nj36dk.

20 Marlin Jeschke et al., "Fixing Church Discipline: What Corrective Love Really Looks like in the Body of Christ," *Christianity Today* 49, no. 8 (August 2005): 30, https://tinyurl.com/y3hr4fmx.

21 Jeschke et al., "Fixing Church," 30.

22 For example, see Carey Nieuwhof, "7 Ways to Grow Church Attendance by Increasing Engagement," careynieuwhof.com, accessed September 19, 2019, https://tinyurl.com/vq83bc3; Rick Warren, "One Way to Increase the Commitment Level of Your Members," pastors.com, December 12, 2017, https://tinyurl.com/y3p7xj8q; and Thom S. Rainer, "Five Reasons Church Members Attend Church Less Frequently," thomrainer.com, May 22, 2017, https://tinyurl.com/yxvevont.

23 Henry Cloud, *The Power of the Other* (New York: HarperCollins, 2016), 111–12.

24 Daniel Im and Todd Adkins, "Episode 211: Leadership Pipeline & Discipleship Pathway," *New Churches Q&A Podcast on Church Planting, Multisite, and Leadership*, accessed September 25, 2019, https://tinyurl.com/yythvxaw.

25 Gilbert R. Rendle, *Behavioral Covenants in Congregations: A Handbook for Honoring Differences* (Bethesda, MD: Alban Institute, 1999).

26 Patterson et al., *Crucial Conversations*, chap. 1, state that "the key to real change lies not in implementing a new process, but in getting people to hold one another accountable to the process."

27 Warren, "Increase the Commitment Level." Saddleback's membership covenant lists the following main covenantal promises: "1. I will protect the unity of my church: By acting in love toward other members; By refusing to gossip; By following the leaders. 2. I will share the responsibility of my church: By praying for its growth; By inviting the unchurched to attend; By warmly welcoming those who visit. 3. I will serve the ministry of my church: By discovering my gifts and talents; By being equipped to serve by my pastors; By developing a servant's heart.

4. I will support the testimony of my church: By attending faithfully; By living a godly life; By giving regularly."

28 Gerzon, *Leading through Conflict*, chap. 8, argues that "setting ground rules before you need them . . . offers a measure of safety and trust [which] is essential for dealing with conflicts before they arise."

29 Karen Caldwell and Chuck Claxton, "Teaching Family Systems Theory: A Developmental-Constructivist Perspective," *Contemporary Family Therapy: An International Journal* 32, no. 1 (March 2010): 6, http://doi.org/10.1007/s10591-009-9106-6, present a theoretical model that is worth exploring.

30 I heard Andy Stanley once quip, "We need to marry the mission but date the method."

31 Friedman, *Failure of Nerve*, 12.

32 Friedman, 19.

33 Mike Breen, *Building a Discipling Culture: How to Release a Missional Movement by Discipling People like Jesus Did*, 2nd ed. (Pawleys Island, SC: 3DM, 2011), 54.

Chapter 8

1 McNeal, *Kingdom Come*, chap. 6.

2 Kenneth C. Haugk, *Antagonists in the Church: How to Identify and Deal with Destructive Conflict* (Minneapolis: Augsburg, 1988).

3 Peter L. Steinke, *Healthy Congregations: A Systems Approach* (Herndon, VA: Alban Institute, 2006), 61.

4 Cloud, *Necessary Endings*, 188–89.

5 Leas and Kittlaus, *Church Fights*, 82.

6 As illustration, see McNeal, *Kingdom Come*, chap. 6.

7 See John Holm, "Here's Why Even Benevolent Dictators Need to Collaborate with Their Team," churchleaders.com, June 24, 2014, https://tinyurl.com/y42k864c.

8 Gerzon, *Leading through Conflict*, chap. 1.

9 Coleman and Ferguson, *Making Conflict Work*, introduction.

10 Coleman and Ferguson, chap. 2.

11 Gerzon, *Leading through Conflict*, chap. 1.

12 Cloud, *Necessary Endings*.

13 Haugk, *Antagonists in the Church*.

14 Paul Meier, *Don't Let the Jerks Get the Best of You: Advice for Dealing with Difficult People* (Nashville: Thomas Nelson, 1993).

15 Daniel A. Brown, "The Spirit of Jezebel: A Controlling Spirit That Splits Churches," CTW, accessed September 17, 2019, https://tinyurl .com/yxurbhjg; Francis Frangipane, *The Jezebel Spirit: Unmasking the Enemies of the Church* (Cedar Rapids, IA: Arrow, 1991); and John Paul Jackson, *Unmasking the Jezebel Spirit* (Flower Mound, TX: Streams Ministries International, 2002), Kindle, for example.

16 Cloud, *Necessary Endings*, 143.

17 Meier, *Jerks*, 55.

18 Meier, 55, 70.

19 Gerzon, *Leading through Conflict*, chap. 1.

20 Meier, *Jerks*, 73–75.

21 Cloud, *Necessary Endings*, 144.

22 Cloud, 144.

23 Jackson, *Unmasking the Jezebel*, chap. 1.

24 Jackson, chap. 1.

25 Gerzon, *Leading through Conflict*, chap. 1. See also Jackson, *Unmasking the Jezebel*, chap. 2.

26 Brown, "Spirit of Jezebel."

27 Jackson, *Unmasking the Jezebel*, chap. 4.

28 For additional references, see M. Scott Peck, *People of the Lie: The Hope for Healing Human Evil*, 2nd ed. (New York: Touchstone, 1998), as well as Cloud, *Boundaries for Leaders*.

29 Gerzon, *Leading through Conflict*, chap. 1. See also Cloud, *Power of the Other*, 40.

30 Cloud, *Necessary Endings*, 144; Meier, *Jerks*, 76.

31 Cloud, *Necessary Endings*, 138.

32 For illustrations, see Patterson et al., *Crucial Conversations*, chap. 3.

33 Coleman and Ferguson, *Making Conflict Work*, chap. 2.

34 Gerzon, *Leading through Conflict*, chap. 6.

35 F. Wesley Shortridge, "Codependency in Church Systems: The Development of an Instrument to Assess Healthy Church Leadership" (DMin diss., Assemblies of God Theological Seminary, 2016), 136, https:// tinyurl.com/y5hf7fn6.

36 Matthew 7:15. For an interesting read, check out Thomas Brooks, "Seven Characteristics of False Teachers," Union Theology, accessed October 15, 2019, https://tinyurl.com/yy6884m7. Thomas Brooks (1608–80) was an English Puritan preacher and writer.

37 John Townsend, *Leadership beyond Reason: How Great Leaders Succeed by Harnessing the Power of Their Values, Feelings, and Intuition* (Nashville: Thomas Nelson, 2009), 4.

38 This sampling of values is a compilation adapted from several churches with which I have worked.

39 Cloud, *Power of the Other*, 190.

40 McNeal, *Kingdom Come*, chap. 6.

Chapter 9

1 Linda Moerschell, David K. Banner, and Teresa Lao, "Complexity Change Theory: Improvisational Leadership for Complex and Chaotic Environments," *Leadership & Organizational Management Journal* 2013, no. 1 (March 2013): 24–47, https://tinyurl.com/y3mj5b2q.

2 Moerschell et al., "Complexity Change Theory," 40–41; Friedman, *Failure of Nerve*, 53, 93.

3 For a family systems framework, see Friedman, *Failure of Nerve*, 188–94.

4 See Leas, *Moving Your Church*, chap. 1.

5 Tim Keel, *Intuitive Leadership: Embracing a Paradigm of Narrative, Metaphor and Chaos* (Grand Rapids, MI: Baker, 2007), 174. Keel reminds us that "confusion is not the enemy of the spiritual life, but the reality of a people seeking to be faithful to God when they're in over their heads."

6 Moerschell et al., "Complexity Change Theory," 28.

7 Friedman, *Failure of Nerve*, 89–93, 203.

8 Moerschell et al., "Complexity Change Theory," 40–41, suggest that "since organizations behave in dynamic, unpredictable, and unstable patterns, [one should] accept and adapt to organizational instability rather than attempting a goal of stability. In other words, get accustomed to dancing on moving floors."

9 Bridges, *Managing Transitions*, 43.

10 Friedman, *Failure of Nerve*, 203.

11 Gerzon, *Leading through Conflict*, chap. 3, writes that "unless violence or other immediate danger is involved, the first tool required in a conflict is not about doing. It is about witnessing—seeing the whole."

12 Friedman, *Generation to Generation*, 51–53.

13 Gerzon, *Leading through Conflict*, chap. 3 and appendix, suggests that when in a situation of conflict, the first thing one needs to do is "absolutely nothing" and "listen to everything, but respond selectively."

14 Moerschell et al., "Complexity Change Theory," 40, suggest that the best strategy is to "keep moving."

15 Gerzon, *Leading through Conflict*, chap. 7.

16 Hagberg and Guelich, *Critical Journey*, 138–40.

17 Hagberg and Guelich, 133–34, describe such surrender as part of the process of spiritual formation, specifically "stage 5."

18 There are several good resources from the business community. For example, Bob Kulhan, *Getting to "Yes And": The Art of Business Improv* (Palo Alto: Stanford University Press, 2017); Andrew Bright, *Improv(e) Leadership: A Comedian's Guide to Effective Leadership in an Unscripted Workplace* (Lynden, WA: Panic Squad, 2017); and Karen Hough, *The Improvisation Edge: Secrets to Building Trust and Radical Collaboration at Work* (San Francisco: Berrett-Koehler, 2011). The principles of improvisation that I discuss are reframed from those within the common domain of these various resources.

19 Garvey-Berger, *Unlocking Leadership Mind Traps*, chap. 3, for example, highlights the positive impact of listening actively as a solution to getting trapped in limiting paradigms.

20 Patterson et al., *Crucial Conversations*, chap. 5, challenge us to look for "mutual purpose."

21 Gerzon, *Leading through Conflict*, chap. 7.

22 Gerzon, chap. 7, states that "true listening involves entering into the perspective of another human being."

23 Cloud, *Boundaries for Leaders*, 126.

24 See Gerzon, *Leading through Conflict*, chap. 10, for example.

25 Coleman and Ferguson, *Making Conflict Work*, chap. 1.

26 Patterson et al., *Crucial Conversations*, chap. 5, call this "agree to agree."

27 Patterson et al., chap. 5; Leas, *Moving Your Church*, chap. 1; Barthel and Edling, *Redeeming Church Conflicts*, loc. 152 of 3758; and Leeman, *Surprising Offense*, chap. 1.

28 See Barthel and Edling, *Redeeming Church Conflicts*, loc. 155 of 3758, for a shared perspective.

29 Gerzon, *Leading through Conflict*, chap. 10, argues correctly that "generating new information . . . reframes the conflict more constructively."

30 Patterson et al., *Crucial Conversations*, chap. 5. Here, I am reframing their concept of "mutual purpose."

Works Consulted

Achtemeier, Paul J. *Romans*. Interpretation: A Bible Commentary for Teaching and Preaching. Louisville, KY: Westminster John Knox, 1985.

Anderson, Sherry. "Women as Stewards of Social Change: The Narratives of American Baptist Women Who Held Senior Leadership Positions as Pastors, Deacons, and Teachers." DA diss., Franklin Pierce University, 2014. https://tinyurl.com/y6fz46kj.

Anyanwu, Christian Ndubueze. *Creative Strategies for Conflict Management and Community Building*. Bloomington, IN: AuthorHouse, 2009.

Augsburger, David W. *Caring Enough to Confront: How to Understand and Express Your Deepest Feelings toward Others*. Scottdale, PA: Herald, 1973.

Ball, R. Glenn, and Darrell Puls. *Let Us Prey: The Plague of Narcissist Pastors and What We Can Do about It*. Eugene, OR: Cascade, 2017.

Barthel, Tara Klena, and Judy Dabler. *Peacemaking Women: Biblical Hope for Resolving Conflict*. Grand Rapids, MI: Baker, 2005.

Barthel, Tara Klena, and David V. Edling. *Redeeming Church Conflicts: Turning Crisis into Compassion and Care*. Grand Rapids, MI: Baker, 2012. Kindle.

Bauer, Walter, William F. Arndt, F. Wilbur Gingrich, and Frederick W. Danker. *Greek-English Lexicon of the New Testament and Other Early Christian Literature*. 2nd ed. Chicago: University of Chicago Press, 1979.

Beebe, R. S. "Predicting Burnout, Conflict Management Style, and Turnover among Clergy." *Journal of Career Assessment* 1, no. 2 (2007): 257–276. https://doi.org/10.1177/1069072706298157.

Bonhoeffer, Dietrich. *Letters and Papers from Prison*. New York: Macmillan, 1972.

———. *Life Together: A Discussion of Christian Fellowship*. San Francisco: Harper & Row, 1954.

Bowen, Murray. *Family Therapy in Clinical Practice*. 3rd ed. New York: Jason Aronson, 1985.

Breen, Mike. *Building a Discipling Culture: How to Release a Missional Movement by Discipling People like Jesus Did*. 2nd ed. Pawleys Island, SC: 3DM, 2011.

Bridges, William. *Managing Transitions: Making the Most of Change*. Reading, MA: Addison-Wesley, 1991.

Bright, Andrew. *Improv(e) Leadership: A Comedian's Guide to Effective Leadership in an Unscripted Workplace*. Lynden, WA: Panic Squad, 2017.

Brueggeman, Walter. *The Land: Place as Gift, Promise, and Challenge in Biblical Faith*. 2nd ed. Minneapolis: Fortress, 2002.

Caldwell, Karen, and Chuck Claxton. "Teaching Family Systems Theory: A Developmental-Constructivist Perspective." *Contemporary Family Therapy: An International Journal* 32, no. 1 (March 2010): 3–21. http://doi.org/10.1007/s10591-009-9106-6.

Carson, Donald A. "On Abusing Matthew 18." *Themelios* 36, no. 1 (May 2011): 1–3. https://tinyurl.com/yxhf4x7d.

Chand, Samuel R. *Leadership Pain: The Classroom for Growth*. Nashville: Thomas Nelson, 2015. Kindle.

Cloud, Henry. *Boundaries for Leaders: Results, Relationships, and Being Ridiculously in Charge*. New York: HarperCollins, 2013.

———. *Necessary Endings: The Employees, Businesses, and Relationships That All of Us Have to Give Up in Order to Move Forward*. New York: HarperCollins, 2010.

———. *The Power of the Other*. New York: HarperCollins, 2016.

Coleman, Peter T., and Robert Ferguson. *Making Conflict Work: Harnessing the Power of Disagreement*. Boston: Mariner, 2015. Kindle.

Colón, Gaspar F. "Incarnational Community-Based Ministry: A Leadership Model for Community Transformation." *Journal of Applied Christian Leadership* 6, no. 2 (Fall 2012): 10–17. https://tinyurl.com/y2vc9730.

Cosgrove, Charles H., and Dennis D. Hatfield. *Church Conflict: The Hidden Systems behind the Fights*. Nashville: Abingdon, 1994.

Doucet, Olivier, Jean Poitras, and Denis Chênevert. "The Impacts of Leadership on Workplace Conflicts." *International Journal of Conflict Management* 20, no. 4 (September 2009): 340–354. http://doi.org/10.1108/10444060910991057.

Dreyer, Yolanda. "Transcending Fear and Anxiety: The Great Cleanup." *Pastoral Psychology* 67, no. 5 (October 2018): 475–491. https://doi.org/10.1007/s11089-018-0819-z.

Dungy, Tony. *The Mentor Leader: Secrets to Building People and Teams That Win Consistently*. Carol Stream, IL. Tyndale House, 2010.

Easum, Bill, and Bill Tenny-Brittian. *Dinosaurs to Rabbits: Turning Mainline Decline to a Multiplication Movement*. Scotts Valley, CA: CreateSpace, 2018.

Edwards, Lloyd. *How We Belong, Fight, and Pray: The MBTI as a Key to Congregational Dynamics*. Bethesda, MD: Alban Institute, 1993.

Ellison, Christopher G., Matt Bradshaw, Kevin J. Flannelly, and Kathleen C. Galek. "Prayer, Attachment to God, and Symptoms of Anxiety-Related Disorders among U.S. Adults." *Sociology of Religion* 75, no. 2 (Summer 2014): 208–233. http://doi.org/10.1093/socrel/srt079.

Everist, Norma Cook. *Church Conflict: From Contention to Collaboration*. Nashville: Abingdon, 2004.

Fisher, Roger, and William Ury. *Getting to Yes: Negotiating Agreement without Giving In*. New York: Penguin, 1991.

Frangipane, Francis. *The Jezebel Spirit: Unmasking the Enemies of the Church*. Cedar Rapids, IA: Arrow, 1991.

Friedman, Edwin. *A Failure of Nerve: Leadership in the Age of the Quick Fix*. New York: Seabury, 2007.

———. *Generation to Generation: Family Process in Church and Synagogue*. New York: Guilford, 1985.

———. *What Are You Going to Do with Your Life?* New York: Seabury, 2009.

Garlington, Don B. "'Who Is the Greatest?'" *Journal of the Evangelical Theological Society* 53, no. 2 (June 2010): 287–316. https://tinyurl.com/y3xg995e.

Garvey-Berger, Jennifer. *Unlocking Leadership Mind Traps: How to Thrive in Complexity*. Palo Alto: Stanford University Press, 2019. Kindle.

Gauger, Robert W. "Understanding the Internal, External, and Spiritual Factors of Stress and Depression in Clergy Serving the Southside of Jacksonville, Florida." DMin diss., Regent University, 2012. https://tinyurl.com/y5yyrr5m.

Gerzon, Mark. *Leading through Conflict: How Successful Leaders Transform Differences into Opportunities*. Boston: Harvard Business School Press, 2006. Kindle.

Gill, Jesse. *Face to Face: Seven Keys to a Secure Marriage*. Bloomington, IN: WestBow, 2015.

Gordon, Sarah Barringer. "The First Wall of Separation between Church and State: Slavery and Disestablishment in Late-Eighteenth-Century Virginia." *Journal of Southern History* 85, no. 1 (February 2019): 61–104. https://doi.org/10.1353/soh.2019.0002.

Hagberg, Janet O., and Robert A. Guelich. *The Critical Journey: Stages in the Life of Faith*. 2nd ed. Salem, WI: Sheffield, 2005.

Halverstadt, Hugh. *Managing Church Conflict*. Louisville, KY: Westminster John Knox, 1991.

Handley, Valerie A., Spencer D. Bradshaw, Kaitlyn A. Milstead, and Roy A. Bean. "Exploring Similarity and Stability of Differentiation in Relationships: A Dyadic Study of Bowen's Theory." *Journal of Marital & Family*

Therapy 45, no. 4 (October 2019): 592–605. https://doi.org/10.1111/jmft .12370.

Harris, Otto D. III. "Transforming Race, Class, and Gender Relationships within the United Methodist Church through Wesleyan Theology and Black Church Interpretive Traditions." PhD diss., University of North Carolina at Greensboro, 2014. https://tinyurl.com/y27z8858.

Haugk, Kenneth C. *Antagonists in the Church: How to Identify and Deal with Destructive Conflict*. Minneapolis: Augsburg, 1988.

Horney, Karen. *Neurosis and Human Growth: The Struggle toward Self-realization*. New York: W. W. Norton, 1970.

Hough, Karen. *The Improvisation Edge: Secrets to Building Trust and Radical Collaboration at Work*. San Francisco: Berrett-Koehler, 2011.

Hunsinger, Deborah van Deusen, and Theresa F. Latini. *Transforming Church Conflict: Compassionate Leadership in Action*. Louisville, KY: Westminster John Knox, 2013. Kindle.

Huttenlocker, Keith. *Conflict and Caring: Preventing, Managing and Resolving Conflict in the Church*. Newburgh, IN: Trinity, 1988.

Hylen, Susan E. "Forgiveness and Life in Community." *Interpretation: A Journal of Bible & Theology* 54, no. 2 (April 2000): 146–157. https://doi.org/ 10.1177/002096430005400204.

Illian, Bridget. "Church Discipline and Forgiveness in Matthew 18:15–35." *Currents in Theology and Mission* 37, no. 6 (December 2010): 444–450. https://tinyurl.com/y6hy7gho.

Im, Daniel, and Todd Adkins. "Episode 211: Leadership Pipeline & Discipleship Pathway." *New Churches Q&A Podcast on Church Planting, Multisite, and Leadership*. Accessed September 25, 2019. https://tinyurl.com/yythvxaw.

Jackson, John Paul. *Unmasking the Jezebel Spirit*. Flower Mound, TX: Streams Ministries International, 2002. Kindle.

Jeschke, Marlin, Mark Galli, John C. Ortberg Jr., David Neff, and Ken Sande. "Fixing Church Discipline: What Corrective Love Really Looks like in the Body of Christ." *Christianity Today* 49, no. 8 (August 2005): 30–36. https://tinyurl.com/y3hr4fmx.

Johnson, Susan. *Attachment Theory in Practice: Emotionally Focused Therapy (EFT) with Individuals, Couples, and Families*. New York: Guilford, 2019.

Keel, Tim. *Intuitive Leadership: Embracing a Paradigm of Narrative, Metaphor and Chaos*. Grand Rapids, MI: Baker, 2007.

Kierkegaard, Soren. *The Concept of Anxiety: A Simple Psychologically Oriented Deliberation in View of the Dogmatic Problem of Hereditary Sin*. Translated by Alistair Hannay. New York: Liveright, 2014.

Konstam, Varda, Miriam Chernoff, and Sara Deveney. "Toward Forgiveness: The Role of Shame, Guilt, Anger, and Empathy." *Counseling & Values* 46, no. 1 (October 2001): 26. https://doi.org/10.1002/j.2161-007X.2001.tb00204.x.

Kuepfer, Tim. "Matthew 18 Revisited." *Vision: A Journal for Church and Theology* 8, no. 1 (2007): 33–41. https://tinyurl.com/yybppeqz.

Kulhan, Bob. *Getting to "Yes And": The Art of Business Improv.* Palo Alto: Stanford University Press, 2017.

Kurtz, Arnold. "The Pastor as a Manager of Conflict in the Church." *Andrews University Seminary Studies* 20, no. 2 (Summer 1982): 111–126. https://tinyurl.com/y4lp6t2y.

Lane, Patty. *A Beginner's Guide to Crossing Cultures: Making Friends in a Multicultural World.* Downers Grove, IL: InterVarsity Press, 2002.

Lara, Jessica A. "The God of Anxiety." *Journal of Psychology & Theology* 46, no. 2 (Summer 2018). https://doi.org/10.1177/0091647118767984.

Law, Eric H. E. *The Wolf Shall Dwell with the Lamb: A Spirituality for Leadership in a Multi-cultural Community.* St. Louis: Chalice, 1993.

Leas, Speed. *Discover Your Conflict Management Style.* Rev. ed. Lanham, MD: Rowman & Littlefield, 2014.

———. *Moving Your Church through Conflict.* Bethesda, MD: Alban Institute, 1985. Kindle.

Leas, Speed, and Paul Kittlaus. *Church Fights: Managing Conflict in the Local Church.* Philadelphia: Westminster John Knox, 1973.

Leeman, Jonathan. *The Church and the Surprising Offense of God's Love: Reintroducing the Doctrines of Church Membership and Discipline.* Wheaton, IL: Crossway, 2009. Kindle.

Lingenfelter, Sherwood G. *Leading Cross-Culturally: Covenant Relationships for Effective Christian Leadership.* Grand Rapids, MI: Baker Academic, 2008.

Lyon, K. Brynolf, and Dan P. Moseley. *How to Lead in Church Conflict: Healing Ungrieved Loss.* Nashville: Abingdon, 2012. Kindle.

Maxwell, John C. *The 21 Irrefutable Laws of Leadership: Follow Them and People Will Follow You.* 10th anniversary ed. Nashville: Thomas Nelson, 2007.

Maxwell, Mark D. "God in the Marital System: A Theory of Covenant Attachment." PsyD diss., Alliant International University, 2013. https://tinyurl.com/y2hcos23.

May, Rollo. *The Meaning of Anxiety.* New York: W. W. Norton, 1977. Kindle.

McCusker, Bryan Patrick. "A New Consultative Tool Measuring Conflict and Climate: A Study Utilizing NILT Survey Data to Assess Conflict Dealing with the Current Climate of Northern Ireland since the Brexit

Referendum." PhD diss., Benedictine University, 2018, https://tinyurl
.com/y2uk7ans.

McNeal, Reggie. *Kingdom Collaborators: Eight Signature Practices of Leaders Who Turn the World Upside Down*. Downers Grove, IL: InterVarsity Press, 2018. Kindle.

———. *Kingdom Come: Why We Must Give Up Our Obsession with Fixing the Church—and What We Should Do Instead*. Carol Stream, IL: Tyndale Momentum, 2015. Kindle.

Meier, Paul. *Don't Let the Jerks Get the Best of You: Advice for Dealing with Difficult People*. Nashville: Thomas Nelson, 1993.

Moerschell, Linda, David K. Banner, and Teresa Lao. "Complexity Change Theory: Improvisational Leadership for Complex and Chaotic Environments." *Leadership & Organizational Management Journal* 2013, no. 1 (March 2013): 24–47. https://tinyurl.com/y3mj5b2q.

Mohler, R. Albert Jr. "Moralistic Therapeutic Deism—the New American Religion." *Christian Post*, April 18, 2005. https://tinyurl.com/yxdg7uwm.

Moore, Christopher W. *The Mediation Process: Practical Strategies for Resolving Conflict*. San Francisco: Jossey-Bass, 2014.

Mulholland, M. Robert Jr. *Invitation to a Journey: A Road Map for Spiritual Formation*. Downers Grove, IL: InterVarsity Press, 2016.

Nichols, Michael. *Creating Your Business Vision: A Step-by-Step Guide for Designing the Work You've Always Wanted to Do*. Scotts Valley, CA: CreateSpace, 2013.

Northouse, Peter G. *Introduction to Leadership: Concepts and Practice*. 2nd ed. Los Angeles: Sage, 2012.

———. *Leadership: Theory and Practice*. 8th ed. Los Angeles: Sage, 2018.

Nouwen, Henri. *The Wounded Healer: Ministry in Contemporary Society*. New York: Image Doubleday, 1972.

Nouwen, Henri, Michael J. Christiansen, and Rebecca J. Laird. *Spiritual Formation: Following the Movements of the Spirit*. New York: HarperOne, 2010.

Ogden, Greg. *Transforming Discipleship: Making Disciples a Few at a Time*. Downers Grove, IL: InterVarsity Press, 2003.

Orrison, David. *Narcissism in the Church: A Heart of Stone in Christian Relationships*. Independently published, 2019.

Ovetz, Robert. "Turning Resistance into Rebellion: Student Movements and the Entrepreneurialization of the Universities." *Capital & Class* 17, no. 58 (Spring 1996): 113–152. https://tinyurl.com/y6rafcb7.

Parrott, Les III. *The Control Freak: Coping with Those around You, Taming the One Within*. Wheaton, IL: Tyndale, 2000.

Patterson, Kerry, Joseph Grenny, Ron McMillan, and Al Switzler. *Crucial Conversations: Tools for Talking When Stakes Are High.* 2nd ed. New York: McGraw-Hill, 2012. Kindle.

Patton, John. *Is Human Forgiveness Possible? A Pastoral Care Perspective.* Lima, OH: Academic Renewal Press, 2003.

Peck, M. Scott. *People of the Lie: The Hope for Healing Human Evil.* 2nd ed. New York: Touchstone, 1998.

Peterson, Eugene. *A Long Obedience in the Same Direction: Discipleship in an Instant Society.* 2nd ed. Downers Grove, IL: InterVarsity Press, 2000. Kindle.

Physics Classroom, 1996–2018. "Newton's Third Law." Accessed September 26, 2018. https://tinyurl.com/ycaguhqs.

Pierre-Louis, Nadine. "Theory of Conflict Resolution Behavior: Dimensions of Individualism and Collectivism and Perception of Legitimacy of Power and Ideology; a Hermeneutic Comparative Analysis." PhD diss., Nova Southeastern University, 2016. https://tinyurl.com/yxrggufg.

Puls, Darrell. *The Road Home: A Guided Journey to Church Forgiveness and Reconciliation.* Eugene, OR: Cascade, 2013.

Rah, Soong-Chan. *The Next Evangelicalism: Freeing the Church from Western Cultural Captivity.* Downers Grove, IL: InterVarsity Press, 2009.

Ramshaw, Elaine. "Power and Forgiveness in Matthew 18." *Word & World* 18, no. 4 (Fall 1998): 397–404. https://tinyurl.com/y5eqs4qh.

Rendle, Gilbert. *Behavioral Covenants in Congregations: A Handbook for Honoring Differences.* Bethesda, MD: Alban Institute, 1999.

Reynoso, Peggy. "Formed through Suffering." In *The Kingdom Life: A Practical Theology of Discipleship and Spiritual Formation*, edited by Alan Andrews, 165–193. Colorado Springs: NavPress, 2010.

Richardson, Ronald W. *Creating a Healthier Church: Family Systems Theory, Leadership, and Congregational Life.* Minneapolis: Fortress, 1996.

Ross, Lee, and Richard E. Nisbett. *The Person and the Situation: Perspectives of Social Psychology.* 2nd ed. London: Pinter & Martin, 2011. Kindle.

Sayers, Tony. *Narcissistic Personality Disorder: How to Spot the Subtle Signs of a Narcissist and Continue to Thrive after an Encounter.* Independently published, 2019.

Scazzero, Peter. *Emotionally Healthy Spirituality: It's Impossible to Be Spiritually Mature While Remaining Emotionally Immature.* Updated ed. Grand Rapids, MI: Zondervan, 2017.

Shawchuck, Norman. *How to Manage Conflict in the Church: Understanding and Managing Conflict.* Vol. 1. Leith, ND: Spiritual Growth Resources, 1983.

Shortridge, F. Wesley. "Codependency in Church Systems: The Development of an Instrument to Assess Healthy Church Leadership." DMin diss., Assemblies of God Theological Seminary, 2016. https://tinyurl.com/y5hf7fn6.

Smedes, Lewis B. *Shame and Grace: Healing the Shame We Don't Deserve.* New York: HarperCollins, 1993.

Steinke, Peter L. *Congregational Leadership in Anxious Times: Being Calm and Courageous No Matter What.* Herndon, VA: Alban Institute, 2006.

———. *Healthy Congregations: A Systems Approach.* Herndon, VA: Alban Institute, 2006.

Sweet, Leonard, and Frank Viola. *Jesus Manifesto: Restoring the Supremacy and Sovereignty of Jesus Christ.* Nashville: Thomas Nelson, 2010.

Tahaafe-Williams, Katalina. "Churches in Ecumenical Transition: Toward Multicultural Ministry and Mission." *International Review of Mission* 101, no. 1 (April 2012): 170–194. https://doi.org/10.1111/j.1758-6631.2012.00093.x.

Thomas, K. W. "Conflict and Conflict Management." In *Handbook of Industrial and Organizational Psychology,* edited by M. D. Dunnette, 889–935. Chicago: Rand McNally, 1976.

———. "The Conflict-Handling Modes: Toward More Precise Theory." *Management Communication Quarterly* 1, no. 3 (February 1988): 430–436. https://doi.org/10.1177/0893318988001003009.

Townsend, John. *Leadership beyond Reason: How Great Leaders Succeed by Harnessing the Power of Their Values, Feelings, and Intuition.* Nashville: Thomas Nelson, 2009.

Tuckman, B. W. "Developmental Sequence in Small Groups." *Psychological Bulletin* 63, no. 6 (1965): 384–399. https://doi.org/10.1037/h0022100.

Tuckman, B. W., and M. A. Jensen. "Stages of Small-Group Development Revisited." *Group & Organization Management* 2 (1997): 419–427. https://tinyurl.com/y8r7vhff.

van der Kolk, Bessel. *The Body Keeps the Score: Brain, Mind, and Body in the Healing of Trauma.* New York: Penguin, 2014. Kindle.

Waldecker, Gary T. "Organizational Learning from Cross-Cultural Experiences: An Ethnomethodological Case Study Examining the Relative Importance of Social Structure and Cultural Values during Dynamic Interaction." EdD diss., George Washington University, 2011. https://tinyurl.com/ybnhzn40.

Willard, Dallas. *Hearing God: Developing a Conversational Relationship with God.* Downers Grove, IL: InterVarsity Press, 2012.

Wise, Terry S. *Conflict in the Church: Practical Help for Understanding and Dealing with Conflict.* Newburgh, IN: Avalon, 1994